*THE AMPHIBIOUS
CAMPAIGN
FOR WEST FLORIDA
AND LOUISIANA*

THE AMPHIBIOUS CAMPAIGN FOR WEST FLORIDA AND LOUISIANA, 1814–1815

A Critical Review of Strategy and Tactics at New Orleans

WILBURT S. BROWN

UNIVERSITY OF ALABAMA PRESS

UNIVERSITY, ALABAMA

TO HONOR PROFESSOR BROWN,
WHOSE DEATH OCCURRED AS THIS VOLUME
WAS BEING PREPARED FOR PRESS,
THE FIRST THREE COPIES WERE HAND BOUND IN BLUE MOROCCO
AND WERE PRESENTED BY THE PRESIDENT
OF THE UNIVERSITY OF ALABAMA TO
MRS. WILBURT SCOTT BROWN,
TO THE PRESIDENT OF THE UNITED STATES, AND
TO THE COMMANDANT OF THE UNITED STATES
MARINE CORPS.

First Printing

Copyright © 1969 by University of Alabama Press
Standard Book Number: 8173-5100-0
Library of Congress Catalog Card Number: 68-10992
Manufactured in the United States of America

TABLE OF CONTENTS

MAPS

PREFACE

During the winter of 1935–1936, the writer, then a captain in the United States Marine Corps, was a student at the Marine Corps Schools at Quantico, Virginia. A historical study of the Battle of New Orleans was presented by a member of the school's staff, who treated the battle as an amphibious operation. The writer was greatly impressed by the lecture, and began reading about important battles of history, especially amphibious ones.

The writer was born in Massachusetts and received his primary and secondary schooling there prior to World War I. He does not allege that his teachers deliberately tried to conceal the truth about Jackson's great victory, but he does recall that as late as 1935 he was entirely unaware of its very great significance. He believed that Jackson was an uncouth, almost illiterate, backwoods Indian-fighter who had the good luck to be in command of American forces at New Orleans at the moment that a very arrogant British general threw away his forces and certain victory by assaulting a prepared, heavily fortified, and quite impregnable position. The British general had lost his own life in the disaster, and Jackson had gone on from there to become president of the United States—thereby introducing the "spoils system" and much more that was evil (almost nothing that was good) to the conduct of the federal government—and for no other reason than the accident of his happening to be in command of the impregnable American line upon which Sir Edward Pakenham committed hara-kiri on a massive scale, a full two weeks *after* the war was over. The battle itself, therefore, for all its heavy British casualties, was sound and fury, signifying nothing.

Twenty years after hearing that lecture, the writer, having completed his career in the Marine Corps, decided to reexamine Jackson's repulse of the British at New Orleans in December and January of 1814–1815. He soon found himself asking the question implied by Professor H. C. Hockett's statement, "What has passed for history has often been little more than fiction agreed upon."

The New Orleans campaign is a classic example of an amphibious operation in which the defenders were almost stripped of naval strength before the operation was begun, while the attacker's naval strength remained overwhelming. The objective of the assault was known to the defenders, but it was so difficult of access directly from the sea that they considered it almost certain that another locality would be selected as the beachhead. For that reason the limited military strength of the American defenders had to be scattered until the British intentions became known. A concentration to meet the British at the point of their choosing was the best that could be planned and hoped for, but in this unsettled country of few and very poor roads and of very limited animal transport and forage, the attendant time and space problems were colossal.

The British, for all their preponderance of strength, encountered grave logistical problems. Changes in the plans of the political high command confounded and handicapped the amphibious force commander increasingly as the moment of attack approached. In the end he committed the fortunes of the entire campaign to what he thought would be a quick victory through a surprise of the main objective itself, using a route of approach previously unknown. He discarded all plans for an intermediate objective of a shore base of operations, easily supported by the navy, and thus he saddled the navy with a tremendous task of supply and evacuation between the fleet anchorage and the beachhead about seventy miles away.

The defending commander, fortunately for him, happened to be inspecting New Orleans itself, the objective of the attacker's first landing attack, just when that attack took place. Jackson had come to New Orleans simply to reassure himself and its inhabitants that the city's defenses were impregnable. He expected the British attack to fall on the Gulf Coast, at Pascagoula or Mobile. The British landing force commander, Lieutenant General Sir Edward Pakenham, was not so fortunate. Through no fault of his own, his arrival on the scene was delayed, and when he actually did arrive he found that a most unsatisfactory beachhead had already been established for him, and that his entire landing force was already ashore by order of the naval commander of the joint attack force.

In a sense, the story of the battle is a record of General Pakenham's various attempts to extricate himself from his predicament, and to mount a drive on to victory. This unfortunate young officer is certainly more to be pitied than censured, for the defenders, under Jackson's leadership, were able to counter his every move. The last effort, made after Pakenham had been heavily reinforced, was the grand assault of Jackson's lines on January 8, 1815—a fantastic mélange of occurrences that seem as though they could not all have happened, certainly not all at once, at the same hour on the same day. It ended in almost complete disaster for the British expedition, and it was fatal for the young British general, for his second-in-command, and for a great many of his officers and men.

Evaluation of all the events of the story has been attempted by the writer in the light of his own training for, and experience in, amphibious battles and campaigns, and in extensive research on the New Orleans campaign. The British plans and orders (and modifications of them in the course of the operation) are considered in some detail, in order to assess the significance that the British attached to their Gulf Coast expedition and, by implication, the historical importance of the outcome of what was the greatest joint amphibious expedition ever to leave England up to that time, and coincidentally the last Anglo–American passage of arms. The writer also attempts to answer the question, was Andrew Jackson truly a great military leader, or was he merely a lucky opportunist? Any study of the battle necessarily involves Andrew Jackson's personality and his strategic and tactical military acumen. Some of the writer's preconceptions had to be altered in the light of all the evidence adduced.

The Manuscripts Division of the Library of Congress contains the very important Jackson and Morgan Papers, and photostats of British Public Record Office documents relating to the campaign. The National Archives yielded the army and navy records of the period, including the excerpts from secret British records that were made and deposited in the Navy Department's Historical Archives by Rear Admiral A. T. Mahan, U.S.N., during the 1890's. The writer has carefully examined every available eyewitness account of the battle, both British and American. Much of the biography and history consulted is not even listed in the bibliography of the present work. There were some thirty-four biographies of Jackson in English and two in French, for example, but only those cited in footnotes are mentioned in the bibliography.

Every effort has been made to cull out of the story the accumulation of myth, tradition, and patriotic or imaginative fiction that has come to be accepted as fact in general histories. A lie can be embalmed into truth by constant repetition. The facts of what happened have been sought by meticulous reading and comparison of all known eye-witness accounts, frequently in the light of personal experiences of the writer and other participants in similar situations. In addition, all available previous analyses of the campaign have been weighed and compared to the writer's conclusions. Some of them have supplanted his own initial findings.

The list of persons in the Library of Congress and the National Archives to whom the writer feels indebted for their unstinted assistance is far too long to give here, and he is reluctant to single out any one, two, or three individuals because he cannot do that fairly. The staff at the Howard Tilton Library at Tulane University was very cooperative during a week of research there, and in lending books subsequently. The staff of the University of Alabama Library makes up another list that defies the singling out any one person or even a half dozen. The writer's gratitude to all of these people is very deeply felt and is herewith acknowledged.

Finally, the writer must acknowledge that without the constant assistance and encouragement of his beloved wife, this project would have been given up long ago.

WILBURT S. BROWN
Major General, U.S.M.C. (Ret'd)

University of Alabama
January, 1967

*THE AMPHIBIOUS
CAMPAIGN
FOR WEST FLORIDA
AND LOUISIANA*

INTRODUCTION

Dramatis Personae (in order of appearance)

So as not to interrupt the narrative of the stirring events that are about to be related, biographical information about the more important participants in the drama is given here.

Major General Andrew Jackson
(1767–1845), United States Army

Andrew Jackson was born somewhere in the Waxhaw settlement between the Carolinas. His father, also named Andrew Jackson, had come to the Carolinas in 1765 from Carrickfergus, a small town on the north coast of Ireland, with his wife, Elizabeth Hutchinson Jackson, who was by all accounts a most remarkable woman. She delivered her third child, Andrew, in a rude log cabin on the border, the exact location of which has never been determined, about a month after her husband had died very suddenly as a result of some internal injury sustained when he tried to lift a log that was too heavy for him.

Elizabeth Jackson retained title to her husband's lands and managed to rear her three sons and educate them in the available elementary country schools of the day. Andrew, though the aptest of the three children in school lessons, was never brilliant. He was rather frail, too light to wrestle, but he would fight at the drop of a hat, no matter what the odds. He was a reckless horseman. Like other boys of the frontier, he used a musket from the time he could lift one.[1]

When the Revolutionary War for Independence came to the Carolinas, Andy's eldest brother, Hugh, joined an American militia company in 1779, at the age of sixteen, and died at the Battle of Stono Ferry. The next year, Andy, aged thirteen and a half, and his other brother Robert, then sixteen, joined the dragoons of Colonel William R. Davie, and participated in the very rugged campaign against Cornwallis and Tarleton. Very little quarter was given by either side, and the Tory leader, Tarleton, gave none. Andy was for a time mounted orderly to Colonel Davie, one of the ablest of the

American partisan leaders. His influence on the course of Andy's life, though hard to define precisely, was nonetheless profound.[2]

Andy and his brother were captured on April 10, 1781, while straggling, a necessary expedient in partisan warfare. That same day a British officer ordered Andy to clean his boots, which he promptly refused to do. The officer struck a violent blow at the boy's head with a sword. Andy tried to parry the blow with his left hand, which was cut to the bone. Another gash on his head left a scar that Jackson carried the rest of his life. But he would get his revenge; that British officer's cruel arrogance brought little profit to any Britisher.[3]

Shortly after that Elizabeth Jackson rode to Camden and succeeded in getting her two sons, both of whom were wounded, released into her care by the British commander. Both boys were suffering from smallpox, and Robert died of it on the journey home. His mother's constant care saved Andy, and as soon as he was out of danger, she went to Charles Town to nurse other American sick and wounded who were prisoners there. She herself died in the epidemic she had come to help fight, sometime in November of 1781. Her grave has never been found, though Jackson spent much effort over it after he became President.[4]

As an orphan, Jackson was apprenticed by an uncle for six months to learn the saddler's trade. A small legacy from his grandfather in Ireland enabled him to escape that fate, and he began reading law in Salisbury, North Carolina. He was admitted to the bar in 1787 and began practicing as a traveling lawyer in Tennessee (then western North Carolina) in the year following, at the age of twenty-one.[5]

Within the year he was appointed public prosecutor, an office requiring a certain reckless courage in that time and place, and he was soon widely known and grudgingly respected. He later moved to Nashville and set up an active and remunerative practice there. In 1796, he sat as a delegate to a convention at Knoxville to frame a constitution for Tennessee, which was soon to become the sixteenth state of the Union. He was appointed Tennessee's first representative in Congress, and was elected to the Senate of the United States the following year.

Jackson disliked living in Washington, however, and in 1798 resigned his seat in the Senate to accept an appointment as justice of the Tennessee Supreme Court, an office he was to hold for six years. On the frontier, the office was no sinecure, and even as a judge he relied on the *code duello*.[6]

In 1801, he was elected commanding general of the Tennessee militia, in which he took great pride and interest, and he held that position until transferred to the regular army in 1814. He was a very enthusiastic "citizen-soldier" and read whatever came his way about the military art and science. He was particularly interested in the career of Napoleon Bonaparte, and he fraternized a great deal with veterans of the Revolutionary War.

Jackson hoped to be appointed governor of the new Louisiana Territory in 1803, but he really had no chance of it, since President Jefferson had taken a dislike to him while he was in the Senate. Jackson made no public comment on his disappointment, because William C. C. Claiborne, whom Jackson had considered his friend ever since they had met in Washington, was appointed instead.

Jackson's personal fortunes in Tennessee waxed and waned. He was a planter with varied interests, an inveterate gambler (especially over horses), and a land speculator. He made many bitter enemies. His killing of young Charles Dickinson in a duel in 1806 was regarded as scandalous by some, though Dickinson had provoked the duel by slandering Jackson's wife and had grievously wounded Jackson in the encounter. As a friend of Aaron Burr, Jackson became involved innocently in the early stages of that very odd "conspiracy," and he was called as a prosecution witness when Burr was tried for high treason at Richmond, Virginia. However, Jackson made no secret of his disapproval of President Jefferson's handling of the *Chesapeake* and *Leopard* affair; this, coupled with his sweeping condemnation of General James Wilkinson, the prosecution's star witness, led to Jackson's being released from his subpoena.

The incident confirmed the enmity toward Jackson of all of Jefferson's friends, including James Madison, who succeeded Jefferson as President. With the coming of the War of 1812 Jackson was rejuvenated with hope of avenging the scar he had carried on his head for thirty-two years, and of gaining military renown in battle, but he could not get active duty.[7]

Through Governor Willie Blount of Tennessee, Jackson offered in 1812 to lead 2,500 of his militia into Canada or Florida. The secretary of war, Dr. William Eustis, courteously refused that offer in a letter to Governor Blount; but in October of the same year Eustis asked Blount for 1,500 militiamen to support General Wilkinson's invasion of West Florida, preferably without Jackson. Because of Jackson's popularity in the militia (plus his promise to fight under Wilkinson's orders so long as he got a chance to fight), Blount ignored the secretary of war's preference and sent Jackson to Natchez, Mississippi with 2,700 men.[8]

Jackson took to field soldiering most readily. Leaving Nashville on January 7, 1813, in one of the coldest winters on record in those parts, he reached Natchez 39 days later, with his ruggedly individualistic Tennessee frontiersmen well in hand and in good shape. Wilkinson directed him to stay at Natchez until further orders. Then the new secretary of war, John Armstrong, a firm friend of Wilkinson, ordered Jackson, under date of February 6, 1813, to disband his troops at Natchez and to return in person to Tennessee. The men could either enlist in the regular army or make their own way home without transportation, food, or pay!

Jackson received those orders in March and promptly refused to obey them. He barred Wilkinson's recruiting officers from his camp, and brought his troops home overland on his own responsibility at his own expense (it cost him more than $1,000, an expenditure that he could ill afford). He marched the entire 800 miles on foot, giving his personal mounts to temporarily disabled soldiers. This won him the affection of his troops and enhanced their already considerable respect. He was given the nickname of "Old Hickory" during this trip, and made many enduring friendships, especially those with John Coffee and William Carroll, two of his colonels.[9] President Madison, on hearing soon after of Jackson's personal expenditures (from Colonel Thomas H. Benton, one of the Benton brothers of Nashville), ordered the federal treasury to reimburse him in full.[10]

In passing, it should be noted that while in Natchez Jackson had exchanged correspondence with his old congressional friend Governor Claiborne concerning the work then being started on the defenses of New Orleans. On the basis of the governor's letters Jackson seems to have been under the erroneous impression, prior to his arrival in New Orleans in December, 1814, that the powerful defenses described by Claiborne had been completed.[11] This, of course, affected his planning.

A few weeks after his return to Nashville as a minor hero, Jackson found himself in a feud with the Benton brothers, mentioned above. His temper led him into a taproom brawl on September 4, 1813, in which he sustained two severe bullet wounds, in his left arm and shoulder, that nearly cost him his life. While he was still in bed recovering at his plantation, the Hermitage, he received news of the Creek uprising and the Indian massacre at Fort Mims on August 20, 1813. Jackson swore vengeance on the Creeks, called out the militia without waiting for the state legislature to authorize it, and promised to lead them into battle. He did just that, most creditably, but the physical suffering it cost him was very great. The penalty that he had to pay for his puerile tavern brawl was bitter—he carried the ball in his shoulder the rest of his life—but he paid it unflinchingly.[12]

Jackson's contribution to the destruction of the Creek Nation's power and influence along the Gulf Coast was very great. Though he served loyally throughout that campaign under command of Major General Thomas Pinckney of the regular army, he was always in command on every battle-field where Tennesseans fought, except in the first engagement at Tallas-ahatchee on November 3, 1814, in which John Coffee commanded.[13]

He had long planned a war against the Creeks, partly as an outgrowth of his and John Coffee's land speculations. His plans were well laid, including much "intelligence" information concerning terrain and routes of advance that had been collected over the years by traders to the Indians.[14]

Jackson's service of supply, which he had to entrust to others, proved to be a great disappointment. His logistic planning was good, but the execution of the plans by his supply agencies was far from that. Only Jackson's strong leadership kept the Tennesseans in the field throughout the autumn and winter of 1813–1814.[15] In the final attack on Horseshoe Bend, however, the supply situation was greatly improved.

Jackson also faced serious disciplinary problems, which put him to tests that few if any American military leaders have had to deal with. But he did maintain discipline—by being tougher than the toughest frontiersman under his command.

Jackson fought his first battle at Talladega on November 9, 1813.[16] This victory, coupled with Coffee's victory of November 3, might have brought the war to a quicker conclusion, except for the failure of his service of supply. In time, his hungry men began to insist on returning to civiliza-tion for supplies, and when that failed they claimed that their term of service was ended.[17] Even the governor of Tennessee failed Jackson, there and then, by letting them go home. But Jackson managed to get a new (but not numerous) batch of recruits in January, 1814, and again took the field, rather recklessly.

He was attacked very heavily at Emucfau Creek on the morning of January 22 and was forced into retreat on the next day. He was again at-tacked at Enotochopko Creek, early on the morning of January 24. This came near to being another "Indian massacre" such as that of the River Raisin a year earlier, or Harmon's defeat in 1790 and St. Clair's in 1791 (all attributable to terrified militia). Jackson's rear guard broke and fled. With the aid of the badly wounded John Coffee, William Carroll, and about twenty other stalwarts, Jackson himself led in the restoration of the battle, and the Indians were eventually driven off. It was a costly and very narrow victory. Even Davey Crockett, who was in Jackson's ranks that day, called it a "damn tight squeeze."[18]

The "victory," such as it was, encouraged recruiting in Tennessee, and Jackson was able to take the offensive again on March 14, 1814, with a force of some 5,000 men, including a new regiment of regulars. Jackson publicly executed a mutineer just before the army moved out—in a chastened mood —at high noon. The supply problem was ended.[19]

The Battle of Tohopeka, or Horseshoe Bend, was Jackson's greatest victory over the Indians. He chose to assault the Creek fortress instead of besieging it, and he personally led the assault, which was spearheaded by the regulars. American casualties, though high, were justified by the results. When the battle was over, 557 Indian dead were counted on the ground, and the river was thought to hold some 200 more. Coffee was convinced that no less than 900 hostile Indians had been killed. Jackson had predicted such an outcome to Pinckney.[20]

The important part was that the power of the Creek Nation was broken forever—and just in time. Had the Creek leaders been able to restrain their braves until the summer of 1814, when the British army and navy were on the Gulf Coast, the subsequent course of American history might well have been changed substantially. The Creek War and Jackson's admittedly harsh treaty (which the Indians had no choice but to accept) played a most important part not only in Jackson's subsequent command decisions but also in the British plans and orders in the campaign that we are about to examine. The Creek war also uncovered and developed Jackson's natural ability as a military leader and made him the only logical person to whom the defense of the Gulf Coast against the British could be entrusted—no matter how the powers in Washington felt toward him personally.[21]

Vice-Admiral Sir Alexander Forrester Inglis Cochrane (1758–1832), British Navy

Alexander Cochrane, as the younger son of the eighth earl of Dundonald, had his own way to make in the world. He entered the Royal Navy at an early age, becoming a lieutenant in 1778 (in those days, it is worth noting, all naval promotions in the junior ranks up to captain were purchased), and was wounded in a naval action off Martinique in 1780. Nevertheless, he continued on duty in the West Indies under the famous admiral, Sir George Rodney, during the remaining years of the American Revolution. By one account, he lost a very good friend at Yorktown and bore Americans much ill will thereafter, but he did not have a bad disposition in general. On the contrary, he is frequently described as rather courtly and very much a gentleman, especially after he reached senior flag rank.

Following the Revolutionary War, Cochrane went on half pay—another British naval custom of the time—and remained on this status until 1790, when he was given command of a frigate, on which he cruised with distinguished success against French commerce.

During the Egyptian campaign, 1798–1801, he rose to command of H.M.S. *Ajax*, an 80-gun ship of the line. He superintended the landing of troops in Egypt and served in close support of the troops after they were ashore by operating a flotilla of armed boats on Lake Marotis. For this service he won high praise from both the naval and military high commands, and he was marked for future amphibious warfare assignments.

After the Peace of Amiens, Cochrane went on inactive status again, and entered Parliament. Upon the resumption of the war with Napoleon, he returned to active duty and was promoted to rear admiral on April 23, 1804. In command of five ships of the line and three frigates, he pursued a French squadron to the West Indies in 1805. He did not make contact with his quarry, but he did join and serve with Lord Nelson in the West Indies, and before Nelson returned to Europe he made Cochrane commander-in-chief of the Leeward Islands. In that role he remained afloat in his flagship, H.M.S. *Northumberland* (74 guns), and served in the West Indies continuously from this time until the autumn of 1813. He was senior naval commander in several amphibious operations, including Martinique in 1807, where Sir Edward Pakenham commanded a regiment of the landing force.

Cochrane gained high honors for his part in the naval battle of San Domingo on February 6, 1806. His flagship was called on for some very fierce fighting, in which the majority of his crew were casualties. Cochrane became a Knight of the Bath as a result of this action.

He was promoted to vice-admiral on October 25, 1809 and then commanded the large amphibious attack force at Guadeloupe, the last French stronghold in the West Indies, from January to March, 1810. He remained in Guadeloupe after its surrender, serving as governor of the island until he was told of his coming appointment to the command of the entire North American naval station. He relieved Vice-Admiral Sir John Borlase Warren at Bermuda on April 1, 1814, with his flag in H.M.S. *Tonant* (80 guns), having spent the previous winter in England participating in the joint army–navy planning of the forthcoming campaign in North America. In furtherance of those plans, Cochrane was present at all operations in Chesapeake Bay in the summer and fall of 1814, and of course at the landing attack at New Orleans in December. It appears that he was selected to command the latter project because of his long and continuous cooperation with the amphibious landing forces of the British Army and his acquaintance with the Caribbean Sea and the Gulf of Mexico.

Cochrane was made G.C.B. in January, 1815, was promoted to full admiral on August 12, 1819, and was appointed commander-in-chief at Plymouth in 1821—facts indicating that he was not considered disgraced by the unfavorable outcome of the New Orleans expedition.[22]

William Darby (1775–1854)

Darby, a self-educated son of Irish immigrants, came to the Mississippi Territory in 1799 and became a surveyor. In 1809, at his own expense, he began extensive explorations of the Louisiana and Mississippi Territories, completing his map in New Orleans in 1814, just in time for it to be available to Jackson, on whose topographical and engineering staff Darby served (under Major Howell Tatum). Darby built a fort for Jackson at the junction of Terre aux Boeufs and Lake Lery, covering the Terre aux Boeufs and the Rivière aux Chênes, but he saw no action in the siege of New Orleans itself.

The map of the area that was published in his book, *Geographical Description of the State of Louisiana and the Southern Part of the State of Mississippi, and the Territory of Alabama* (New York: James Olmstead, 1817), was endorsed by Andrew Jackson himself, on April 5, 1815, as being accurate and valuable. This book, which is a very graphic and picturesque geographical description of the area, is of even greater use to modern historians, since the terrain is now quite different from what it was in Darby's time. Between July 9, 1805 and May 7, 1815, Darby traveled 20,000 miles, mostly on foot, working on his map. In his book he deplored the treatment being accorded the Creoles of Louisiana by many of the Anglo-Saxons who had come to Louisiana after its purchase. It is unpleasant to relate that because Darby could not copyright his famous map he made no pecuniary profit from his ten years of effort. In history, however, he now gets credit for his very valuable work.[23]

Master Commandant Daniel T. Patterson
(1781–1839), United States Navy

Patterson was twenty-nine years of age when he met his opposite number, Major General Andrew Jackson, at New Orleans on December 1, 1814. Fourteen of the twenty-nine years had been spent in the navy. Early in his career, he had made two cruises against the West Indian pirates, and in 1804 he had been aboard the U.S.S. *Philadelphia* operating against the Barbary Coast pirates when she ran aground in the harbor of Tripoli. As one of that unfortunate ship's crew, he had been imprisoned for some nineteen months, and his subsequent animosity toward pirates in general is quite understandable.

For over a year after his return to the United States, he served his first tour of duty at the New Orleans Naval Station in 1806–1807. During this period he married a New Orleans girl—but an American like himself, not a Creole. He was serving at that time under Captain—later Commodore—David Porter.

After another tour at sea, Patterson was sent back to the Mississippi River area to command a flotilla of twelve gunboats based at Natchez, Mississippi, from January, 1810 to February, 1811. He then became second-in-command, under Captain John Shaw, of the New Orleans Naval Station. He lived through all of the horrors of the single army-navy command regime of General Wilkinson, and, with the remainder of the naval forces, writhed at the overbearing audacity and impunity of the Baratarians under the naval command regimes of both Porter and Shaw.

Patterson was promoted to master commandant (then the grade just below that of captain in the navy) on July 24, 1813, and in December he relieved Shaw as commanding officer of the naval station. As had his predecessor, Porter, Shaw had demanded relief—neither he nor Porter could foresee anything but defeat and disgrace if the war ever came to New Orleans—and he even threatened to resign his commission unless relieved. Captain Charles Ludlow, who was then ordered from Philadelphia as a relief for Shaw, shared Porter's and Shaw's pessimistic view, and he actually did resign from the navy in order to avoid duty at New Orleans. Nobody else would go, it seemed, and so it had to be Patterson—if Shaw were to be kept in the navy. The assignment could not be considered, then or now, as any special mark of confidence in Patterson.

Before meeting Jackson in person, Patterson had convinced the general, by exchange of several letters with him at Mobile, of the command relationship established between the secretary of war and the secretary of the navy in January, 1813. There was no longer a senior commander, as there had been under Wilkinson and Shaw. Cooperation between equals in command was thereafter the practice.

Patterson was also the first commandant of the New Orleans Naval Station to whom the Navy Department provided forces adequate for dealing with the Baratarian pirates. The U.S.S. *Carolina* was sent to him in August, 1814 for that express purpose. (Porter and Shaw had begged for such authority, but in vain.) Patterson broke up the Baratarian den of iniquity in September, 1814 and brought a considerable number of small piratical craft and much naval stores back from the freebooters' lair. At the time of Jackson's arrival in New Orleans the admiralty courts had yet to make a judgment in the premises, and the captured matériel was all at the Navy Yard.

It is worthy of noting that the file of Master Commandants' letters to the secretary of the navy contains a remarkably prophetic letter from Patterson, dated November 18, 1814, in which he foretold a landing of the British on the banks of the Mississippi and their progress toward the city along a narrow strip of land between the river and the swamp. This advance would be defeated, he predicted, by his larger vessels, the U.S.S. *Carolina* and the U.S.S. *Louisiana* (if he could get a crew for the latter), acting from the river in support of the American army on shore. Patterson must have expected the British fleet to force a passage up the river, but he might also have thought of a British penetration through the swamps. Be that as it may, there is no record of his having communicated this premonition to Jackson, and so it is a matter of passing interest only. In no way did it affect the course of the battle.[24]

William Charles Coles Claiborne (1775–1817), First Governor of the State of Louisiana

Claiborne had been a friend—a genial acquaintance, anyway—of Andrew Jackson during the latter's service in Congress between 1796 and 1798, and over the years the two men had exchanged considerable correspondence concerning New Orleans. Claiborne was a most prolific letter-writer, and his letters were often prolix. They indicate that he was alternately optimistic and pessimistic about the loyalty to the United States, or lack of such loyalty, of his Louisianians of Latin descent.

Claiborne was a man who placed his own notions of dignity and personal integrity above all other considerations. Commodore David Porter, the first commandant of the naval station, considered him to be obnoxiously vain, and Jackson eventually came to share this opinion.

As the first governor of the Territory of Louisiana, appointed by his fellow Virginian Thomas Jefferson, Claiborne served under great handicaps, personal and official. He spoke no French when appointed, and it appears that during the next twelve years he never took the trouble to learn any. As governor of Mississippi Territory he had acted for Jefferson as one of the two commissioners who accepted Louisiana from France in 1803, and he was the President's proconsular representative thereafter until his appointment as governor. General James Wilkinson was one of the trials he had to bear, the Burr Conspiracy was another, and then there was the problem of the Baratarian smugglers or pirates, a problem that worsened steadily as time went on. It has been truly said that Claiborne achieved an honorable record of service on a disturbed frontier during a transitional period of uncertainty and turmoil. There can be no doubt that he was a man of good motives and mild temper, and that he was scrupulously honest, diligent, and a loyal servant of the republic. And he did manage to win election by the voters of Louisiana as their first state governor in 1812. But this did not mean that he had won the hearts of the Creoles. *That* he never did.[25]

Judge François-Xavier Martin, a contemporary civil servant in New Orleans, thought Claiborne irresolute at times, and a man inclined to magnify his difficulties. To Claiborne, any opposition seemed treasonous. His correspondence shows that he was changeful in his impressions and wavering in the expression of his opinions.

After Jackson's arrival in New Orleans, his friendly feeling for Claiborne was soon dispelled. The erroneous information about the defenses of New Orleans that Claiborne sent to Jackson at Natchez in 1813 may have been part of it. But of greater importance, probably, was Claiborne's insistence on sharing Jackson's authority, even the military command, in spite of his complete lack of military knowledge and experience. Claiborne actually took to the field and claimed command authority subordinate only to Jackson, and direct command of all of his state's militia. He wrote to the secretary of war on December 9, 1814, asking for a confirmation of that peculiar command relationship, but in vain.

In his handling of Claiborne's pretensions Jackson displayed sagacity, tact, and considerable leadership ability. Rather than challenge the governor directly, he simply put Claiborne in command of the militia troops on the Plain of Gentilly—and left him there. Claiborne's writings show that he was far from happy over this, and there is no record of anything but coldness between Jackson and Claiborne after December 22, 1814.[26]

Of course, it should also be remembered that Edward Livingston became an aide of Jackson, and there is no question that he was Claiborne's enemy before he was Jackson's counsellor.

One of the traditions of the Battle of New Orleans revolves around Claiborne—that he did not understand the Creoles and misrepresented them to Jackson with unfortunate results. On the contrary, it seems that he may have understood some of them only too well, and that Jackson was well advised to depend chiefly on his regulars and Tennesseans. Even so, the uniformed companies of New Orleans and the majority of Creoles conducted themselves in a manner that was above reproach. Claiborne's doubts were justified only in respect to certain individuals and some militia.

Arsène Lacarrière Latour

Major Latour served as a volunteer on Jackson's staff section of engineers during the New Orleans campaign. He was a Frenchman who had emigrated to Santo Domingo about 1793, and moved to New Orleans in 1810 as one of a great many French refugees from the French islands. Guadeloupe, the last French colonial holding in the West Indies, fell to Vice-Admiral Cochrane and Major General Sir George Beckwith in March of that year.

In 1813 Latour helped a Major Bartholomew Lafon make a map of the vicinity of New Orleans for Brigadier General Thomas Flournoy, Jackson's

predecessor in command of the District of Louisiana and Mississippi. Latour was recommended to Jackson by Edward Livingston, and he seems to
have served the general well throughout the battle. Latour was a friend and
associate of the Baratarian pirate Jean Laffite, and it was he who introduced
Laffite to Jackson on December 18, 1814. Subsequent to the War of 1812,
according to Edwin H. Carpenter, Latour and Laffite were both to be
agents of the king of Spain in the southwest United States.

Latour wrote in French and published in English a most useful *Historical
Memoir of the War in West Florida and Louisiana, 1814–15* (Philadelphia,
1816). It is a source book for the battle, written by an eyewitness who was
close to Jackson, and though it can be contradicted successfully in places, it
is, in the main, excellent basic history and includes much pertinent and
valuable information about the planned and the actual defenses on the west
bank of the Mississippi that Latour designed on Jackson's orders.[27]

Major General John Keane (1781–1844)
British Army

John Keane was the son of a baronet member of Parliament who must have
had powerful family friends indeed, since Keane's assignments of duty from
the moment of his entrance into the army, in 1794, as a captain at the age
of thirteen, were light and congenial, consisting of a series of home staff
assignments. He saw active duty for the first time in 1809, when as a colonel
he served without distinction under the Duke of Wellington in Spain.
Nonetheless, he was promoted to major general on June 4, 1814, and
somehow he contrived to get himself placed in command of the first group
of reinforcements ordered to Major General Robert Ross' command in
September, 1814.

With Admiral Cochrane, Keane and the reinforcements arrived at Negril Bay, Jamaica, on November 25, 1814, where he found himself, quite by
accident, in command of the landing troops—Ross having been killed in
action at Baltimore. In fact, owing to his peculiar orders from the War
Office, Keane was a stooge for Cochrane. The War Office apparently did not
consider him qualified for independent command, and his orders allowed
him no initiative in dealing with Cochrane. When Lord Bathurst learned of
the death of Ross he made every effort to get Keane superseded in command
by Major General John Lambert, pending the arrival of Lieutenant Gen-

eral Sir Edward Pakenham. Considering the importance of the expedition, it is very difficult for this writer to understand how the War Office could have risked the possibility of Keane's ever assuming command responsibilities as a result of misadventure.

As it happened, Cochrane personally determined the location of the landing beachhead, with or without Keane's concurrence (which Cochrane would have had to obtain from Ross or Lambert or Pakenham). And it was Cochrane who assembled the landing force from its various transports at Pea Island in Lake Borgne. General Keane reviewed the army there on December 21, 1814 and organized it for landing. The following morning, he commanded the advance party of about 1,000 troops, accompanied by a rocket battery and two pieces of light field artillery.

Keane was able to advance all the way to the left bank of the Mississippi River before disclosing himself and his men, whereupon he fatefully elected to await reinforcement before advancing further. This may have been the most colossal blunder of the entire campaign, for Jackson promptly snatched the initiative from him by attacking on the night of the 23rd.

Subsequently, Keane commanded, without distinction, one of the two brigades into which Pakenham divided the army soon after his arrival on Christmas Day. Keane was badly wounded on January 8, 1815, and so took no further part in the operations at Mobile.[28]

Lieutenant General Sir Edward Michael Pakenham (1778–1815), British Army

General Pakenham was a second son and his education was rather perfunctory, but the fact that he entered the army at the age of sixteen partly explains that, and in any case his lack of learning does not seem to have harmed his military career: he fought as a lieutenant in the Irish Rebellion and was promoted to the rank of major before his seventeenth birthday. Unlike Keane, Pakenham began acquiring solid battle experience while very young. He became a lieutenant colonel of the 64th in 1799, at the age of twenty-one, and led it to the West Indies in a series of amphibious operations against the Swedish and Danish islands. Upon resumption of the war with Napoleon in 1803, Pakenham's excellent experience in the conduct of amphibious operations was put to use at St. Lucia, but he was badly wounded in the combat on June 21. He then served for a short time in Nova Scotia.

By 1805 he had recovered from his wound and was brevetted to colonel, with permanent rank as lieutenant colonel of the 7th Royal Fusiliers, which he led ashore in the amphibious campaign at Copenhagen. In 1807, he and his regiment participated in the amphibious attack on Martinique, where Rear Admiral Cochrane was the senior naval commander. That the two met there is certain, but Lieutenant General Sir George Beckwith was the senior troop commander. Again Sir Edward was wounded, the second wound correcting a cock of the head caused by the wound he had sustained at St. Lucia.

Pakenham did not join his sister's husband, the Duke of Wellington, until just after the Battle of Talavera (July 20, 1809), but his reputation as a leader in battle was already well established before he went to Spain. He was assigned as assistant adjutant general for a time after his arrival, but in 1810 he led a brigade (his own elite, veteran 7th Fusiliers and the Cameron Scotch Highlanders) at the battles of Busaco and Fuentes d'Onoro. He was made a major general in 1811, and in the Battle of Salamanca, on July 22, 1812, he commanded the Third Division, Wellington's center. The Iron Duke afterward called that battle the best maneuvered battle of the war. By a dashing though costly attack at exactly the right moment, Pakenham broke the French line and covered himself and his division with glory. The story of his gallant assault is told by Sir William Napier in great detail in his account of the Peninsular War. John W. Cole tells of Sir Edward's early career in great and glowing detail, too. Wellington said of him, "Pakenham may not be the brightest genius, but my partiality for him does not lead me astray when I tell you he is one of the best we have."

After Salamanca, Sir Edward went back to staff duty for a time, and he seems to have become quite good at it. (Wellington was to deplore his absence at Waterloo, where he thought the British staff work was terrible.)

Pakenham was again in active command of his division for the invasion of France, and added considerably to his battle honors there. He was made a Knight of the Bath in 1813, and a G.C.B. in 1815, though he never learned of that last honor.

He was appointed to command the expedition to New Orleans on October 24, 1814, with explicit secret instructions that he was not to suspend hostilities on account of any report of a peace treaty until he had positive information of ratification, which would only come to him by a special emissary of the prince regent himself.

The appointment of Pakenham to command was well received every-where. Sir Edward Codrington, Cochrane's "captain of the fleet" (in modern naval parlance, chief-of-staff), said that Pakenham was "the next to look to after Wellington." The contention has often been made by some American writers that Sir Edward Pakenham was merely a nepotic selection of Wellington, just a staff general, thoroughly inexperienced in independent command, with no knowledge of America, no real military knowledge, or education, arrogantly proud of British might, and on the whole quite incompetent, however "brave" he may personally have been. Thus critics of Andrew Jackson, and they are numerous, allege or insinuate that Pakenham lost the battle, and that Jackson and his men cannot be given much credit for winning it. The facts do not lend much support to this view.

Pakenham sailed from England on the frigate H.M.S. *Statira*, which had an unlucky reputation in the fleet, on October 28, 1814, accompanied by his excellent staff and his second-in-command, Major General Sir Samuel Gibbs. The captain of the vessel, venerable and anything but an incautious sailor, *insisted*, despite all remonstrances, on shortening sail every night. But for that, and the fact that the captain's navigation was not of the best, Pakenham might well have arrived as many as ten days sooner than he did. And had he done so, the entire course of events at New Orleans would almost certainly have been quite different than it was, for not only Pakenham's own talents and experience, but also those of his staff officers, would have been brought to bear on the battle in its early stages.

Pakenham's staff included Colonel Alexander Dickson as chief of artillery, Colonel John Fox Burgoyne as chief of engineers, and Major Harry Smith (later a famous general in his own right) as his assistant adjutant general. All three were Peninsular War heroes, having served on the Duke of Wellington's superb staff, and all three were later to serve very brilliantly under Wellington at Waterloo. And Pakenham's second-in-command, Major General Gibbs, was an experienced officer with battle honors won in India and Java, and with experience in amphibious warfare in the latter campaign.

The *Statira* arrived at Negril Bay to find that the expedition was already on target, but they did encounter General John Lambert's brigade of reinforcements there. Pakenham had been told in England that the 40th Foot, and the field artillery train as well, had already been ordered to his command, even before Lambert's brigade had received its orders.

Pakenham hastened on to his rendezvous with death, arriving at the Villeré plantation on Christmas Day, 1814 to find his entire landing force ashore in a cul-de-sac on the left bank of the Mississippi, already badly shaken by Jackson's night attack of December 23, and with its camp under constant bombardment by two American warships in the river.

American writers have asserted that Sir Edward had been promised an earl's coronet for his expected conquest of Louisiana. No British source has been found to confirm this, and it is probably just another American myth, as false as Alexander Walker's story of a Lady Pakenham waiting offshore to become the first lady of Louisiana and a countess. Sir Edward was most definitely unmarried.

What little remained of this unfortunate young man's too short life was spent in trying to recover control of a bad situation that was not of his making. He died in the attempt on January 8, 1815, at the age of thirty-six.[29]

Colonel Alexander Dickson (1777–1840), British Army

Dickson attended the Royal Military Academy in Woolwich, entering the Royal Artillery from there in 1794. He served overseas almost constantly during the Napoleonic Wars, and he so distinguished himself while serving with the Portuguese army in 1810 that he was brevetted to command the artillery of that army, which made him outrank many British artillery officers in the Portuguese service. Wellington was never happy with his artillery until, in 1813, he chose Dickson as his artillery chief, when his rank (less his brevet title) was that of a mere captain. Dickson not only handled the job to the satisfaction of the Iron Duke, but also to the satisfaction of his artillerymen, many of whom were senior to him in permanent rank. He was marked in Spain as a great artilleryman and a most industrious and methodical collector and registrar of details which came under his notice. Just a glance at the journal of his American campaign (finally published in 1929) proves that this reputation was well justified by the facts. He was selected to accompany Sir Edward Pakenham to New Orleans as his chief of artillery.

Sir Alexander Dickson and Sir Harry Smith had served in the disastrous British landing at Buenos Aires in 1806 before going to the Peninsula, and were no strangers to fields of bloody slaughter. Dickson would later be the Iron Duke's chief of artillery at Waterloo, and would serve his country with great distinction as an artillery inspector and chief until his death. He was especially noteworthy for the tremendous loyalty and affection that were accorded him by associates and subordinates throughout his life. He was truly an artillery genius of his day.[30]

Colonel John Fox Burgoyne (1782–1871), British Army

As the illegitimate son of an unsuccessful and eventually unpopular general, "Gentleman Johnny" Burgoyne (the man who planned, organized, led, and lost the Saratoga campaign in North America in 1777), John Fox Burgoyne could hardly expect any special consideration in a military career. He had to make his own way on his own merits, and he did so amazingly well. The legitimate successor to his father's title sent John to Eton and then to the Royal Military Academy at Woolwich, from which he was gazetted to the Royal Engineers in 1798—in itself a remarkable achievement for a bastard son in those days. The engineers and artillery, the elite branches of the army, were the only services that received any military education. Burgoyne served overseas almost constantly from 1798 until the end of the Napoleonic Wars at Waterloo. He served in Malta, Sicily, and Egypt (where he was made commanding engineer as a second captain). He was in Portugal in 1807 and in Sweden the following year, and then became chief engineer for the immortal Sir John Moore at Corunna, where he covered that masterly retreat in brilliant fashion. Burgoyne joined the Iron Duke in Portugal, 1809, and was the engineer who built the impregnable lines at Torres Vedras. He conducted the engineering at the siege of Badajoz in 1811, for which he was brevetted to lieutenant colonel. He served with distinction at Vittoria, and was royal engineer at the sieges of San Sebastian and Bayonne. Nevertheless, preference was given in honors at the end of the war to a much less able engineer, a member of the nobility whose coat of arms would never carry a bar sinister. Burgoyne was gazetted a C.B. (but not a K.C.B.) in 1814, but he was proud enough to refuse civil knighthood, since he considered it a slight to his profession. He did accept the Order of the Tower and Sword from the king of Portugal.[31]

Major General John Lambert (1772–1847), British Army

John Lambert was commissioned as an ensign in the First Foot Guards on July 27, 1791, at the age of nineteen, promoted to captain on October 9, 1793, to lieutenant colonel on May 14, 1801, and to colonel on July 25, 1810. Along the way, he saw active duty in the Irish Rebellion of 1798, in the expedition into Holland in 1799, and in Portugal and Spain in 1808. He was present with Sir John Moore in the Corunna campaign. He next commanded the light companies of the Guards in the rugged Walcheren Expedition of 1809. Thus Lambert was obviously a seasoned veteran before he ever joined the Iron Duke in Spain, which he did with the Third Battalion of the First Foot Guards at Salamanca. (By then he had already been in Spain since the summer of 1811, at Cadiz and Carthagena.)

He was promoted to major general on June 4, 1813 and put in command of a brigade of the Sixth Division of the Iron Duke's army. He and the brigade served gallantly at the battles of Nivelle, Nive, Orthes, and Toulouse, being especially mentioned in dispatches at Nivelle and Toulouse. For this he would eventually receive the thanks of Parliament, be awarded a gold cross, and become a Knight Counsellor of the Bath on January 2, 1815, while at New Orleans.

He commanded a brigade of reinforcements, the 7th Fusiliers and the 43rd, which reached Sir Edward Pakenham's army below New Orleans on January 6, 1815.

Upon the deaths of Pakenham and his second-in-command on January 8, 1815, Lambert succeeded to command at New Orleans and made the decision to withdraw the army from that city. He successfully resumed the offensive at Fort Bowyer, but was there informed of the exchange of ratifications of the Treaty of Peace and returned soon after to Europe with his troops, arriving in time to join Wellington in Belgium, where the Iron Duke was facing Napoleon.

Lambert commanded the 10th Brigade at the Battle of Waterloo, where he lost two-thirds of his command in the very fierce fighting at La Haye Sainte, the heaviest casualties of any brigade in the battle. He was commended by the Duke of Wellington, and received high honors from Parliament, with additional decorations from Russia and Austria.[32]

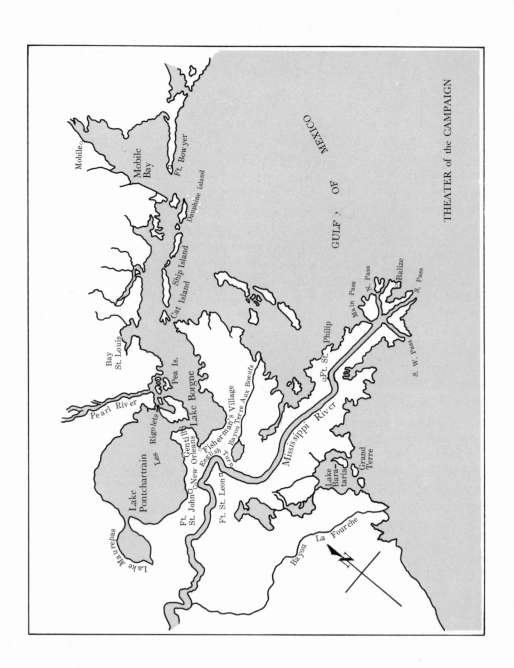

THEATER of the CAMPAIGN

Map   1

1. STATUS OF WAR
WITH GREAT BRITAIN IN
THE SOUTHWEST
IN 1814

On May 22, 1814, Andrew Jackson was put in command of the Seventh Military District (Louisiana, Mississippi Territory, and Tennessee), succeeding Brigadier General Thomas Flournoy. On the same day Jackson was promoted to the rank of brigadier general in the regular army of the United States, and six days later he was promoted to the rank of major general.[1]

Even if these items of news had been immediately disseminated throughout Europe, they probably would have attracted little or no attention. Too much else was happening. Just a little more than a month before, Napoleon Bonaparte had been forced to abdicate (April 11, 1814). Then, with Bonaparte safely installed as "emperor" of the island of Elba, the Treaty of Paris was signed on May 30 and the French monarchy was restored in the person of Louis XVIII. Thus, for the first time since the Wars of the French Revolution had begun in 1792, Europe was at peace—at least for the moment.

Great Britain, which had been at war with France continuously since 1803, could now turn her full attention to the "American War of 1812." British merchants at home and Russia abroad were united in urging peace, and the British cabinet was also quite ready for peace, but only on its own terms—after the Americans had been properly chastised. The British press, never friendly to Americans, had become increasingly bitter and contemptuous toward them during the first two years of the war, and early in January, 1814, a large part of the press had begun a campaign of intense vilification and misrepresentation of the United States.[2]

The initial demands of the British government at the peace conference were entirely in accord with the vindictive sentiments of the press. The demands were set forth by Foreign Secretary Lord Castlereagh in a document prepared for Lord Bathurst who, as Secretary of War and of Colonies, was acting for Castlereagh while the latter was at the Congress of Vienna.[3]

In essence, the British demanded:

(1) the establishment of a new boundary line from Nova Scotia and

New Brunswick through northern Maine along the forty-seventh parallel, plus the islands in Passamaquoddy Bay;

(2) that the American–Indian boundary established by the Treaty of Greenville in 1795 be made permanent, with all the Northwest Territory north of the line to be an Indian reserve guaranteed jointly by the two powers, this provision to be a *sine qua non* of any treaty;

(3) the renewal of Article III of Jay's Treaty, whereby navigation rights of all lakes, rivers, and waters of the interior of the continent (except for territory of the Hudson Bay Company) were to be reciprocal (and specifically stipulating British navigation rights on the Mississippi River);

(4) the prohibition of United States war vessels on the Great Lakes, and the cession to Canada of Michilimackinac and a strip of land on the east side of the Niagara River;

(5) that the international line extend straight to the source of the Mississippi, if a boundary from Lake Superior could not be obtained; and

(6) termination of the American right of fishing in British territorial waters and of drying on British shores.[4]

This document, which had been published in England and in Canada, was quoted by an American periodical (from a Canadian source), and shows still another British demand of great interest to this discussion:

(7) The Americans not to be allowed to incorporate the Floridas with their republic; and the cession of New Orleans to be required in order to insure to us the enjoyment of our privileges to navigate the Mississippi; and here it may also be a question, in how far the arrangements made between Spain, France, and America, respecting Louisiana, can come into discussion.[5]

These designs were republished widely by newspapers and periodicals in the United States. Whether or not they reflected the unalterable will of the British government is uncertain—and unimportant, since continued American resistance to British encroachments was motivated not so much by Britain's actual war aims as by what Americans believed those aims to be.

When the fall of Napoleon freed the British army and navy from most of their commitments elsewhere, the British government sent some 20,000 troops to North America. Their plan was to invade the United States in 1814 successively from Niagara, Lake Champlain, Chesapeake Bay, and New Orleans, and simultaneously to raid the United States coast at various points under cover of a strict blockade. The main effort was to be an amphibious invasion at New Orleans, to be accomplished during the mild weather of the late autumn.[6]

The American high command at first ignored the British threat to New Orleans. Secretary of War John Armstrong, on June 25, 1814, assured Jackson that there would be no more fighting on the southern front. Rumors of Spanish or British agents inciting the Indians were utterly incredible, he said, and a report of a British naval force on the Gulf Coast was of nearly the same character. Jackson was instructed to dismiss all but a thousand of his men.[7] Fortunately, however, Jackson remained alert to the British menace on the Gulf Coast. He flatly contradicted Armstrong's estimate of the situation, and he asked for authority to attack Pensacola.

The British knew that the United States government was not worried about any threat to New Orleans. They also believed, erroneously, that Jackson himself was unaware of their projected venture, and that he was concerned about the Georgia coast but little else.[8] Jackson was still an unknown quantity to them. The British troops in America who had heard of him at all thought of Jackson as an untutored general of militia whose only battle experience was that gained against the Creek Indians.

The regular army component of the Seventh Military District, according to a War Department general order, was to be the 2nd and 7th Infantry Regiments plus a few artillerists, dragoons, and riflemen. The 3rd Infantry, which had been ordered from the Seventh to the Eighth District (Kentucky, Ohio, and the Northwest Territory) when Flournoy took command, had been retained for his use in the Creek War. The 3rd still remained under Jackson's command after that war. Meanwhile, the War Department had recruited two new regular regiments in the Seventh District, the 44th in Louisiana and the 39th in Tennessee. The 39th had served gallantly against the Creeks at Horseshoe Bend, and had then proceeded to Mobile.[9]

American naval strength at New Orleans consisted of a sloop, the U.S.S. *Louisiana* (which had no crew and could not enlist one), and six of Thomas Jefferson's ridiculous gunboats, "which could go to sea only if they put their guns in the hold."[10] The authorized strength of the five army regiments assigned to Jackson's Seventh Military District was 2,378 men in five regiments, plus 350 artillerists scattered through the district.[11] All of the regiments were understrength, however, and only the 39th and a part of the 3rd had ever been in battle—and then only in the Creek War.

This was a dangerously small force with which to defend the entire South-

west—a vast, sparsely populated area in which there were almost no prepared fortifications, few (and very poor) roads, and no manufacturing
facilities to provide arms for its scant militia, but having perhaps more than
its share of serious Indian and Negro "problems." The Louisianians, who
had lived in dread of a major slave revolt ever since the one in Haiti, had already experienced several minor revolts, including one as recently as January, 1811. The Louisianians themselves were a racial and linguistic potpour-
ri, and the loyalty of many of them to the United States was open to serious
doubt. General Flournoy had asserted to the secretary of war on January 24,
1814, that in the event of war not one Louisianian in twenty would fight for
the United States.[12]

On August 22, 1814, General Jackson arrived at Mobile with the 3rd Infantry—531 strong—and set about preparing to defend the Gulf Coast
against the British and their allies. He had expected the British to land in
the vicinity of Mobile, to drive inland to Walnut Hills (now Vicksburg) in
order to close the river there, and then to descend on New Orleans from the
north.[13] Now, however, after personally reconnoitering the coastal area, he
realized that the British might well choose to land at Pascagoula, with a view
to closing the river at Baton Rouge. Still another possibility was a shore-to-
shore landing across Lake Pontchartrain from a base in Pascagoula. The
British could probably secure enough horses from the Spaniards to supply a
column that would advance through the intervening few miles. Captain
Hugh Pigot of the Royal Navy had so reported to the British high command, following a prolonged reconnaissance on shore during the previous
May. Pigot believed that horses were so plentiful on the Gulf that the British, if they provided accoutrements, could even mount Indians as cavalry-
men, with quite enough horses left over for transport. The plan actually
adopted by the British, following their failure at New Orleans, was the one
first considered by Jackson: invasion by way of Mobile. Admiral Sir Alexander Cochrane, as late as September 2, 1814, wrote to Lord Bathurst that
he proposed landing the British forces at Mobile, taking New Orleans first,
and then the rest of Louisiana—all of which could be accomplished, he predicted, by March, 1815.[14]

However, the British offensive in the North did not go entirely according to plan. In May, 1814, about 10,000 of Wellington's veterans left Bor-

deaux for Canada to launch the Lake Champlain offensive. On June 2, Major General Robert Ross left the Gironde with 3,000 more, to join Cochrane at Bermuda. That summer, while Jackson was en route to Mobile, the United States suffered grievous and humiliating losses in the Chesapeake Bay area. But the critical British attack on Baltimore was repulsed in September, and the invasion from Canada was positively turned back by Captain Thomas MacDonough's astounding naval victory on Lake Champlain, September 11, 1814.

Cochrane had landed Ross and his veterans at the mouth of the Patuxent River in Chesapeake Bay in August, 1814. Their triple mission was to destroy the gunboats of Commodore Joshua Barney, to raid Washington and Alexandria, and to capture Baltimore. On August 22, Barney destroyed his own gunboats to prevent their seizure, and led his sailors and marines as a naval brigade to join Brigadier General William H. Winder's 7,000 militia, who were supposedly defending the capital. But at the Battle of Bladensburg, on August 24, only Barney's naval brigade stood to fight.

Paradoxically, the conduct of Winder's army, disgraceful and deplorable though it was, may ultimately have proved beneficial to the American cause in the Southwest. The utter contempt in which all those British veterans, army and navy, held American arms was based in large measure on the behavior of Winder's militia, and the British who faced Jackson's forces at New Orleans confidently expected another Bladensburg rout.

Colonel William Thornton and his 85th Light Regiment, later important at New Orleans, carried Barney's position with a reckless attack, albeit with heavy losses. Several public buildings in Washington were burned by the direct order—indeed under the personal supervision—of Admiral Sir George Cockburn and General Ross, whereupon the British boarded their transports to descend on Baltimore, fully expecting to win tremendous prize money from the capture of that port city.

Unfortunately for the British, however, General Samuel Smith's defense of the city withstood Ross' landing attack of September 12. British casualties were generally quite heavy and included Ross himself, who died in the battle. The British naval bombardment of Fort McHenry was also unsuccessful, after which the army made a rapid withdrawal to the transports, and the joint force finally left Chesapeake Bay for Jamaica on October 14.

One supposed reason for abandonment of the enterprise at Baltimore was the next objective: the city of New Orleans. Bathurst had, however, on orders of Prime Minister Lord Liverpool, ostensibly authorized abandonment of the New Orleans objective if something better could be accomplished at Baltimore.[15] A dispatch from Bathurst to the British landing force commander with Admiral Cochrane, dated September 22, 1814, authorizing the abandonment of the New Orleans objective, did not arrive in America until after the 40th Foot reached New Orleans in mid-January, 1815. The fact that Bathurst entrusted delivery of the message to the commanding officer of the 40th Foot suggests strongly that Bathurst did not want the commanding general in America to have the alternative objective, since the 40th Foot was ordered directly to New Orleans, and its sailing date was delayed several times.

The American government, impoverished in general and now temporarily paralyzed by the raid on the Chesapeake, did not awaken to the danger to New Orleans until late September, and even then it did almost nothing to aid Jackson. Letters were sent from the War Department to governors of Tennessee and Georgia (September 25, 1814) and to the governor of Kentucky (October 10, 1814) asking them to help Jackson, and all three responded affirmatively, but Jackson and the westerners were left with the responsibility. Washington did not even order guns and ammunition sent to New Orleans from Pittsburgh until November. On September 5, 1814, Secretary of War James Monroe called for Jackson to organize all the friendly Indians into his army instead of militia because it was feared that the Choctaws had become disaffected. "Indians must be . . . made to fight," he said. On September 27, 1814, Monroe informed Jackson that the attack would come against Louisiana through Mobile, that Spain would probably attack from Texas, and that a slave insurrection would paralyze the Louisiana militia. On October 28, 1814, Monroe forbade operations against Pensacola, and stated that the first British objective would probably be New Orleans. But this last letter was not received until after the end of the war, and like Bathurst's dispatch of September 2 it may never have been intended as a directive to be obeyed.[16] Jackson had already received a contradictory opinion from the War Office. The procurement agency of the Ordnance Department at Pittsburgh sent forward a vital War Department requisition with criminal slowness, in order to save money. At that time there were a number of Americans, especially in New England, who were quite indifferent to the fate of New Orleans. Indeed, some of them appear to have hoped not for an American victory in Louisiana, but for another defeat that could be held against the Madison administration.

Vice Admiral Sir Alexander Cochrane assumed command of the British naval forces in North American waters on April 1, 1814. He had been in London during the previous winter, and had participated in the British government's planning of the American campaign of 1814, which then tentatively expected to culminate in the seizure of New Orleans by an amphibious assault, to be conducted by Cochrane when ordered.

The admiral had promptly sent Captain Hugh Pigot, R.N., to the mouth of the Apalachicola River in April, 1814, to rouse the Creek Indians to a new uprising. Pigot reported that the Indians were highly enthusiastic at the prospect—not only the Creeks but other tribes as well—and that horses were plentiful in the Southwest for whatever use the British high command might have for them. Upon receiving Pigot's report, Cochrane asked the Admiralty for an execute order on the projected New Orleans expedition.

On his own initiative, Cochrane ordered the occupation of Pensacola by British forces. In late July, Major Edward Nicholls of the Royal Marines (with an acting rank of colonel) and a cadre of about 100 soldiers and marines were landed by Captain Sir William H. Percy's squadron. Nicholls' orders were to organize and arm the Indians.[17]

Jackson's excellent intelligence operatives, friendly Indians and frontiersmen whom he had retained in service since the Creek War, kept him very well informed of Pigot's and Nicholls' missions. Jackson passed the information along to Secretary Armstrong, who did not credit the reports. Colonel Benjamin Hawkins, the American Indian agent with the Creek Nation, sent out friendly intelligent Indians as Jackson's scouts.[18] A considerable English force was reported to be in the Bay of St. Rose, distributing muskets and ammunition to the Indians, and the British had sent runners to the different tribes to invite them to the coast. In July, from Fort Jackson, Jackson sent his chief of scouts, John Gordon, with a letter to Governor Don Mateo Gonzales Manrique at Pensacola demanding both the surrender of two fugitive Creek leaders reported to be at Pensacola and an explanation of the British activities on Spanish territory. Manrique told Gordon that Jackson was impertinent and that the chiefs were entitled to protection, but he did not formally answer Jackson's letter until much later.[19] Gordon reported to Jackson that the British were establishing a large base at the mouth of the Apalachicola and that a bigger British fleet was expected to reinforce the men-o'-war then off the coast.

As early as June 27 Jackson had written Armstrong that it would be necessary to seize Pensacola in order to put a stop to British and Spanish incitement of the Indians; he asked for authority to do so, or permission to use his own judgment in the circumstances.[20] The October 28 letter from Monroe to Jackson, mentioned above, forbade action against Pensacola, but its very tardy preparation and very slow dispatch indicate that it may not have been really intended to stop Jackson. It seems obvious now that the government wanted the attack to be made upon Pensacola, but on Jackson's personal responsibility.

This responsibility Jackson was quite willing and even eager to accept, but he had to have troops to do it. He quickly set about getting the best he knew, writing early in July to Brigadier General John Coffee, his second-in-command in the Creek War, that the British were arming Indians and bringing black troops from Jamaica.[21] Shortly after this he wrote to Governor William Blount asking for Coffee's Tennessee troops, specifically to deal with Pensacola.[22] He also ordered his adjutant general, Colonel Robert Butler, who was then in Nashville on court martial duty, to begin enlisting volunteers there, and to stay and continue recruiting when the court martial was over, until sent for.[23] It is important to note that all of the Tennesseans supplied to Jackson before General William Carroll's arrival in December were sent by their governor to fight the Spaniards first, and the British only later, if need be.

The burning of Washington meant that the War Department would be all but paralyzed for weeks, but if it could not help Jackson, neither would it interfere. However, it did mean that throughout most of the following campaign Jackson and his quartermaster would receive almost no federal government funds.

Meanwhile the British continued to recruit, arm, and equip the Indians and runaway slaves.[24] Nicholls hoped to recruit whites, too. All the British leaders, at this point, seemed to have been bemused with the idea that all the settlers on the Gulf Coast and trans-Allegheny area, not only the French Creoles and Spaniards but also the Anglo-Saxons in the West, would flock to the British standard against the discredited and humbled national government.[25]

Events were to show that there was a measure of disaffection in Louisiana, but it was not at all on the scale that the British expected. In any event, Jackson would never allow the British to exploit it. The British seem to have been influenced by their own propaganda. Nicholls' proclamation of August 29 was addressed to Spaniards, Frenchmen, Italians, and British settlers, but he aimed a couple of paragraphs at the Kentuckians as well.[26] It was an extraordinary production, all in all, and it did bring Indians flocking into town to get muskets and British uniforms. Nicholls set them to drilling in the British Army manual of arms, and the Cross of St. George was unfurled alongside His Catholic Majesty's standard at Pensacola.[27]

American sympathizers had made Jackson well aware of the Irish "colonel's" activities ever since the latter had appeared in Havana, about a month before his descent on Pensacola. Nicholls loved to talk. His announced plan was to occupy Pensacola as a base, and then to seize Mobile, close the mouths of the Mississippi, and march on Baton Rouge. He counted on many slaves joining his Jamaican black regiments, on an Indian uprising, and on help from the Louisiana and West Florida Creoles, and he even affected to believe that the Kentuckians and Tennesseans would join the British.

Nicholls was apparently a man after Cochrane's heart in boastfulness. Cochrane to Bathurst, July 14, 1814, relates the admiral's own grandiose plan of campaign from Maine to Louisiana. He said that he "had it much at heart to give them [the Americans] a complete drubbing before peace is made—when I trust the northern limits will be circumscribed and the command of the Mississippi wrested from them."[28]

With the British landing already accomplished at Pensacola, Jackson moved fast to block their next move to Mobile. His predecessor, Flournoy, had begun to build Fort Bowyer at the entrance to Mobile Bay, but had later recommended that it be dismantled as indefensible. Jackson, however, sent Major William Lawrence with 160 men to repair the fort—and hold it. The major worked night and day and did wonders with very little. He was given more time to prepare because the British naval commander on station, Captain Sir William H. Percy, who was to attack the fort, had a previous assignment: to collect if possible under the British banner another group of recruits—the pirates, smugglers, and privateers at Barataria Bay, led by Jean Laffite.

A British mission led by Captain Nicholas Lockyer, R.N., accompanied by Major Nicholls, R.M., was sent to Barataria under a flag of truce on September 3, 1814. The freebooters were offered an amnesty provided they surrendered their ships and stronghold to British naval control and joined forces with the British in their attack on New Orleans. Though naval rank and pay were offered to those participating, the British offer was actually an ultimatum, signaling the end of the Baratarians' freebooting days. Their only hope of survival in their nefarious racket was for the United States to retain control of the Gulf waters, although they already knew of the federal government's intentions to destroy their lair.

Laffite promised an answer in two weeks, and the British mission departed. Almost immediately afterward, Laffite informed the American authorities in New Orleans of the British offer, and thereby hangs a long tale that must here be told.

2. JEAN LAFFITE,
THE BARATARIANS, AND
THE LOUISIANA
CREOLES

In the historical imagination of many Americans, Jean Laffite and his men, the "Baratarians," were a romantic lot, comparable in some respects to "Robin Hood and His Merry Men" in the hearts of many Englishmen. Though living outside the law, it is rather commonly supposed, the Baratarians were really "good" folk at bottom—witness their "heroic" and "patriotic" contribution to the defense of New Orleans. Indeed, romantic and imaginative stories about Laffite, the last and most famous of the Gulf of Mexico freebooters, have often been cited as fact by professional historians.

Most such stories can safely be discounted as largely or entirely fictitious, but the undeniable fact does remain that Laffite, for one reason or another, did play a part, and without doubt an important one, in the defense of New Orleans in 1814–1815. It is possible that Jackson might have defended the city successfully without the aid of the Baratarians, but it is probable that he could not have done so if Laffite and his men had accepted British offers of amnesty, alliance, and bribe money and had thrown their weight against the American defense. In Laffite's own opinion, set down in his "journal" some thirty-odd years after the battle, the names of Andrew Jackson and all of the other officers would have been completely "forgotten like that of General Winder in Washington"—if Laffite and his associates had accepted the "alluring" offers and promises of the British.[1]

Aside from Laffite's memoir, written long after the events treated in it, there is no real proof that the idea of joining the British was ever seriously entertained by Jean Laffite or any other member of the Baratarian brotherhood, and it is hard to imagine the pirates interpreting the British offer as "alluring." The piratical brotherhood were summoned to surrender their ships and stronghold to British naval authority and to cease molesting Spanish and all other shipping forever. They would receive amnesty and escape further immediate prosecution, but only by surrendering. Those who joined the British armed forces against the Americans would get some special consideration in rank and pay. Jean Laffite himself would have received a sum estimated at about 30,000 pounds—or so he said: there is nothing to prove that any such offer was made—but presumably he would have been expected to share that bribe with the other leaders of the brotherhood.

The international struggle for the Gulf Coast was a part of the larger struggle for the Caribbean Sea area. Since the days of the Elizabethan sea dogs—Drake, Hawkins, Frobisher, etc.—privateering and piracy had gone hand in hand. "Dead men tell no tales," a somber but apt expression that comes to us from those days, was a guide to conduct among pirates, and when death mercifully released captive women, many far more gruesome tales were kept from the telling. Apparently this did not greatly disturb the many British merchants, aristocrats, and even members of the royal family who invested in piratical and "privateering" ventures at various times. Desperate men of all nations and races served as shipmates and crews for Blackbeard, Morgan, L'Olonnois, and many other infamous scoundrels. Some of the pirates fared well: Morgan was pardoned and even knighted by the British monarch. But many others, such as Blackbeard, ended on the gibbet.

Not until the latter half of the eighteenth century did the British government turn its navy's attention to ridding the seas of piracy, and subsequently other nations joined in the effort. However, during the Wars of the French Revolution and the Napoleonic Wars there was a resurgence of piracy— masked as privateering—in the Caribbean and Gulf of Mexico. The British could spare only limited forces to police the western areas, and after Trafalgar the French and Spanish navies ceased to exist, for any practical purpose, in the Caribbean and the Gulf. The infant navy of the United States had been generally emasculated by Jefferson's naval policy, and it was a complete farce in the Gulf of Mexico. Nevertheless, under the command of such officers as David Porter, John Shaw, and Daniel T. Patterson the navy's official policy of enmity toward pirates remained constant. In accordance with an Act of Congress dated March 1, 1807, the secretary of the treasury looked to the secretary of the navy to suppress piracy and smuggling, and on at least one occasion the secretary of the navy bitterly rebuked the naval commander at New Orleans for his failure to cope with the problem.[2]

Eventually—in 1825—the United States Navy (with some British help) would eradicate piracy in all its forms from the Gulf of Mexico and the

Caribbean,[3] but during the period with which the present chronicle is concerned piracy was still a major factor in the life of the region. During the first decade of the nineteenth century the wars of France had filled the Gulf of Mexico with her privateers—and with pirates claiming to be privateers. Though they were commissioned by France to act against British ships and shipping, the real prey of the international brotherhood of pirates was Spain's rich commerce in the area. The "privateers" operated out of Guadeloupe and Martinique, claiming the protection of the French tricolor. The English drove them out of there by conquering those islands, finally, in February, 1810, and "the French privateers were as homeless then as Noah's raven."[4]

Before 1810 the Baratarians were chiefly sailors and fishermen of the coastal islands who had maintained themselves in no great luxury by smuggling throughout the French and Spanish domination, avoiding payment of import and export duties to the government. These were very petty malefactors in comparison with the later inhabitants of Barataria, led by Laffite.

The real Creoles of Louisiana, during this period at least, were the Louisiana-born children of the French settlers of the early years of eighteenth century—the original French-speaking, native ruling class. The name implied a certain excellence of origin among themselves, and soon came to include any native of French or (later) Spanish-French descent by either parent, whose non-alliance with the slave race entitled him to social rank.[5] The proud love of freedom that characterized all white settlers of the North American wilderness also marked these Creoles, but so did the enervating and "luxurious" climate, and the habit of commanding an abject slave class encouraged their rather free expression of a fierce "Latin" imperiousness of will and temper.

In 1776, when the very young Don Bernardo de Galvez became governor of Spanish Louisiana, he found the people, though still French in feeling, somewhat more reconciled to Spanish rule than they had been in 1763–1768. Galvez did much to placate and conciliate the Creoles still further, because he needed their support in his war against the British. He gave the colony the right to trade with France, for instance, and he permitted and encouraged immigration from, and trade with, the French West Indies.

He also opened the trade of New Orleans with east coast cities, and Anglo-Saxon immigration into Louisiana—and later into Spanish Florida

—began. The later exploits of Galvez in conquering Florida were brilliant, but he could not have succeeded without the support of the Creoles, who displayed discipline, fortitude, ardor, and impetuous fury, all of which Galvez generously praised. Thus a British plan to seize New Orleans in 1779 was foiled, largely by the efforts of the Creoles. The Creoles continued their support of Don Bernardo in his conquest of Mobile in 1780, and of Pensacola in 1781.[6] They did some very rugged battling in both places, demonstrating their excellent fighting capabilities fully thirty-five years before Jackson's famous defense of New Orleans. They also established a precedent for subsequent Creole resistance to British designs on New Orleans and Louisiana—a precedent that would be overlooked by the British in 1814, when by some mysterious thought process—perhaps as simple as "wishful thinking"—they convinced themselves that the Creoles would welcome them! However, the significance of the violent Creole reaction against the threat of British domination in 1788 and after has also been rather consistently overlooked by American writers prior to and ever since the time of Governor William C. C. Claiborne.

The change over to American (i.e. "Anglo-Saxon") rule in 1803 was naturally a very rude and completely unexpected shock to the sensitive and volatile Latins of the Crescent City. Indeed, it shook them to their very foundations—especially when, in 1804, the importation of African slaves into Louisiana was prohibited by the United States government more than four years before Congress passed a similar prohibition for the entire country. As early as 1804, then, if not before, a number of Creoles were yearning for the return of Spanish rule, and the Spaniards still firmly ensconced in nearby Florida encouraged Creoles of such mind to hope for, and even to expect, such a change once Napoleon's fall had been accomplished.

Spain had vigorously protested to both France and the United States against Bonaparte's violation of the French promise not to alienate the province of Louisiana.[7] While Spain was under the rule of Charles IV, who was completely dominated by Napoleon, there was no further action taken or contemplated in 1803. But even under Charles IV Spain began to cling fiercely to every foot of the Floridas, much to the dismay of Jefferson, who understood that New Orleans was not defensible, and that navigation of the Mississippi River could not be secure, so long as West Florida remained under Spanish rule. Whatever Napoleon's scheme concerning West Florida may have been, he found it politically necessary, in order to soften Spanish opposition to his having sold Louisiana to the United States, to support Spain's contention that none of West Florida was involved in the sale. Nevertheless, the Spaniards continued to nourish bitter feelings about the matter for the next fifteen years.[8] The British government was also overwrought, and the transaction was severely condemned in Parliament during the discussion of the Treaty of Amiens. It was said in debate that the interests of England were essentially wounded by the sale, since New Orleans was the key to Mexico.[9] Whatever the merits of that notion, Britain fully endorsed Spain's refusal to add West Florida to Louisiana.[10]

The West Florida controversy that ensued was of great interest to the men of the West who were advocating various measures to assist American settlers in West Florida to win their independence from Spain, with a view to making the area part of the United States before Britain could seize it from Spain.[11] The British minister in Washington advocated such a seizure in 1804, and the British had contemplated such an action even earlier, in 1793–1795 when Spain was an ally of France.[12] The possibility of the British taking over West Florida was of grave concern to all well-informed Americans west of the Appalachians, and was also prominent in the thoughts of the Spaniards in Florida and the Creoles of Louisiana.

In 1808, as the European holocaust wore on, the Spanish people revolted against the usurpation of their throne by Napoleon's brother, Joseph, and set up a revolutionary regency for their rightful king, Ferdinand VII, who was a prisoner in France. The United States refused to recognize the regency, and diplomatic relations with Spain were, in effect, severed.

That refusal permitted the ceremonious seizure of West Florida on December 10, 1810 by the governors of the territories of Orleans and Mississippi, armed with President James Madison's proclamation on the subject. The feeble Spanish government in Florida, almost totally lacking in military resources, was easily overwhelmed by a group of border ruffians from Mississippi Territory. The Spanish governor fled to Mobile without a fight, for which act of eminent good sense he was later imprisoned in Havana, where he died without ever being brought to trial. When Louisiana was admitted to the Union in 1812, the area seized in 1810 became the toe of Louisiana east of the Mississippi to the Pearl River. Thus, at long last, the United States held not only New Orleans and the Mississippi River, but also adjacent lands that were necessary for effective defense of the city.[13]

Spain bitterly resented the seizure, of course, but in 1810 neither she nor her ally Great Britain was in a position to go to war with the United States. Spain and England were deeply involved in their war against Napoleon on the Iberian Peninsula, and both countries depended on the United States for grain with which to feed their armies. They had to content themselves with filing vigorous protests with the United States government—and with a private agreement to take the matter up "later."[14] The Spaniards in Pensacola, meanwhile, confidently predicted that West Florida and Louisiana would be returned to Spain eventually. The Creoles of New Orleans heard such talk constantly, and some of them came to believe it.

The first American governor of Louisiana, soon renamed Orleans Territory, was William C. C. Claiborne, a Virginian who could not speak even a word of French when he assumed office and never saw fit to learn that "foreign" language. Claiborne was much like the hapless hen that has hatched duck eggs. The strange character of the Creoles perplexed and wearied him. He never quite understood them, never entirely trusted them. Since he did not speak, and did not care to speak, their language, he could know little of their history. More than ten years after his appointment, he wrote Jackson: "I have a difficult people to manage."[15]

For Claiborne, loyalty to the state meant strict obedience to its laws. The Creoles saw things differently. Most of them, of both high and low estate, considered smuggling in general and the African slave trade in particular to be lucrative parts of their very economic existence; both practices were of very long standing under two governments, and the consciences of the Creoles were not at all troubled by them.[16] This being so, it is not surprising that the act of prohibiting the introduction of slaves into Louisiana, passed in 1804, transformed the Baratarian smugglers, comparatively small operators before this, into big-time "bootleggers" of Negro slaves—a fact that may be surprising and disconcerting to some of those who imagine the Baratarians to have been "good" folk at heart.[17]

Between 1804 and 1810 the population of New Orleans doubled. By the 1810 census, the total population, including suburbs, was 24,552, of which number only about 3,200 were Americans.[18] Most of the newcomers were French settlers who had fled to Cuba to escape the Negro revolt in Haiti, and were later forced to move again because of renewed war between France and Spain in Europe in 1808. Still others had fled British rule on the recently seized islands of Guadeloupe and Martinique. Whites, "men of color" (free mulattoes), and black slaves came to New Orleans in almost equal numbers, and nearly all of them settled permanently in the city. They were absorbed into the native Creole community, soon doubling the number of French-speaking Louisianians, most of whom were determined to resist "Americanization."

Following the Burr Conspiracy—during which the Creoles, through their legislature, washed their hands of any part in that alleged treason— Claiborne's letters continued to dwell on what he considered the sad cultural mixture in his territory. England had her partisans, he said, Ferdinand VII some faithful subjects, and Bonaparte his strong admirers; but there was "a fourth class of men, commonly called 'Burrites,' who would join any standard which would promise rapine and plunder."[19]

In the summer of 1810 there was serious trouble among the smugglers of Barataria. The native inhabitants of those islands, somewhat lackadaisical fishermen and *contrabandiers*, found themselves brought into competition with the newly arrived "privateersmen" from Martinique and Guadeloupe —the "Burrites" to whom Claiborne referred. Within the year the islands of Grand Isle and Grand Terre, adjoining each other at the seaward side of Barataria Bay, doubled in population. The newcomers and the native smugglers formed two distinct groups that were soon warring against each other.

With plunder in hand and a market in New Orleans at their door, the Baratarian pirates required a leader, an agent, and a banker. Enter one Jean Laffite, who became their agent in New Orleans. Laffite was an energetic and efficient businessman, fluent in English, French, Spanish, and Italian, who had a gift for making phrases in all four languages and "a conscience as elastic as any politician could wish for."[20] With such eminently desirable qualifications for their special needs, Laffite was soon chosen to be the leader of the united Baratarians.

Jean Laffite and an older brother, Pierre, began operating a blacksmith shop in New Orleans, using slave labor, in 1810 or thereabouts. They had come from Port au Prince, Haiti, where Jean, the youngest of eight children, was born in 1782. The Laffites had fled to Haiti from Spain to escape the Inquisition. Jean's maternal grandparents were Jewish, and his grandfather was a victim of the Inquisition. His maternal grandmother reared Jean after his mother's death, which occurred when Jean was very young. The grandmother instilled in Jean, he was to claim later, an abiding hatred of Spain and all things Spanish. The oldest brother, Alexander (later known by the name of Dominique You), entered the Caribbean privateering profession early in life, and by Jean's own account he and Pierre also became privateersmen in 1800 or soon thereafter, learning the business under their second cousin, Renato Beluché, whom they called "Oncle." Beluché was a native of New Orleans (born 1780), and the Laffite family began assembling in Louisiana about 1804.[21]

The Baratarian commune of smugglers, slave runners, slave-ship hijackers, privateersmen, and pirates claimed legitimacy and protection from hanging on the basis of letters of marque from the revolutionary party in Cartagena,[22] the first city of New Granada to declare its independence from Spain. The revolutionists were always welcome to the "glory," it seems, while Laffite himself disposed of the proceeds.[23] Though the Baratarians were supposedly commissioned to prey only upon Spanish commerce, they also took defenseless British and American prizes when they could.[24] Apologists for the Laffites have vociferously asserted that this accusation is untrue, of course, because it was never proved in court,[25] but in view of the fact that the Laffites were pardoned by President Madison *before* trial, that is at best negative evidence. No apologist for these scoundrels has ever satisfactorily explained away the jewelry recovered during Patterson's expedition against Barataria that was identified as belonging to people on an American ship reportedly lost at sea.[26] This revelation, which came to light after the Battle of New Orleans, finally cost the Laffites their popularity in the city.

It is surely significant in this connection—but it is constantly (and perhaps deliberately) overlooked—that those professional "privateersmen" and "patriots" of Barataria would not and did not apply for United States letters of marque to sail in the service of the United States against British merchantmen. Only six letters of marque were issued in New Orleans throughout the War of 1812, and only one of these was issued to a Baratarian, Renato Beluché, and he brought in only one British vessel to prize court.[27] The other Baratarians sailed only under Cartagena colors, secure in the knowledge that no accounting would ever be required of them by those unorganized insurgents.

Lord Nelson said, "All privateers are no better than pirates,"[28] and there is ample supporting evidence in both British and American naval records.

Mawkish sentimentalists have spilled gallons of ink in an attempt to prove that the Baratarians, under their Cartagena letters of marque, were in legitimate business. It is too often ignored that the Baratarians' own records show that while they were quite often overstocked with captured vessels and booty, they were seemingly never embarrassed by any need to care for the prisoners—if they ever took any.[29] Dead men and women told no tales. The unvarnished story of West Indian piracy and privateering, often plainly told for those who care to read it, is one of revolting cruelty throughout; and though the Spaniards were most frequently the victims, they were also, in their turn, merciless sea and coastal robbers.[30]

The Baratarians sold their booty in or near New Orleans and at points up the river, in flagrant disregard of both the United States revenue laws and American neutrality in Spain's war with her rebellious colony of New Granada. The government in Washington found itself powerless to cope with the situation, even before the War of 1812 began, so weak were the federal revenue service and the navy. And certainly there was no condemnation of the Baratarians by the native Louisianians. The merchants and planters of the Mississippi Delta, profiting from the activities of the pirates, with the connivance of the general public, screened the contrabandists and defended their character.[31]

Some of the proudest names in New Orleans were owners of privateering ships.[32] David Porter of the navy, later a famous commodore but then only a master commandant, was indignant at this open flouting of the law and reported that "the District Attorney apparently winked at piracies committed in our waters and at the open communication kept up between these depredations and the citizens of New Orleans."[33] The territorial authorities seem to have left the matter to the federal men until the slave revolt of January, 1811. Official investigation after that somber event brought to light the fact that Laffite's agents were raiding remote coasts for slaves, stealing them for sale in Louisiana, and that it was these stolen slaves who were the principal instigators of the uprising. Governor Claiborne, fearing another revolt, at last decided that the Baratarians simply had to go, and he asked the territorial council for men and money to attack the pirate stronghold. The Creole council, however, declined to assist the effort.[34]

The Baratarians, under their "bos" Jean Laffite, reached the height of their power and arrogance in 1813 and, as the Spanish-French historian

Gayarré remarked, "their morals and general behavior declined in proportion to their gain in wealth and power."[35] The Laffites had by then become outlaws. Claiborne, having failed to win the support of the territorial council, prevailed upon the federal customs officials to call in the army in the shape of 40 dragoons under Captain Andrew H. Hunter. On the night of November 16, 1812, the dragoons captured the Laffite brothers and a number of their men with a fleet of pirogues filled with contraband, and took them under guard to the city.[36]

The Baratarian chiefs had no difficulty in arranging bail for themselves —and of course they jumped it—but they were now outlaws, officially as well as in fact, and the contest between the smugglers and the customs men grew more heated, soon amounting to a small war. On November 24, 1813, Claiborne, under federal pressure, offered a $500 reward for the arrest of Jean Laffite. Three days later, the impudent fugitive issued his own "proclamation" offering $5,000 bounty to the person who delivered Claiborne to him at Cat Island (on Mississippi Sound).[37] The American federal authorities were all but speechless with rage and frustration—and the citizens of New Orleans laughed all the louder at each new development.

The public conscience finally began to awaken in January, 1814, however, when the Baratarians attacked a group of revenue officers, killing one of them (John B. Stout), seriously wounding two others, and making prisoners of the rest—an incident that later apologists for Laffite neglect to mention.[38] As a result, on July 27, 1814 a federal grand jury finally indicted the Laffites on several counts of piracy.[39] A few days later Pierre Laffite, careless or overbold, was arrested on the streets of New Orleans, jailed without bond, and put in irons, while a number of indictments were prepared against him. Jean now began to realize that the end of his immunity to legal sanctions, if not at hand, was surely in sight. He was very fond of his brother, and he secured the services of the attorney Edward Livingston to defend Pierre and the Laffite interests.

At about this time Master Commandant Daniel T. Patterson received explicit orders from the secretary of the navy to disperse the Baratarians and was informed that the schooner U.S.S. *Carolina*, en route to New Orleans, would give the naval station the reinforcements it needed for the operation. She arrived on August 10, 1814. Patterson had stated his case against the smugglers upon relieving Captain John Shaw, as mentioned above. Colonel George T. Ross, commanding the regular army infantry in New Orleans, was directed by the War Department in Washington to assist Patterson. On September 3, when the British made their overtures to Jean Laffite, the *Carolina* had already arrived, and Laffite well knew that preparations for a joint army–navy assault on Barataria were being made.[40]

Ironically but unquestionably, the Baratarians' having made such preparations necessary was one of their outstanding contributions to the defense of New Orleans. Had it not been for the provocations of Laffite and his pirates, the *Carolina* would not have been at New Orleans to help against the British invasion. The *Louisiana*, which was already stationed there, was without a crew until the second day of the battle, the navy having been unable to obtain recruits in New Orleans, where it was no secret that the navy was committed to the destruction of the maritime pirates.

The letters of all of the naval commandants at New Orleans—those of Porter, Shaw, and Patterson—constantly reported to the secretary of the navy of their absolute inability to get recruits for the navy. Porter wrote in his memoirs that "naval officers were looked upon as the tools of an oppressive government." Some historians and others writing about the Baratarians seemed to believe that the naval officers, especially Patterson, moved against the Baratarians because of personal animus and hope for prize money. The officers were in point of fact required to suppress piracy, by an Act of Congress dated March 3, 1807, and in 1814 they were specifically ordered to attack as they did.[41]

Laffite's associates in New Orleans were also well aware of the mission of the *Carolina* and of the preparations that the army and navy were making.[42] The federal customs authorities now had sufficient forces to establish national authority over revenue, and the Laffites' career of crime—at New Orleans at least—was about run. Claiborne, now governor of the State of Louisiana, was no longer a federal official (as he had been when he was territorial governor) and his vacillation and weakness could no longer be relied upon by Laffite's lawyers. Claiborne did want to stop Patterson's expedition just before it left, but he had no authority over Patterson or Ross, and Jackson was fully in sympathy with the decision to suppress piracy.

At this critical moment the British overtures to Jean Laffite looked like a great stroke of luck for him. He immediately saw the advantages that he and his brothers and friends might gain from this. He put off his answer to the British for two weeks and through a friend, one Jean Blanque, wrote immediately to Governor Claiborne,[43] telling of the British offer, and tendering the services of himself and his men in the defense of New Orleans—provided that he secure "an act of oblivion for himself and all his adherents."[44] This was the sum of Laffite's "patriotism," the *sine qua non* of his offer of support to Claiborne and later to Jackson. He saw that no matter who might win the impending struggle for New Orleans, his own free-wheeling racketeering in and around the city would not be allowed to continue. Quite obviously, neither the British navy nor the American navy would tolerate the Baratarians any longer. But the British offer gave him a chance to drive a shrewd bargain and at least obtain for both himself and Pierre a pardon from the United States. Perhaps he might even forestall Patterson's expedition,[45] for his adherents included a group of New Orleans citizens (perhaps they could be classed as "business associates," but it was a most illegal and nefarious "business," as the "associates" well knew), among them members of the legislature and a number of other men of wealth and social prominence.

Governor Claiborne, who was by then grasping at straws to get some— any—native Louisianian to defend the state, was impressed by Laffite's offer, and forwarded it to Jackson, recommending acceptance. Major General Jacques Villeré, commanding general of the state militia, agreed with Claiborne, but of course neither of them had any authority to stop Patterson's raid.

The expedition went off as ordered, on September 16,[46] and encountered no resistance from the Baratarians. They had an amnesty in prospect for all their various crimes, and resistance would have been utterly idiotic, and anyway, the pirates of this period (as of all periods) were not noted for their courage. (They *never* attacked an armed merchantman, only the defenseless ones.) In any case, Patterson and Ross now had too much power to be resisted successfully by the Baratarians. Jean and his brother Pierre (who had, of course, escaped from jail in New Orleans!) were not at Grand Terre Island. They had taken refuge elsewhere. But the pirates' installation on the island, south of Lake Barataria, was burned and half a million dollars worth of stolen goods (and about 80 prisoners) were carried by the federal forces to the prize court in New Orleans. Most important for the safety of New Orleans, Patterson brought back several vessels, twenty naval guns, and much powder and shot. (There was, however, a great deal more powder and shot belonging to the Baratarian pirates in scattered caches that Patterson did *not* find and that would be very significant in later bargaining by Jean Laffite with Jackson.)

None of the information provided Jackson by Laffite (through Claiborne) in September, 1814 added anything to his strategic intelligence, but it showed him how far the British were prepared to go in an attempt to take New Orleans. At that moment, from Mobile, Jackson repudiated the Baratarians as "hellish banditti," much to the distress of several historians ranging back from Dr. de Grummond via Marquis James to Gayarré.[47] The last named said that the British must have considered the Baratarians as belligerents or else they would not have applied for their support,[48] but Gayarré overlooked the fact that the British of 1814 were not at all squeamish. Fomenting a Negro slave revolt, with its many horrors for all concerned, was considered seriously in their planning, and so were Indian uprisings and all of *their* unrestrained excesses—even to the buying of scalps. The British record in failing to control their own soldiers in Spain was deplored by Wellington himself.[49] And in point of fact, the British severely criticized Jackson after the battle for having employed the "pirates" against them.[50]

The Baratarians' concern for themselves and their New Orleans friends was real, for reasons given by a state supreme court judge of Louisiana, Judge François-Xavier Martin, who was an eyewitness to events in New Orleans during that period, and who can be considered one of the better authorities on this matter:

Among the papers of Laffite, which had been lately taken at Barataria, had been found letters of several merchants, who had hitherto sustained a good character, affording evidence of their being accomplices of that man, Lafitte, and prosecutions had been instituted against some of them. The stern impartiality of the judge, Dominic Hall, District Judge of the United States in New Orleans had induced a belief that they had much to apprehend: the counsel, whom they had employed, were generally the opponents of Claiborne.[51]

3. GULF OPERATIONS
TO DECEMBER 1,
1814

On August 30, 1814, Governor Don Mateo Gonzales Manrique of Pensacola, emboldened by the presence of British armed forces in the immediate vicinity, finally answered Andrew Jackson's letter of the early summer.[1] Manrique's reply put a great deal of emphasis on the matter of protection afforded the Baratarian pirates on United States territory while they plundered Spanish ships and sold their booty in New Orleans.[2] Jack-

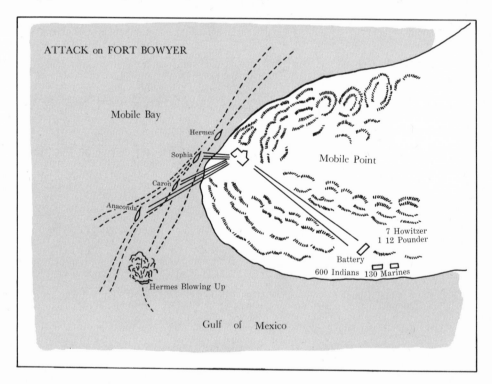

Map 2

son's reply was characteristic of the man: he was no diplomat swapping words, he would listen to no criticism of his government, and his next message would be from the mouths of his cannon.[3]

Captain Percy, finally despairing of aid from the Baratarians, undertook an amphibious assault on Fort Bowyer as the first step toward the capture of Mobile. On September 12 Major Nicholls landed in the rear of Fort Bowyer with his marines and Indians (about 120 men in all) and a howitzer.[4] On the day following, the naval force of four small vessels, commanded by Captain Percy, moved into the pass. Percy's total armament was seventy-eight guns.[5] Except for pivot guns, no more than half the guns on any ship (those on the engaged side) could be brought to bear at any one time. Because of shallow water two of the ships could not close to the effective range of their carronades and so played no part in the action. Major Lawrence, the American defender, had only twenty guns, and not all of these would bear or shoot. Finally, on September 16, Percy launched his attack by land and water.[6]

Few actions in the war caused the British greater humiliation. Nicholls' Indians, in their British red coats, made many frightening noises, but they were held completely in check by the defender's judicious use of grapeshot. The seaborne attack was also beaten off with comparative ease. The flagship H.M.S. *Hermes*, her cable cut by a shot, drifted into the full raking fire of the American batteries[7] and then ran into shoal water, whereupon her commander set the vessel on fire and blew her up. The British squadron then withdrew to Pensacola, while Nicholls' force retreated overland. The American loss was 4 KIA and 5 WIA.* The British loss, as officially reported, was 27 KIA and 45 WIA, including Nicholls, who lost an eye.[8]

The British account of the action is undoubtedly accurate. Captain Percy had to face a grim naval court of inquiry into reasons for the loss of one of His Majesty's ships, and all the circumstances of the action and damages received were mercilessly sifted, according to the court record. The court exonerated the captain and condoned his losses on the ground that the strategic situation justified the attack. The reasoning of the court is very significant, because it shows that Mobile was considered vital to the main

---

* The abbreviations KIA (killed in action), WIA (wounded in action), MIA (missing in action), and DOW (died of wounds), now used in all official American casualty reports in all the military services, are used throughout this work.

British plans as late as September, 1814. Mahan elaborates on this, citing a letter from Cochrane to the Admiralty dated October 3, 1814.[9]

Judged in the light of modern principles of amphibious warfare, Percy's decision to attack, without having a much larger and better trained landing force than he had, was foolhardy. The expectation that all Americans would "break and run" in the manner of Winder's militia at Bladensburg, undoubtedly influenced the British decision to undertake the action. As it turned out, however, Major Lawrence and his men were American regulars, and Lawrence in particular was a great credit to his profession. The American garrison fought coolly, bravely, and efficiently, and deserved all the plaudits they afterwards received. There can be no question that Lawrence's victory had a great morale-lifting effect on all Americans in the Southwest. And the strategic importance of this victory, attributable ultimately to Jackson's military astuteness in having restored Fort Bowyer in time to forestall the British descent on Mobile, was very great.

When the action commenced, Jackson was en route by boat across Mobile Bay to inspect the fort. He returned to Mobile to hurry reinforcements, but they did not reach the fort until the fight was over.[10] The British defeat came as a surprise to British sympathizers in Mobile, and the first reports received were that the fort had been blown up. The correct information, that the explosion had occurred in H.M.S. *Hermes*, greatly relieved Jackson, but threw the Spanish and British sympathizers into consternation. Jackson then knew himself to be surrounded by spies who were reporting his slightest move to the enemy.[11] This realization finally convinced Jackson of the need to drive the British menace from Pensacola, which he knew to be the center of the very keen British intelligence system in the Gulf Coast area.[12]

It was during this period, too, that Jackson first became aware of the problems of command relationship in joint operations—that very tender subject between armies and navies since history began. With respect to this problem, the navy's experience at New Orleans had been a most unhappy one since the beginning of the war in 1812. Secretary of the Navy Paul Hamilton had evinced a great personal devotion to the President, but by 1811 he was well known to be a drunkard and was suspected of revealing state secrets when in his cups.[13] One of the secretary's more colossal blunders had been to direct Captain John Shaw, the naval commandant at New Orleans at the beginning of the war, to place himself under the command of General James Wilkinson.[14] As a result, army–navy relations at New

Orleans were marked by dissension throughout the remainder of Shaw's tour of duty. Wilkinson had promptly demanded and eventually gained authority over all naval funds, as well as personnel and matériel, but he generously left the accounting responsibility with the senior naval officer. Under this peculiar arrangement Wilkinson was able to squander naval funds on almost anything that suited his fancy—and that did not include maintenance of naval equipment. It was over this issue that Shaw began demanding relief from command. His reports tell of serious disputes between army and navy personnel of all ranks, army courts-martial of naval personnel, and generally poor morale among naval personnel on the station.[15]

President Madison finally requested Hamilton's resignation and appointed William Jones, a Philadelphia merchant with some experience at sea, to replace him in late January, 1813.[16] The sorry command-relations situation at New Orleans was promptly renegotiated by the secretary of war and the secretary of the navy, and a new statement of policy reached New Orleans by late spring. But nothing could immediately undo the very serious damage that had been done to the already feeble naval arm on the Gulf. Naval expenditures—extravagant under Wilkinson, but chiefly into his own pocket—were rigidly curbed by Secretary Jones in 1813, who proceeded to deny Shaw (and later Patterson) even the funds that were needed for naval operations on the Gulf. Effective naval strength at New Orleans and on the Gulf was all but nonexistent.

Jackson wrote to Patterson in August, 1814, asking him to bring all his available naval strength to Mobile to assist in its defense. Patterson refused —very politely it is true, but positively—in a letter dated September 2, 1814.[17] He insisted that New Orleans would be the British point of attack, and that all of his naval forces should be kept there for defense of the river and the city. He pointed out that if he went to Mobile he could very easily be blockaded in Mobile Bay and prevented from getting back to New Orleans. He discussed the importance of the fort at the Rigolets and said that he planned to use his gunboats to try to stop an invasion through Lake Borgne, but that eventually he would have to concentrate the gunboats near the fort, to help hold at least that critical position, since he did not have enough gunboats to command the lake. He insisted, throughout, that New Orleans, not Mobile, should be given priority in naval defense planning.

Jackson wrote to the War Department from Mobile on September 8,

1814, reporting that he had twice written to Patterson for naval support and had yet to receive an answer. He asked the secretary of war if he (Jackson) could exercise command over the naval forces. Actually, as we have seen, Patterson had answered Jackson's question, and in the same letter he had told Jackson of his intention to set out to attack Barataria on September 6. And with the letter, Patterson had enclosed a copy of the agreement between the secretaries of war and the navy concerning employment of the joint forces of the two departments that had been drawn up when William Jones assumed office in January, 1813. The upshot of it all was the fact that Jackson could not command the forces of the two services. It would have to be a joint operation, one of cooperating commands.[18]

Jackson, never having seen a gunboat, had some odd notions about what could be done with them. In his letter to the secretary of war on September 20, Jackson asked him to notify the secretary of the navy that if he (Jackson) had had just two of Patterson's gunboats at Fort Bowyer, all four of the vessels in Percy's squadron would have been captured! Jackson's letter neglected to say just how he would have accomplished that fantastic feat. If evidence was needed to show that Jackson should not be allowed to command the naval forces, this letter surely supplied it.[19]

In October, following Patterson's expedition against the Baratarians, Jackson sent a very sharp letter to Patterson on the subject of foodstuffs from New Orleans that were reaching the enemy in Pensacola. The navy had to destroy that commerce, he said, and maintain communication with Mobile. Patterson agreed fully, and cooperated with Lieutenant Colonel William McRae, then the senior army officer present in New Orleans, in putting a stop to the traffic.[20]

A few days later Jackson wrote Patterson in a rather friendly vein, acknowledging receipt of a letter from Patterson dated October 17 in which the case for the navy presented in the letter of September 2 was restated, and which made more clear the serious weakness of naval forces in the area. Jackson said that he now understood the command relationships, and that all he had ever wanted was friendly cooperation. He had learned elsewhere of naval ordnance that was being lent to the army in New Orleans, and he thanked Patterson for it.[21]

Jackson's correspondence with various other persons in New Orleans while he remained at Mobile or its vicinity was voluminous, and some of the letters from this period are most interesting and revealing. Jackson has been severely criticized by some historians for not proceeding to New Orleans sooner than he did, but he considered the defense of Mobile and the expulsion of the British from Pensacola to be more immediately imperative than any inspection of New Orleans—and rightly so in the judgment of historians with a better grasp of military matters than that of most of Jackson's critics. Though Governor Claiborne, an indefatigable correspondent with Jackson during this period, frequently expressed a desire to see the general at New Orleans, his letters show that even he and his Louisiana friends wanted Jackson to take care of the Pensacola matter first. So do the letters of Governors Willie Blount of Tennessee and David Holmes of the Mississippi Territory. Only Edward Livingston, secretary of one of the two committees of public safety in New Orleans, and Lieutenant Colonel William McRae, chief of artillery for the Seventh Military District and senior military staff officer present in the city, were impatient for Jackson's immediate presence in New Orleans. But there was no chance of that. The West wanted an attack made on Pensacola, and Jackson's own heart was set on it. The attack would occur as soon as possible after the arrival of Coffee's brigade of Tennessee Mounted Volunteers.

Claiborne's letters, meanwhile, reiterated again and again his belief that the Louisianians were unreliable, and perhaps totally disaffected, and that regular troops and the militia of the other western states would have to be relied upon to defend New Orleans if it were attacked. He also feared a slave revolt. Much later, when defending his decision to proclaim martial law in New Orleans, Jackson cited Claiborne's letters of August 8, 12, and 24 and September 8 and 19,[22] but in addition to those 5 letters, Claiborne wrote 2 more in August, another in September, 8 more in October, and 7 in November—all addressed to Jackson and all to the effect that the people of New Orleans could not be counted upon in the event of a British attack. But in none of these letters, or others written during this period, did Claiborne disabuse Jackson of his erroneous information concerning the fortifications of the city, which Claiborne had described in an earlier letter, written in 1813, as being extensive and nearly completed. This misinformation continued to influence Jackson's estimate of the situation until his arrival at New Orleans.[23]

In the meantime, Jackson was informed by McRae that the defense establishment in New Orleans suffered from badly divided command relationships within the army itself, and that lamentable conditions existed in the quartermaster and paymaster departments. Jackson remedied these matters of detail by means of a series of general and special orders. McRae, as senior artilleryman, was appointed to command of all forts, given responsibility for all ordnance and ordnance supply, and put in command of all artillerymen in Greater New Orleans, including Fort St. Philip. The 7th Infantry was concentrated in New Orleans under command of Colonel George T. Ross. The district paymaster quickly found out who was in charge when he demurred about paying Indians, men of color, and militia units. He was also jolted out of his complacency by being made to purchase artillery horses and to make a complete overhaul of the ordnance stores. Louisiana militiamen, to the number of 1,200, were called out to garrison critical points around the city, and work on new fortifications was started. McRae reported a large supply of artillery ammunition in store.[24]

Jackson's inspector general, Colonel Arthur P. Haynes, was sent early in November to inspect what had been accomplished and was, therefore, already in New Orleans ready to report when Jackson arrived.

Jackson also corresponded with members of a committee of public safety in New Orleans, including the committee's secretary, Edward Livingston. In sum, Jackson did not neglect to include the defense of New Orleans in his plans prior to his going there in person—all assertions to the contrary notwithstanding.

Coffee and his brigade of Tennessee Mounted Volunteers finally arrived on the scene, and halted not far from Fort St. Stephens, where Jackson joined him on October 26.[25] Owing to a lack of adequate forage en route to Pensacola, part of Coffee's brigade had to be dismounted for his next march. He had about 2,800 men under his command, but not all of them were in condition to proceed further. By this time Jackson had private assurance that President Madison would approve of the Pensacola expedition.[26] Using his own limited funds and personal credit, Jackson supplied the rations for the trip, and took up the line of march on November 2, 1814. He had a total of about 4,000 men, consisting of 700 regulars, Coffee's brigade, and other volunteers.[27] By November 6 he had reached Pensacola, where his arrival was expected by both the Spaniards and the British.

Major Henry B. Peire of the 44th Infantry was sent forward, under a flag of truce, to demand that the Spanish forts—Barrancas, St. Rose, and St.

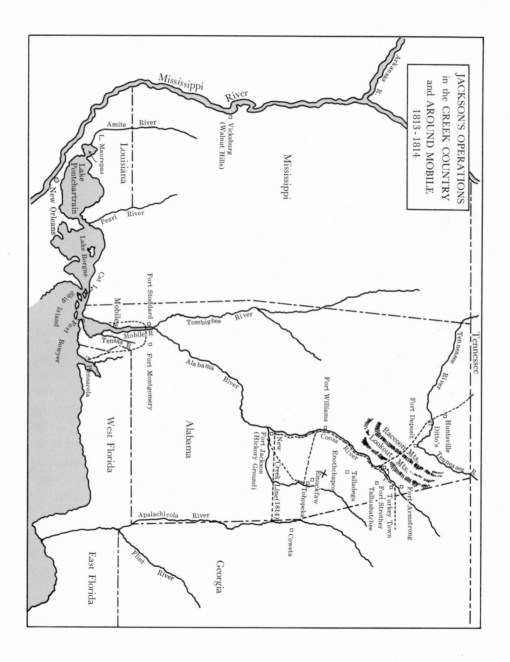

JACKSON'S OPERATIONS
in the CREEK COUNTRY
and AROUND MOBILE
1813-1814

Map 3

Michael—be immediately surrendered to the Americans, to be garrisoned by the United States until such time as Spain could preserve unimpaired her neutral character.[28] The flag of truce was fired upon,[29] but Jackson was still anxious to avoid unnecessary bloodshed and the possible crippling of his new army—he was well aware of the risks he was taking almost entirely on his own responsibility. Accordingly, he sent another message to the governor that evening, this time using a captured Spanish corporal as the messenger. Governor Manrique replied promptly: The flag of truce had been fired on by the British without his authority, and he would receive any overtures that Jackson wanted to make. At a late hour Major Peire presented Jackson's terms and the governor's council met promptly, but the terms proved to be unacceptable to the Spaniards.

On the morning of November 7, Jackson moved forward to take the town by storm. An American demonstration was made by 500 men along the shore approach to the town. The British responded by forming their vessels across the bay with their guns ranged and bearing on that approach, whereupon Jackson led his main forces in an attack from the north. His regulars were on the left, with the 3rd, 39th, and 44th abreast; Coffee's dismounted volunteers and the Choctaw Indians were on the right. Only one company of the 3rd Infantry, the advance guard, met sharp action: they took a Spanish battery with the bayonet. The regulars then poured into town, fighting from house to house. The governor soon put an end to the killing by personally coming to Jackson under a flag of truce, asking for mercy for his city, and promising to consent to whatever terms Jackson demanded. Even after the battle, the conduct and discipline of Jackson's irregular and regular forces deserved commendation. Their restraint was most remarkable.

The British ships stayed in the bay, but they did send armed boats in towards the shore to fire on any Americans who might come into their range. American artillery of greater range, emplaced on the beach, drove the boats back far enough to put an end to this threat.

Jackson was now most anxious to secure the British stronghold at Fort Barrancas before it could be reinforced.[30] It was situated some 14 miles to the west of the town, and Fort St. Michael lay in between. Despite the governor's capitulation, however, the Spanish commander at St. Michael temporized and delayed surrendering the fort until the Americans were formed

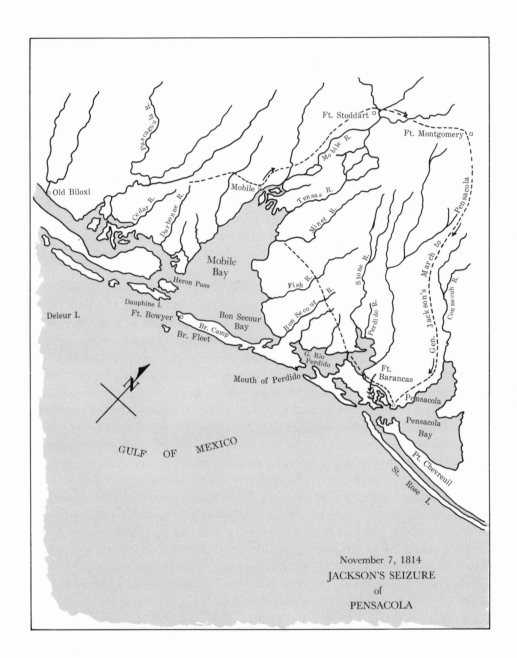

November 7, 1814

JACKSON'S SEIZURE

of

PENSACOLA

Map 4

to assault. Only then did he surrender, and by that time the day was spent, forcing Jackson to defer his plans for Fort Barrancas until the next morning. But even before the Americans were well en route on the morning of November 8, they heard a series of explosions from Barrancas. The British had destroyed the fort and were sailing away. Captain Percy reported later that he had destroyed the guns of the fort, three hundred double barrels of gunpowder, a large magazine of every sort of ordnance stores, and two stores of provisions.[31] According to Percy's report, these victualling stores, enough to feed 500 men for a month, were located so far outside the fort that the fort could not have been held. These had to be British stores, not Spanish, since the latter's poverty was so abject. Jackson's casualties were 7 KIA and 11 WIA.[32] He was back on the Tensas at Fort Montgomery on November 13.

Captain Percy's report to Admiral Cochrane of the events at Pensacola, and the latter's to the Admiralty, are hard to reconcile with the American version of what happened.[33] It is established that the British were in Pensacola as early as July, when Nicholls' proclamation was issued from there.[34] Percy reported officially that he arrived early in November, and that he brought his ships to Pensacola only at the urgent request of Governor Manrique. But when Percy arrived there on November 4, the governor refused to allow him to land sailors and marines, either to help garrison the forts or to meet and drive off the Americans who were en route to the city. (It is significant that Percy said that he had promised the Spanish governor-general in Havana that he would enter Pensacola only on invitation of its governor.) Manrique eventually changed his mind, according to Percy, and asked for armed help, but by then the British had moved Nicholls and his Indians to the eastern side of the harbor, from where they could proceed overland to their camp at the Apalachicola, and the governor's request for help was accordingly refused. Percy admitted that on his arrival the Spaniards had asked him to remove British ensigns from Spanish forts in the city, and this he did, but his report does not reveal when the ensigns were raised there or by whom (one assumes that probably Nicholls did it).

Percy also said that he took 200 Spanish soldiers with him, but he did not say to what destination. This seems very curious indeed, and is hard to credit, in view of evidence of a pitiful lack of Spanish military strength in Florida at the time.[35] The Spanish authorities claimed that the British carried off 400 slaves,[36] and it is probable that Percy's "Spanish soldiers" were Spanish-owned Negroes who were forcibly conscripted for service in the West

India regiments or colonial marine battalions. Cochrane reported to the Admiralty in February, 1815 that he was returning to Pensacola some "Spanish soldiers taken to Apalachicola."[37] Be that as it may, Sir William Percy's report is positively contradicted at many points by American records, and the judicious reader is almost forced to suspect that Percy sought to make as good a case for himself as he could, and that Vice-Admiral Cochrane did not inquire very closely into the details—perhaps because both Mobile and Pensacola ceased to be of much strategic interest to him after these two defeats suffered by Percy. Cochrane's letter of December 7, which enclosed Percy's report, is more concerned with affairs at Jamaica. It is worthy of note, however, and the fact provides food for speculation, that Percy wanted to garrison and defend the Spanish forts against Jackson. Finding them not victualled to withstand a siege, however, Percy claimed that Governor Manrique refused to "invite" him to resist the Americans until it was too late for him to do so.

Jackson was neither equipped nor adequately supplied to conduct a siege. He would have had either to take the forts by storm, and this without any artillery support, or else to retreat. Had he retreated, or been repulsed, he would have lost great prestige among the Spaniards, the Indians, his own soldiers, and his fellow countrymen generally. Even had he succeeded in taking his objectives by assault, he would surely have been so hurt by casualties that his arrival at New Orleans would have been delayed considerably—and even as it was he reached that city none too soon. Thus, the outcome of the action at Pensacola, including the British destruction of the fort (which relieved Jackson from the necessity of garrisoning it), was highly beneficial to Jackson and the American defense generally.

Jackson deserved this extraordinary good fortune, surely, by reason of his energy and enterprise. His strategy in the Pensacola episode was excellent. It *was*, as he had claimed from the outset, a vital step. If Jackson had not subdued the Creeks, Mobile could not have been held. If Pensacola had not been captured, New Orleans could not have been defended as it was. Using Pensacola as a base—it was the best harbor on the Gulf Coast—the British could have landed elsewhere on the coast and taken New Orleans from above. More by luck, perhaps, than design, the British commander was being left with no choice other than to make a direct assault on his objective—to win or lose by a single throw of the dice. Moreover, news of the American victory at Pensacola, coupled with the earlier victory at Mobile, was heartening to the American defenders along the entire Gulf Coast, and it was especially important in winning the support of any wavering Louisianians.

But Nicholls' Indians and the British squadron that was carrying some of them to Apalachicola (the others were proceeding overland) had escaped Jackson, whose intelligence reports indicated that a depot of all necessary supplies had been landed at Apalachicola and that a fort had been built there, all with a view to helping the Indians prosecute the war in their own fashion.[38] Jackson was determined that the Indians "should have no rest or respite from danger, so long as a warlike attitude was preserved."[39]

Accordingly, Major Uriah Blue of the 39th Infantry, commanding 1,000 mounted men and a Choctaw company of 53 warriors led by Chief Pushmataha, which Jackson had mustered into the service on August 17, was sent in pursuit.[40] Albert J. Pickett, who drew much of his material from survivors of the war, says of this expedition:

Major Blue . . . scoured the swamps of the Escambia and all the bays in West Florida. . . . He killed many of the refugee Creeks who fought him in their dense retreats, and captured a large number, besides women and children, whom he constantly sent to Fort Montgomery, guarded by strong detachments. We regret exceedingly that want of space forces us to omit a detailed account of this fatiguing and perilous expedition, taken from the lips of an intelligent surgeon. In some other work we hope to be able to record the brilliant achievements and valuable services performed by Major Blue. We would remark, however, that he was the officer that brought the Creek War of 1813 to a final termination. No official account of this march has fallen into our hands, and we believe that none exists.[41]

The major's detachment endured many privations but saw no action except skirmishes. He did kill some Indians and he captured many others, before finishing his expedition at Fort Jackson, where he arrived with his men and animals in a starving condition but without having suffered any American casualties.

Colonel Benjamin Hawkins, on orders from Jackson, took the field at about the same time as Major Blue, with a force of friendly Creeks under the half-breed General Billy McIntosh. Jackson knew that the Indians were by now experiencing very serious doubts about the valor and military effectiveness of their erstwhile British and Spanish protectors and allies, and he wanted to drive home to them forever the superiority of the Americans in these respects. Thanks to Blue, Hawkins, and McIntosh the point was made very clearly indeed. [42] By terms of the Treaty of Fort Jackson, the Creeks were forced to give up any previous allegiance to the British or Spanish.

After the Battle of New Orleans, the British high command was criticized for not having brought into play some 5,000 Indians that it was then thought would be available.[43] In July, 1814 Admiral Cochrane had sent Nicholls to recruit and arm Indians for use by the British. In December, according to George Gleig, an embassy (including Nicholls) was sent by Cochrane from Lake Borgne to the Apalachicola to bring the Indians to the scene of the battle—but only two Indians came.[44] On the basis of these facts it seems obvious that it would have been a grievous strategic mistake for Jackson not to have followed up his humbling of the Spaniards and British at Pensacola by sending Blue, Hawkins, and McIntosh in pursuit of the Indians. And before leaving Pensacola, Jackson also cautioned the by now much chastened Governor Manrique against having any further dealings with the British, and it would appear that his later relations with Manrique were good.[45]

Jackson's concern for Mobile and Pensacola and the attention he gave to the Indian problem had not led him to neglect New Orleans in his plans, as has so frequently been charged. The 7th Infantry and almost all the artillery and artillerymen in the Military District were in garrison there, and he had also called up part of the militia of the State of Louisiana on that flank. Moreover, he had come to an understanding with his opposite number in the navy and closed all coastwise trade between New Orleans and Pensacola.

The entire operation on the Gulf Coast in the summer and early fall of 1814 was an amphibious campaign. The position in which Jackson found himself was a typical example of the dilemma that a force on the defensive in such an operation encounters when in the presence of superior sea power, especially when there is a long coastline to guard. To protect his line of communication via the Mississippi, Jackson had to guard his left flank against the Indian attack toward Baton Rouge that Cochrane had contemplated and had sent Nicholls to organize and exploit. Jackson countered this move very effectively.

After dispatching Blue and other covering troops to hold the Creek Indians in check, Jackson continued to be concerned about the defense of Mobile. Some of the Georgia militia had already arrived, however, and he knew that more were on their way. He strengthened Fort Bowyer to the point that he convinced himself (erroneously, as later events would prove), as he wrote Brigadier General James Winchester on November 22, "that 10,000 troops cannot take it."[46] In addition, he stationed regulars and militia at Mobile and posts to the northward where they could be quartered and subsisted, and whence they could be thrown where needed in event of attack. He assigned command of the Mobile area to General Winchester, a member of Jackson's Cumberland militia division before the war. "Fort Bowyer . . . is the key of communication between Mobile and New Orleans," Jackson instructed him, and ". . . it must be maintained."[47] Jackson still expected that Mobile (or Pascagoula) would be the prime objective of the British landing, and he clearly expected to return there from New Orleans in order to meet the attack.

To cover New Orleans, Jackson ordered the rest of the Louisiana militia to be embodied, and he now sent Coffee's brigade and Major Thomas Hinds' Mississippi Dragoons to Baton Rouge.[48] Jackson knew that Carroll's Tennessee militia and General John Thomas's Kentucky militia were en route to New Orleans via the Mississippi River. (That both forces were unarmed was not known to Jackson, and certainly it was not his fault that such was the case.) Jackson also ordered from Mobile to New Orleans the 44th Regiment of regulars, originally recruited in Louisiana. As stated above, his inspector-general had already gone ahead to inspect the defenses of the Mississippi and of the city, and to correct reported problems in command relationships.

When news of Winchester's arrival on the Alabama River reached Jackson, on November 22, 1814, he and his staff left Mobile for New Orleans. He knew nothing of any likelihood of a peace treaty being concluded in the near future. On October 15, 1814 his friend Charles Cassidy had written him from the War Department in regard to John Quincy Adams' report of September 5 to the effect that peace negotiations appeared almost certain to fail. "A war of seven years may be expected," Cassidy predicted.[49] Cassidy's letter must have been the last news from Washington that Jackson received before meeting the British in battle.

Thus Jackson rode toward New Orleans as a man of destiny. On the results of his efforts rested the future of the republic he served and of the continent on which it had been born. The Battle of New Orleans would establish finally and forever the United States' title to West Florida, to the mouth of the Mississippi, and to the Mississippi River valley.

4. AMERICAN PLANS
AND PREPARATIONS
DECEMBER 1–20
1814

Jackson's trip from Mobile to New Orleans was not made in haste. For one thing, his health was not good; for another, he wanted to make a personal reconnaissance of the coast. He went slowly, comparing the troublesome topography with a map Governor Claiborne had sent him (but which map this was is not known). He came to the conclusion that the mouth of the Pascagoula River, 30 miles west of Mobile but about 120 miles due east of Baton Rouge, was a likely place for a landing in force by an enemy attacking New Orleans. Considering the geography of the area as it was in 1814, Jackson's estimate of the situation would seem to be quite reasonable. Had he been opposed by a soldier instead of by a sailor in the high command (Cochrane), it is not unlikely that the landing would have been at the mouth of the Pascagoula.

A study of the theater of operations as it was in 1814—we have an accurate description from that year, prepared by William Darby of Jackson's topographical staff of engineers in New Orleans—shows that to the east of the Mississippi River, near its bank, there was a long strip of land heavily timbered because of its rich soil. Farther east, between the Mississippi and the Mobile rivers, the land broke into hills and dales, and many of the valleys contained fresh water most of the year. The Mississippi River valley itself contains many small lakes and swamps. The Mobile River had generally higher banks that were not as subject to inundation as those of the Mississippi were. Between those rivers there were several smaller streams—the Amite, Tickfaw, Tangipac, Pearl, and Pascagoula rivers—which flowed into the chain of lakes that extended from the Amite to the Mobile. Swamps and tracts of high pine were intricately interwoven in this region.[1]

Darby thought that the lakes—Maurepas, Pontchartrain, and the Rigolets at the mouth of the Pearl River—were once a prolongation of Lake Borgne. Actually, this prolongation, uniting the waters of the Mississippi with Mississippi Sound, had once been the river itself, but long before Darby's advent the river had taken a new course to the southwest. In doing so it cut off a portion of its own delta that lay between its new and old channel. This fragment of "half-made" country, comprising something over 1,700 square miles of river banks, swampland, and marsh, was then widely known as Orleans Island, on which the city of New Orleans and the battlefield of that name were located.

In the extensive area that Darby mapped, there were few roads, and in the greater part of it, there were no roads at all. Three of the roads branched out from Natchez, and another one ran north and west from Mobile, but all of them were merely wagon tracks winding through the forests, without cut or fill, following the contours of the land and the fords or ferries of the rivers.

Darby's judgment concerning the defensibility of the routes of approach to New Orleans, representing the perspective of the professional mapmaker, was written long before the British invasion and deserves our attention here:

> The shell banks and deep morasses of Louisiana have always been considered by the writer as a bulwark . . . of the country they enclose. It is an incontrovertible fact, that from the mouth of the Sabine to the mouth of the Atchafalaya, not one spot of ground is found where an army of a thousand men could land with its implements of war and penetrate the interior, except through the rivers; and when the rivers are examined . . . a small body of determined troops could, by choosing its ground, repel very superior numbers. Few places in the range specified could be transversed (except through the bayous and rivers) by any human power, without opening a canal through the fens that everywhere line the coast.[2]

Jackson and his staff arrived in New Orleans early in the morning of December 1, 1814, having crossed Lake Pontchartrain from Covington almost due north of New Orleans. They landed at the mouth of the Bayou St. John and proceeded to New Orleans by way of the road along the bayou. Major David Hughes of the 7th Infantry (Lieutenant Colonel William McRae's adjutant general) and Major Henri Chotard of the 44th Infantry (afterwards Jackson's assistant adjutant general) had joined Jackson's party at Fort St. John, a few miles from New Orleans. Among others in the small party were Jackson's adjutant general, Robert Butler; his aide (and later one of his biographers), John Reid; and Major Howell Tatum, the general's chief topographical engineer, who kept a historically valuable journal of the campaign.[3]

The general breakfasted at the home of J. Kilty Smith. The hostess, according to the story as told by Alexander Walker, was a "nameless" Creole lady, a neighbor of Smith (who was a bachelor). She took one look at Jackson's travel-worn appearance and decided that he was "an ugly old Kaintuck boatman."[4] It seems that all the Americans of the western rivers were then called "Kaintucks" or "Kaintocks" by the New Orleans Creoles, and the nickname was by no means an affectionate one. No compliment to the newly arrived general, the lady's characterization of him was a harbinger of the social cleavage Jackson was to encounter.[5]

As noted above, this story comes to us from Alexander Walker, a newspaperman born in Philadelphia in 1815, who first came to New Orleans in 1840. In gathering material for his well-known work on the battle of New Orleans, published in 1855, he undoubtedly collected many stories about Jackson from eyewitnesses to the events of those stirring days, but his sources were old men whose memories were of doubtful accuracy even when they were trying to be truthful, and who were not above giving him falsehoods, traditions, legends, and complete myths as "truth." All of their stories were grist to Walker's mill, however, for he made no claim to being a historian. Nor was he one, though he is frequently cited—even by historians—as an "authority." Walker claimed that his sole motive in writing was to rescue the "facts" of the battle from the warp and tinge of personal and political animosities and prejudices that grew up after Jackson entered politics, and yet Walker seemingly made no effort whatsoever to document anything he wrote. This is most unfortunate, since his story of the battle is colorful, and much of it is easy—even desirable—to believe. But his book cannot be relied upon, except where it is corroborated by others. Worse, many of his fanciful tales about Jackson, reflecting Walker's patriotic enthusiasm, have been accepted uncritically for so long, and by so many, that it is necessary to refute them in order to set the record straight.

Jackson plunged himself into the New Orleans situation "immediately after breakfast," literally and figuratively, attending a meeting of a number of leading citizens who were to figure prominently in the background of the defense of New Orleans. Among those present was Governor Claiborne, of whom Judge François-Xavier Martin, an eyewitness, said that he was "not unwilling to increase his own merit by magnifying the obstacles he had to surmount." Indeed, according to Martin, Jackson was surrounded from the moment of his arrival (which had been expected) by persons seeking to increase his reliance on them by constantly pricking his sense of danger.[6] In this criticism of Jackson's advisors, Martin evidently refers chiefly to Edward Livingston. As Gayarré has said, Claiborne's correspondence showed how changeable his impressions were and consequently how wavering he was in his opinions.[7]

Edward Livingston, who was secretary of a committee of safety, had chosen the welcoming committee for Jackson.[8] Livingston's position as legal representative of the Baratarians was his strongest bond with some of the Creoles, but he had many enemies among them as well. As early as 1805 Claiborne believed Livingston to be his enemy and thought he was a bad influence in New Orleans.[9] For one thing, Livingston's name had been connected with Burr's in the latter's mysterious conspiracy.[10] For another, he was a leader among the Americans who engaged in the West Florida land speculations and was very prominent in the batture controversy—a dispute over the alluvial lands lying between the levee and the river at the low water stage that had been a sore point in American—Creole relations.[11] John Randolph said of Livingston in later years: "He is a man of splendid abilities but utterly corrupt. He shines and stinks like a rotten mackerel by moonlight." It is now very much open to doubt that Livingston guided Jackson well in his relations with Governor Claiborne and the Creole leaders of New Orleans in December, 1814. Certainly Livingston could have been much more politic in the selection of people to attend this first morning gathering, and also of the guests at his dinner for Jackson that evening.

From this first day in town, then, Jackson was off on the wrong foot with a number of important men, most notably Bernard Marigny de Mandeville, a very influential Creole who was conspicuously absent—since he had not been invited—from both the meeting with Jackson on the morning of December 1 and from Livingston's dinner party for Jackson that evening.[12] Through a letter of introduction, Jackson had previously asked Marigny to be his host in New Orleans. Marigny had received the letter and had prepared to accommodate Jackson sumptuously—and then never heard from him again. Perhaps Jackson received bad advice from Livingston or others, but for whatever reason he seems to have been either rude or simply obtuse in his "dealing" with Marigny. Jackson very soon became suspicious of the Creoles, and he became more so in the course of the battle, even to the point of directing his adjutant to forbid British envoys to use any language except English in talking to Creoles in the American lines.[13]

The Mayor of New Orleans, Nicolas Girod, and a few other Creole gentlemen of Livingston's "committee of public safety" were present at this first conference with Jackson. So was the senior naval officer on the station, Master Commandant Daniel T. Patterson, fresh from his recent Baratarian raid and cordially detested not only by the Baratarians but also by many Creoles —and some Americans—who had long profited from smuggling and piracy.

The next day, Jackson reviewed the city's four companies of uniformed militia. Each company had its distinctive—and gorgeous—uniform, and each made a fine display for Jackson in parade. These militia units later made a good showing in combat as well, standing their ground courageously throughout the battle. Some of the men in the ranks were said to be seasoned Napoleonic veterans, and even the beautiful uniforms proved to be of military significance—albeit of minor significance: the British, in attempting to estimate American strength, assumed that each uniform meant another regiment. It should be noted in passing that Captain Henri St. Gême of the Dismounted Dragoons, a member of a very rich and aristocratic family, was listed as the owner of one of the privateering craft that Patterson had taken at Barataria.[14] St. Gême was to play an important part in the night action of December 23 and again in the fighting on the morning of January 8.

One of Jackson's first concerns was familiarizing himself with the geography and topography of the country around New Orleans. Though he would say later that he was astonished at the ignorance he encountered concerning this important matter,[15] Jackson did have the benefit of Darby's counsel, and also that of Arsène Lacarrière Latour. As for the prevailing "ignorance," there then existed a number of useful maps of the area, notably: (1) a map that was made by Major Bartholomew Lafon for the City of New Orleans in 1805; (2) a British Hydrographical Chart, done in 1764 by Jefferrys, Geographer to his Majesty; (3) a map in Spanish done in 1801 on the order of the Marquis de Casa Calvo; and (4) a French map made in 1803 by J. B. Poisson. It is not known whether all, or even any, of these were available to Jackson and his staff, but is seems likely that some of them were —at least *one* of them!—and it is certain that Jackson had Darby's map, which was quite accurate. From the orders that Jackson issued within his first twenty-four hours in New Orleans, dealing with the building of fortifications and the obstruction and closing of bayous and coulees, it appears that he had collected—from whatever source or sources—all the topographical and hydrographical information that he needed to prepare his defenses effectively.[16]

The city of New Orleans lies 105 miles from the mouth of the Mississippi and has two water approaches, one by the river, and the other (for light draft vessels) by way of Lakes Borgne and Pontchartrain. Lake Borgne opens on Mississippi Sound, which is separated from the Gulf by a chain of small islands extending to the eastward as far as the mouth of Mobile Bay. This is a protected route of communication between the two gulf ports. The two lakes are connected by a narrow channel known as the Rigolets.

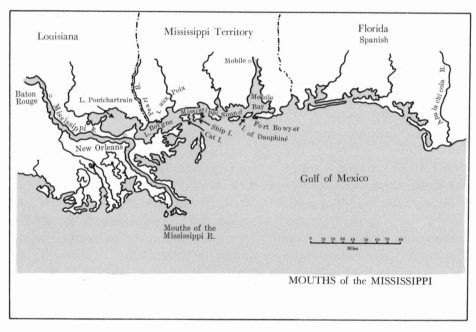

Map 5

Between the river and Lake Pontchartrain is a narrow strip of land upon which the city of New Orleans was built in 1718, fronting on the river. In 1814 the Lake was 4 miles distant. The road between New Orleans and the Rigolets, the Chef Menteur Road, passed through a tropical forest bordered by swamps that were impassable for troops; thus, if the road were blocked by felled trees it could be defended by relatively few men, provided they were not unduly intimidated by greatly superior forces that might be sent against them. Chef Menteur Road followed a narrow ridge of dry ground known as the Plain of Gentilly, and this was thought to be the most likely route for a British attack. In 1814 it was defended by a small fort at the Rigolets known as Petites Coquilles—probably the most strategic spot in Louisiana. It was easily defensible, and formidable if properly prepared. The country around it was bare of trees and was mostly a morass. An amphibious attack against it would encounter grave difficulties indeed.

The main channel of the great river was the most usual approach, but in those days it was quite a difficult one, because there were five comparatively shallow "passes," the most navigable of which was only about 12 feet deep. These passes were not then defended.

To the north of the city, on the shore of Lake Pontchartrain, there was another fort, called St. John, at the mouth of the Bayou St. John. The bayou extended to within a couple of miles of the city in those days, and it was by this route that Jackson and his party had reached the city on December 1. The bayou was navigable for vessels of up to a hundred tons. The water route through the lakes and this bayou ranked next to the Mississippi River as an artery of the city's waterborne commerce. A formidable defense could have been made on this approach.[17]

Fort St. Philip was 50 miles from the mouth at a sharp angle in the river. This was an important fortification, but it was in a state of neglect in the early summer of 1814. Across from Fort St. Philip was Fort Bourbon, but that had been dismantled. Prior to Jackson's arrival, his inspector general, Colonel Arthur P. Haynes, had decided that the forts of this route could be made impregnable to a naval attack in sailing ships, and he had diligently set about making them so. Because of the swamps surrounding them, there was no possibility of landing troops for an amphibious assault on these forts, and the British seem to have conceded their impregnability from the start. They would prove it later, by making a final futile attempt to force the forts in mid-January.[18]

There was still another defense of the river, 65 miles higher up at English Turn. At this point the Mississippi makes so decided a turn that for 3 or 4 miles flows almost due north. Thus, a breeze that would bring a ship to this point in the river would be nearly dead ahead when the ship rounded the curve and bore southward. Here, on the west bank, was another fort, St.

Leon, which was garrisoned at the time of Jackson's arrival by forces led by Brigadier General David B. Morgan of the Louisiana militia.

Unlike those of the Mobile River, the banks of the Mississippi are not high. Then, as now, levees were necessary to confine the river to its course in flood season, so that it would not inundate the plantations and settlements on its banks. The banks near New Orleans were higher than those of the lower river. The ground sloped away from the river banks into swamps, marshes, bayous, coulees, and shallow lakes.

Jackson learned that there were no less than six easily defensible approaches to New Orleans. From west to east, these were:

(1) Bayou La Fourche, a narrow deep stream, actually one of the mouths of the Mississippi, which leaves the parent river between New Orleans and Baton Rouge and enters the Gulf about 60 miles west of the delta.

(2) Lake Barataria, slightly to the east of the mouth of that bayou and about 50 miles west of the delta. Grand Terre Island, at the seaward end of the lake, was the pirate lair. Laffite's pirates had used a series of watercourses, known best to them, to bring their loot from Grand Terre to New Orleans. Defending these waterways against a landing attack on the right bank of the river would have been easy, and the broad river would have been an almost impassable barrier to an army without boats. Jackson never seems to have feared an attack from that direction, nor does it appear that the British ever considered it.

(3) The main channel of the Mississippi River itself.

(4) The Rivière aux Chênes and the Bayou Terre aux Boeufs, east of the river. These were sluggish streams, navigable to small boats. It was on this approach that Darby built his fort for Jackson.

(5 and 6) Lake Borgne, an arm of the Gulf on the east side of the delta, which reached to within 6 miles of the Mississippi at English Turn, 14 miles below the city. From Lake Borgne there were two approaches: one via Bayou Chef Menteur to the Plain of Gentilly, which was described above; the other from Lake Borgne to the river, 6 miles away. Of these 6 miles about 5 were swamp, passable only by a series of finger-like bayous and coulees, which Jackson immediately ordered to be blocked and closed.[19] Between this swamp and the river there was a strip of firm ground. On the east bank of this strip lay the city of New Orleans and plantations south of it. This was the terrain on which the battles for New Orleans were to be fought.

This must have been the area that Jackson had in mind when he com-

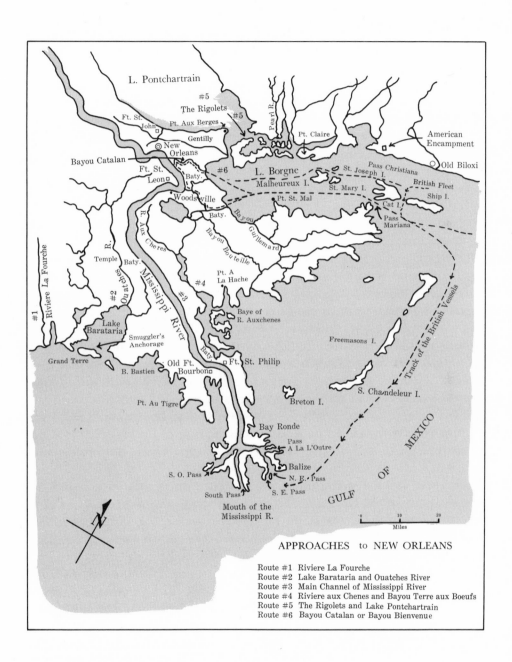

L. Pontchartrain

#5
The Rigolets
#5

Ft. St. John
Pt. Aux Berges
Gentilly
New Orleans

Bayou Catalan

Ft. St. Leon
Baty.

Woodsville
Baty.

Temple Baty.

Riviere La Fourche

#1

#2
Ouatches R.

R. Aux Cheres

Mississippi River

#3

#4

Pt. A La Hache

Baye of R. Auxchenes

Lake Barataria

Smuggler's Anchorage

Grand Terre

B. Bastien
Old Ft. Bourbon
Ft. St. Philip
Baty.

Pt. Au Tigre

Bay Ronde

Pass A La L'Outre

Balize
N. E. Pass
S. E. Pass

S. O. Pass

South Pass

Mouth of the Mississippi R.

Pearl R.

Pt. Claire

L. Borgne
Malheureux I.

St. Joseph I.
Pt. St. Mal
St. Mary I.

Pass Christiana

American Encampment

Old Biloxi

British Fleet
Ship I.

Cat I.
Pass Mariana

Freemasons I.

Track of the British Vessels

S. Chandeleur I.

Breton I.

GULF OF MEXICO

0   10   20
Miles

APPROACHES to NEW ORLEANS

Route #1 Riviere La Fourche
Route #2 Lake Barataria and Ouatches River
Route #3 Main Channel of Mississippi River
Route #4 Riviere aux Chenes and Bayou Terre aux Boeufs
Route #5 The Rigolets and Lake Pontchartrain
Route #6 Bayou Catalan or Bayou Bienvenue

Map 6

plained about the lack of topographic knowledge of those whom he had consulted in New Orleans. Tatum's comment on this point is illuminating. He says, "It appeared that scarcely any person interrogated by him had failed to acquire that knowledge, or if they possessed it [they] did not choose to communicate it, lest it might lead to a discovery of some smuggling passage into the Lakes from the river."[20] Routes through this terrain from Lake Borgne could have been easily blocked and guarded. This seems to have been done on all these routes except one—the one the British took.

Jackson first completed his map reconnaissance and study of the theater of operations. He then ordered emergency work on the forts at the Rigolets and St. Jean. Next he ordered Governor Claiborne to have all routes through the bayous and coulees closed, a task Claiborne properly assigned to his chief of militia, General Jacques Villeré. Jackson then promptly set out on a personal command reconnaissance, beginning with the forts of the lower Mississippi, on which his inspector general, with the help of the artillerymen and the navy, had been working hard to make defensible. Jackson spent five days on the river and upon completion of his tour reported to Secretary of War Monroe that Fort St. Philip and the river approaches were impregnable.[21]

Command reconnaissance is a function of military leadership that is of primary importance to every echelon of command. Times without number a competent command reconnaissance has made the difference between victory and defeat. Jackson seems to have realized that, but he could never get the opportunity to make a personal reconnaissance of the right bank of the Mississippi. In that matter he trusted staff officers, which is a professional hazard in battle, but often necessary as in this case.

Wherever Jackson went, he saw what needed doing and set people hard at work doing it. On December 12, after writing Coffee to keep his brigade in constant readiness to march, he resumed his personal reconnaissance, this time on the Plain of Gentilly and the shores of the lakes.[22] Here old fortifications were being strengthened, new ones begun, and lines of resistance laid out. Patterson had sent five of his six gunboats, under Lieutenant Thomas ap Catesby Jones, to Lake Borgne. Patterson's orders to Jones were to watch for any British advance from that quarter, keep the New Orleans headquarters informed of the enemy's movements, and fall back on the fort at Petites Coquilles to reinforce that point with the cannons of the gunboats if the British began a determined advance up the lakes. Jackson felt certain that if a battle were going to be fought in the vicinity of New Orleans, it would be a fight for entrance through this back door to the city. The British fleet was by then known to be in Mississippi Sound. Jackson was still convinced that the main British attack would be through Mobile Bay, and that any threat via Lake Borgne would be only a feint. His reliance on the ability of the gunboats to be an effective defense on the lake is astonishing; all of his naval officers must have known better, but if anyone told Jackson, there is no record of it. Everything Jackson did at New Orleans in his first two weeks in the city was calculated to leave the British no other alternative but Mobile or Pascagoula for their landing. That was, of course, the way that he had disposed the majority of his own forces to meet them, and the way that Lord Hill or Sir Edward Pakenham would probably have struck. One critical eyewitness, Martin, commented on Jackson's activities:

> His immediate and incessant attention to the defense of the country, the care he took to visit every vulnerable point, his unremitted vigilance and the strict discipline enforced, soon convinced all that he was the man the occasion demanded.[23]

When Jackson set up his headquarters and began to survey other matters, he found his own troops in a woeful situation as far as strength in men, arms, equipment, fortifications, and psychological preparation for combat were concerned. He had a very grave morale problem on his hands, for he found after his return from his reconnaissance that there were racial, class, national, religious, and political divisions within the population of New Orleans and the state of Louisiana, and that there was much factional jealousy and animosity. Some cleavages were very wide and deep, with a long history of both real and fancied injuries to justify them, as has been indicated in Chapter 2.

The Spaniards of the American Southwest were kept aware of the alliance between the British and Spanish governments, and the Spanish governor at Pensacola had even prevailed upon the Creeks not to attack Mobile during the early days of the Creek War because it was a Spanish possession which the Americans would soon be forced to return to Spain.[24]

A British expedition against New Orleans in great force had been predicted by British and Spanish agents all over the Southwest ever since the beginning of the war; and very many people, not just the Louisiana and West Florida Creoles, doubted that such an attack could be repelled by the United States. It would not have been at all strange for many of them to have concluded that the Americans were not there to stay. It is doubtful that any significant number of Creoles would have welcomed British domination; their fathers had fought for Spain against Britain in 1779–1781. While the prospect of returning to Spanish rule may have been attractive to a number of them, there were in New Orleans a great many Latin Americans of all classes who had become patriotic Americans. Unquestionably, they were in the majority.

It seems inescapable, however, to conclude that there were some people in Louisiana in 1814 who believed that big changes would result from the war and that, if the changes happened to concern the land on which they were living, it would be preferable to change rulers peacefully. Some landowners, large and small, must have had a strong impulse to protect their holdings for themselves and their descendants. It should be remembered that Spanish intrigue for return of Louisiana and West Florida to Spain had been unceasing since 1803.

There were frankly pro-British interests in Louisiana, as well as pro-Spanish ones. Some Britishers had lived there ever since the American Revolution, and there were British and West Indian commercial representatives in New Orleans. The British West Indian planters very much wanted New Orleans to be under the British crown, because this would solve all their food supply problems.

The population of New Orleans was polyglot, and disaffection was unquestionably there for Jackson to deal with. Judge Martin mentions that British agents were operating in New Orleans openly long before Jackson's arrival. Claiborne twice brought this to the mayor's attention and urged that something be done, but nothing is recorded of any action by city authorities, nor is it clear even now what they could have done.[25]

At this moment of calm before the storm, the militia had again been called up, but they were arriving very slowly. Only the New Orleans companies were at hand, plus two battalions of men of color, of unknown military quality. Patterson could not get a crew for the *Louisiana*, even though the waterfront was full of idle sailors. Constant efforts were being made by Laffite's lawyer, Livingston, and also by General Villeré and a committee of the legislature headed by Bernard Marigny, to get Jackson to accept the aid of the Baratarians.[26] The first step, of course, the *sine qua non* for the Laffites, was to get a pardon from the President for themselves and all their foreign and American accomplices. Jackson steadfastly refused. Instead, he asked through

Claiborne for a suspension of the writ of habeas corpus by the legislature so that he could impress seamen and handle spy suspects. On December 14 the legislature refused to grant this request.[27]

There is grave doubt that the legislature of any state can suspend the writ of habeas corpus constitutionally, and the Louisiana legislature was not open to censure on this matter. Recollections of General Wilkinson's high-handed procedure in 1806 undoubtedly influenced the legislature's decision, as Claiborne must have remembered that it would. And it would have given the British writers a field day if Jackson had been given his way, since the United States had gone to war over that issue of impressment of seamen. However, Jackson might have justified it as part of his *levée en masse*.

Nevertheless, the fact remains that Jackson's temper was rising fast at this moment: he had at hand fewer than 2,000 militia and only 1,000 regulars, his diminutive naval support was paralyzed for lack of men, and the enemy was known to be off the coast, in Mississippi Sound.

Gayarré, writing fifty years after the event, gives the following graphic picture:

Jackson . . . was emphatically the man for the occasion. . . . He was, above all, preeminently gifted with the precious faculty . . . of subjecting the minds of others to his own by that kind of magnetism which seems to emanate from an iron will. . . . Such qualities were eminently needed for protection of a city containing a motley population, which was without any natural elements of cohesion, and in which abounded distraction of counsel, conflicting opinions, wishes and feelings, and much diffidence as to the possibility of warding off the attack which was threatened by a powerful enemy. Various measures had been discussed, but none effectively executed. Governor Claiborne, Commodore Patterson, the Military Commandant of New Orleans, and a Joint Committee of both Houses of the Legislature, had frequently met on the subject, but their deliberations had led to no practical results. There was a multitude of advice and schemes, but nothing was done, whilst the population was becoming daily more excited and alarmed on hearing the nearer approach of the enemy.[28]

Latour, an eyewitness, takes up the story:

The citizens having very little confidence in their civil or military authorities for the defense of the country, were filled with distrust and apprehensions. Miserable disputes on account of two different Committees of Defence (one of the legislature and the one called together by Livingston) unfortunately countenanced by the presence and influence of several public officers, had driven the people to despondency. . . . Credit was annihilated. . . . Everyone was distressed, confidence had ceased, and with it almost every species of business. Our situation seemed desperate.[29]

Gayarré resumes:

General Jackson found the country he had come to defend in the most defenceless condition . . . For the defences of its extensive shores it had six gunboats and a sloop-of-war, with Fort St. Philip on the Mississippi, and Fort Petites Coquilles on the Rigolets. . . . Both were thought incapable of standing a regular siege. The supply of arms of all sorts and ammunition was very deficient, particularly in artillery.[30]

*   *   *

He (Jackson) did not deplore, in helpless despair, the scarcity of his resources; he did not write to his Government that he could not defend New Orleans with his limited means; he never thought of retreating, of abandoning one inch of territory; he saw that he had to create everything for defence, and everything he did create. In reply to timid insinuations he swore . . . that not one foot of the soil of Louisiana should be permanently held by the English, and he kept that oath to the letter.[31]

Neither Wilkinson nor Flournoy had made any permanent improvements on the fortifications of New Orleans, and Patterson had been ordered by the Navy Department to stop work on a blockship, the U.S.S. *Tchifonte*, the construction of which had been ordered in the Spring of 1813 and from which great things were expected by the navy at New Orleans.[32] This ship would have been completed by May 20 and would have been a formidable bulwark of defense, had it not become another false economy of the Madison administration.

The problem of defending the Mississippi at New Orleans had been initially "solved" by Jefferson's administration by stationing a flotilla of twenty gunboats there. By 1814, all but six of these had been decommissioned. The uselessness of gunboats had come to be generally accepted in the light of experience, but the very rapid deterioration of those at New Orleans was due largely to the lack and the misuse of maintenance funds by General Wilkinson. The plan of defense arrived at in 1814 was to depend on the naval ships based at New Orleans and on the local militia and the few regulars stationed there.

Patterson had six gunboats, of which he used five in Lake Borgne and one at Fort St. Philip. They were all schooner-rigged, but very poor sailers, and each drew about 5 feet of water. The *Louisiana,* a ship sloop, was a merchantman purchased in New Orleans in 1812 and converted to a man-o'-war. She carried sixteen guns—four 24-pounders, eight 12-pounders, and four 6-pounders—was 100 feet long, and had a beam of 28 feet. She had been known as a fast merchant vessel before she received her armament. She had no crew when Jackson arrived, partly because enlistees in the army were being paid a bounty while those in the navy were not, partly because of the navy's opposition to smuggling and piratical privateering—activities in which many citizens of New Orleans participated.

The *Carolina,* the best of the naval vessels at New Orleans, was a schooner, built in Charleston, South Carolina and purchased in November, 1812. She had arrived fortuitously at New Orleans in August, 1814, on specific orders to cope with the Baratarians. She had a seasoned crew of 95 New Englanders and an armament of twelve 12-pounder carronades and three long nines. Her length was 84 feet, her beam 24.

That was the total of Patterson's naval strength. The administration had early in the war decided that there was no danger of attack on the Gulf Coast, so both the War and Navy Departments failed to prepare properly for the defense of New Orleans.[33] The miniscule American navy was fated to take the first British blow, and it would be a hard one.

Two things were necessary to bring order out of the welter of confusion that existed on December 13 in New Orleans: a positive invasion attempt by the British, and a great commander who could offer effective opposition to them. The latter requirement was already met in the person of General Andrew Jackson. On December 14, the British provided the other requisite by capturing the American gunboat flotilla in Lake Borgne.

5. BRITISH PLANS
AND OPERATIONS TO
DECEMBER 20
1814

The decision of Vice-Admiral Sir Alexander Cochrane on December 8, 1814 to assault directly at New Orleans[1] had been kept a deep secret from the British troops—but apparently from nobody else—until the amphibious force arrived at Jamaica.[2] Cochrane reported that all secrecy had been compromised in Jamaica and that many of his logistic plans were awry.[3]

Had Fort Bowyer fallen in September, it is most likely that the Mobile route would have been taken. By December an Indian war would surely have been raging in West Florida on the line of communications to New Orleans. Cochrane was planning a landing at Mobile as late as October, 1814.[4] When he learned that Jackson had driven the British out of Pensacola, Cochrane lost interest in the entire West Florida coast. By then he knew he had to have a quick victory. The British repulse at Baltimore had made the navy's prize money in the American campaign very much less than Cochrane had promised, and the navy men were disappointed. Cochrane knew that he could count upon them to do all in their power to get a chance to loot New Orleans instead. He planned to use them unsparingly, and he did. He completely dominated the temporary commanding general of troops, the very inexperienced Major General John Keane.

Major General Robert Ross had been given explicit orders from the British Army to refuse to undertake any joint operation suggested by Cochrane if Ross did not think it militarily feasible. Keane, who arrived at Jamaica to find himself in command of the entire landing force that he had come to reinforce, had received no such orders. When Major General John Lambert, who would succeed to the command after the death of Lieutenant General Sir Edward Pakenham, set out with his brigade to reinforce Keane, he was given orders similar to those given Ross, and it appears that the War Office must have expected Lambert to arrive in time to supersede Keane prior to any landing. Pakenham had most explicit orders to the same effect, and he actually arrived before Lambert.[5] Instructions given

to Ross in the Gironde in France stated: "You will consider yourself authorized to decline engaging in any operation which you have reason to apprehend will lead either from the probability of its failure to the discredit of
the troops under your command, or to expose them to loss disproportioned
to the advantage which it may be the object of the attack to attain." Bathurst's letter to Ross September 6, 1814, *in re* the expedition against the
Gulf Coast, reiterated the above instructions and told of Keane's reinforcements being en route to him. Bathurst wrote to Keane on September 12,
1814, saying that if should he accidentally succeed to command, he was to
open the dispatches that he was carrying to Ross and be guided by the instructions they contained "and by the counsel and opinion of Vice-Admiral
Sir Alexander Cochrane, to whose views it is the desire of his Majesty's
Government that you should pay every deference." Two letters from Bathurst to Lambert, of October 5 and October 18, 1814, directed him to go
directly to Negril Bay, skipping Bermuda, and relieve Keane of command.
(News of Ross' death reached the War Office on October 17.) Lambert
was to be guided by the same instructions as those issued Ross before he
sailed from Bordeaux. He was told that Pakenham would very soon relieve
him. On October 24, 1814, Bathurst restated to Pakenham the orders given
to Ross concerning the understanding between military and naval forces.

If either Lambert or Pakenham had arrived at Jamaica or Mississippi
Sound before the landing was made, Jackson's guess as to the importance of
Pascagoula or Mobile would probably have been correct. The Duke of
Wellington himself had advised against any direct attack from the sea
through Lake Borgne on New Orleans. Lieutenant General Sir Harry
Smith told of a conversation after the war with the duke, who asked Smith
about the circumstances of the battle. Smith said at the end, "We should
not have landed where we did, my lord." "Certainly not," he said, "I was
consulted about those lakes . . . and I said it is injudicious to use them to
land an army."[6]

The entire blame for the British failure at New Orleans has often been
attributed erroneously to Cochrane, whose lust for prize money is alleged
to have led him and, indeed, the whole navy to urge this ill-fated expedition.[7]
This view ignores the well-established fact that the campaign was planned
in detail in England, by the cabinet itself, during January and February of
1814.

Originally, the amphibious attack force was to assemble secretly at Barbados in the late autumn. A diversionary effort was to have been made against the Georgia–South Carolina coast to draw the defenders there. The main effort was then to have fallen swiftly on New Orleans. Though Cochrane had repeatedly insisted on this diversion, the Admiralty had not carried out those plans. In the interest of economy, they had shifted the advance base from Barbados to Jamaica, thereby giving the show away. The diversionary effort, or cover plan, was not organized in time. It did not, as a matter of fact, strike the Georgia coast until *after* Cochrane had arrived in Mississippi Sound and it was, therefore, completely useless.[8]

Cochrane had recommended the purchase of a number of Dutch *schuyts* for navigation of the shoal waters of the Gulf Coast. These were small sailing craft of bluff bows, rounded sterns, and shallow draft, built for the navigation of the shoal waters of the Dutch Frisian coast. Instead, the Admiralty hired or purchased small craft, of too great draft, at Fort Royal and other West Indian ports, and the publicity surrounding their purchase further served to give the plan away. Cochrane had also urgently—but vainly—asked for warm clothes for his West Indian Negro regiments.

As a result of his superiors' failure to provide shallow-draft small sailing troop carriers with the transports, he also had to contend with a shortage of pulling boats at the scene of operations. Finally, he was faced with a grave shortage of provisions. The Admiralty had elected to purchase these in the West Indies to save the cost of shipping from Europe. This had driven prices up to terrific heights that the disbursing officers were not prepared to meet. There was not sufficient food to be had in the West Indies for so large a force. The search for provisions also further compromised the secrecy of the operation's objective, and made a quick victory essential. Jackson's action in closing the border of Spanish Florida to illicit trade very definitely cut off another British source of provisions, especially beef, from Louisiana. Pensacola had figured in the British plan, as another major supply base, but that was denied them also.

The capture of New Orleans had long been contemplated in British military and naval planning—ever since 1763, as a matter of fact. The available intelligence data in the Admiralty and War Office archives concerning the theater of operations must certainly have been extensive.

It has been well said that strategy and tactics are unchanging in the history of warfare. Only weapons have changed. The strength, disposition, and plans of the enemy, and foreknowledge of the geography, topography, hydrography, etc. in the theater of operations, have been essential elements of military intelligence in all warfare since time immemorial. Most such information is collected during times of peace.

Marine Major Edward Nicholls and Captains Hugh Pigot and Sir William H. Percy of the navy were all primarily intelligence operatives in charge of others working undercover, and they were in continuous correspondence with the admiral. Cochrane learned that Jackson expected an attack on Mobile, and that he had disposed his forces to meet it there. The British agents that Judge Martin and Governor Claiborne knew to be in New Orleans were but a few of the many who actually were there. The efforts of the British agents were primarily directed toward convincing whomever they could that resistance against the overwhelming power of the British would be futile, but they also reported to their superiors on the defenseless condition of the city and the fact that the inhabitants were so convinced that the city was hydrographically and topographically secure against direct attack that they were constructing no fortifications except on the lower Mississippi. Finally, the three Spaniards from New Orleans who were identified as having been in the company of Cochrane (by American prisoners after 'the Battle of Lake Borgne) were most probably not the only ones who aided the British before the landing.[9]

Nevertheless, the British afterwards admitted that they were never able to learn the exact strength of Jackson's army. Jackson's counterintelligence precautions after his arrival in New Orleans are thus shown to have been excellent, especially in respect to concealing his actual strength even from his own people.

The key point in the preliminary British advance was Lake Borgne, and the key man in the American defense there was Lieutenant Thomas ap Catesby Jones. With his small squadron of gunboats—the only type of naval craft in which he had ever served up to this time—he had remained off Ship Island until December 12, keeping the British fleet under surveillance, in accordance with Patterson's orders. Then Jones decided it was safer to retire to a position near Malheureux Island. Moving there, he saw the British light draft flotilla enter Lake Borgne, and rightly concluded that his gunboats were about to be attacked. He had been given no discretion whatever as to where he was to meet and fight the enemy; it was to be off the Rigolets, where his gunboats could reinforce the artillery strength of that fort from positions close to the beach. He immediately got underway, with a view to carrying out those orders.

The British admiral had already discovered him and, realizing that the element of surprise had been lost, he immediately set about disposing of Jones' squadron. The admiral hoped to capture the American vessels intact, if possible, so as to use them in his own later operations. However, the British sailing craft promptly ran aground when they tried to close with the Americans, "who running on, were quickly out of sight."[10]

The British did not know that Jones had also been aground for a time, just a bit earlier. A strong east wind had blown steadily for several days from the lake to the Gulf, reducing the depth of water so that even the deepest channels were too shallow to float the "Jeffs," as these gunboats were called after their protagonist, Thomas Jefferson. Everything that could be spared was thrown overboard to lighten the ship, but to no avail. Just at that moment, on December 13, the tide came in and the Americans were again able to set their course for the Rigolets. But as soon as the tide stopped running, Jones' boats began to ground again and finally, at 1 A.M., they anchored on the west of Malheureux Island to wait for another tide.

The dispatch boat *Sea Horse*, meanwhile, had been sent by Jones to bring a cache of naval stores from the Bayou St. Louis. When the gunboats escaped, this craft was cut off by the enemy barges. She drove off a first attempt by the British pulling boats to capture her, but when the British returned in greater strength her captain saw the hopelessness of the situation and forthwith burned the stores, blew up his ship, and retreated by land. The commanding officer of the *Sea Horse* was Sailing Master William Johnson, who later watched the battle of December 14 from on shore and carried news of it to Patterson. Jones later confirmed that he had given Johnson authority to destroy his ship to prevent its being captured.

The morning of December 14 found Jones' squadron becalmed, while a strong current set toward the Gulf. Then a British flotilla of some forty open pulling boats, each carrying a carronade in the bow, came into view. The flotilla carried about 1,200 veteran British sailors and marines, as compared with the total of 182 Americans divided among the five becalmed gunboats.

The proper thing for the Americans to have done then was to emulate the *Sea Horse*, taking to their small boats and blowing up the gunboats to

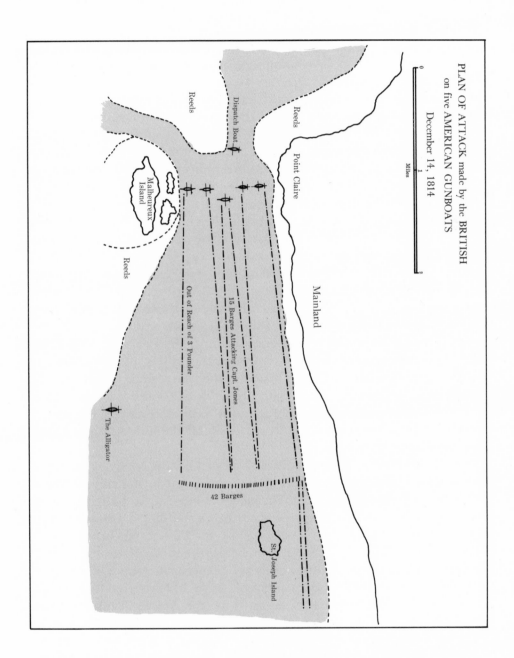

Map 7

keep the British from getting them. No one, strange to say, had foreseen the possibility of a situation developing such as the one that Jones now faced. The decision was up to him. He did have orders to retire to the Rigolets before offering battle, but the vagaries of wind and tide made that impossible. With his honor and that of the navy at stake, so he thought, he concluded that it was incumbent upon him to fight to the last. And who can blame him? No American historian has ever questioned Jones' decision, though one of the British artillery personnel present at New Orleans termed his resistance very quixotic.[11] However, his contemporaries would probably never have forgiven him if he had not fought.

Jackson's critics have said that the use of the gunboats for observation of the British fleet was one of his mistakes. But this was Patterson's error, not Jackson's. Considering the woeful weakness of the defenses at the Rigolets, one can now see that these floating "flatirons-o'-war" should have been sent there at once. Observation on the lake could have been done by smaller, swifter craft, which could have reported British movements quite adequately. If anyone could have seen this in advance it should have been Patterson; he had commanded a squadron of gunboats in those waters in 1810–1811, and he knew what erratic vessels they were, and he surely must have known of the vagaries of wind, tide, and current in the lake region.

Having decided to fight, Jones made proper dispositions for battle. A line was formed, with springs on the cables, and all ships were cleared for action. Unfortunately, the current carried two vessels off the line, and as a result three separate fights occurred.

The British flotilla, under the command of Captain Nicholas Lockyer, moored out of range of the American guns while the men coolly ate their dinner. They then closed with their enemy. They had to pull very hard against the same current that prevented the escape of the gunboats, but they could row their lighter boats against it. They came under quite effective American fire about 10:50 A.M., before their own guns could range, but they came bravely and inexorably on. Some boats were lost, but the British carronades finally began to speak, soon followed by the British marines' musketry. The flotilla bore down on the American line in three boat columns, and closed after an hour's pulling.

The Americans fought bravely, but were overwhelmed by weight of numbers and the *élan* of the British attack. The British had been told to take the gunboats at all hazards, and they did not count the cost, which was heavy.

The American flagship was one of the two that had dragged anchor and drifted out of line. Her capture was thus facilitated and, when her guns were used against them, the others were taken more easily. Jones put up a very brave fight. He was wounded, as was Lockyer. Firing ended at 12:30 P.M.

The Americans admitted 10 KIA, 35 WIA, and 86 captured.[12] The British admitted 17 KIA and 77 WIA.[13] The Americans reported the loss of 23 guns of various calibers,[14] but Lockyer listed 45 as having been captured.[15] The Americans considered the swivel guns as small arms, not naval artillery. In every ship action of that period, the captor always found more armament than the "rating" of the ship specified.[16]

That does not seem to matter much. What did matter was that the British victory was an American disaster. Jackson's sanguine hopes for the security of the lakes, about which he had written to Monroe, were shattered. He was now without lookouts or defenses on Lake Borgne. Patterson could do nothing whatever to provide any substitute boats smaller than the gunboats, because of his personnel shortage. Jackson's naval intelligence was thus nonexistent. Jackson also lost, with the gunboats, much of his defensive gunpower to hold his forts on the Rigolets and Bayou St. Jean. His naval component was reduced to the *Carolina* and one gunboat which was near Fort St. Philip. The *Louisiana*, without a crew, hardly counted.

The only good purpose served by the gunboat action was the erroneous intelligence the British received from their American prisoners in regard to the strength of the American fortifications at the Rigolets and the size of Jackson's army. By lying, even to each other when they seemed to be alone, the prisoners convinced the British that Jackson had "several thousand" men, with "more arriving daily."

As a result Cochrane decided to move all troops to Pea Island in upper Lake Borgne, in open boats, as a preliminary to advancing upon the coast. No intelligence of this ever reached Jackson or Patterson. From the point where even the lightest transports went aground to the island was a distance of about 30 miles. The trip was no holiday for the troops in open boats; there were heavy chilling rains against which cloaks would not furnish protection. Each division, after an exposure of ten hours, landed on a small desert island where Cochrane and Keane determined to collect the entire army before crossing over to the mainland. Meanwhile, constant reconnaissance for a landing place was made. The army was assembled, without tents, huts, or any other covering to shelter them from the inclemency of the weather. Pea Island was incapable of furnishing even fuel enough to maintain fires. To add to the troops' miseries, the rain generally ceased as the night closed and severe frosts set in, freezing their wet clothes to their bodies and leaving little animal warmth to keep their limbs in a state of activity. The consequence was that many of the Negro soldiers, to whom frost and cold were altogether new, actually perished, while the others were rendered unfit for combat and remained so through the entire operation.[17]

It took six days and nights to move the army to Pea Island. The strain on the sailors as well as on the soldiers must have been man-killing, but the doughty Cochrane was relentless. Time was of the essence to him, and he thought the navy would be amply repaid in prize money if they won.

On the morning of December 15, 1814, before the news of the disaster on Lake Borgne had time to reach him, Jackson published a blunt warning in regard to a rumor being circulated in New Orleans to the effect that the object of the British expedition was to return Louisiana to Spain. It is probable, as has already been stated, that at least some of the Spanish-descended Creole gentry would have welcomed that eventuality. Jackson scouted the rumor, and warned that the rules of war stated that the death punishment awaited anyone who held secret correspondence with the enemy.[18]

Jackson then proceeded on a visit of inspection to the Plain of Gentilly. A courier found him there and reported that Jones' gunboats had been taken and that Lake Borgne was, therefore, tactically in the possession of the enemy. This meant that Jackson could not meet the amphibious assault at its most vulnerable moment, while it was still afloat, but would have to surrender all initiative and await the next blow. Jackson galloped back to his headquarters, though almost too ill that day to stand, and set about transforming the frightened city of New Orleans into an armed camp.[19]

The news of the loss of the gunboat flotilla had a tremendous impact on the morale of the citizens of New Orleans and on Jackson's army. At first, panic threatened to overwhelm the city. At long last the enemy was known to be actually "at the gates," and a direct assault upon the city was expected "hourly." This was the psychological moment for Jackson to seize complete control of the city and the countryside, and to put an end to all bickering with the civilian authorities. This he promptly did.

The man and the hour had met.

A battalion of Santo Dominican men of color, under Major Pierre La Coste, was sent to reinforce the Chef Menteur defenses. Another such battalion—which had, at Jackson's unpopular orders, been recruited by Major Jean Daquin and Captain Baptiste Savary—was in the city. To Jackson they were gladiators, not a social problem. As he saw it, an old Serbian proverb applied: "You can walk with the devil as far as the bridge." The men of color were willing to fight, and Jackson had a fight in which to put them. Orders went to the forts at Petites Coquilles, St. Jean, and St. Philip to resist to the last. Navy guns were being mounted on Gentilly Plain. Orders to come immediately to New Orleans went to John Coffee at Baton Rouge, William Carroll on the Mississippi, and Thomas Hinds at Woodville, Mississippi. Another was hopefully sent to John Thomas and his Kentucky militia, who were much farther up the river, to hasten them to New Orleans.

Coffee received Jackson's dispatch on December 17, took 800 of his best mounted men, and came 120 miles in three days. Hinds and his Mississippi Dragoons came 230 miles in four days.[20] Brigadier General James Winchester at Mobile was informed of this new development, but he was still warned to be ready for an attack on Mobile. If the enemy's attempt to land through the lakes were repulsed he would have to resort to Mobile, and Jackson thought all routes through the swamp towards New Orleans from Lake Borgne were closed.

The legislature's refusal to suspend the writ of habeas corpus was ameliorated by its voting $6,000 to Patterson to use as bounties to secure recruits for his unmanned ships, and an embargo law was passed to deny stranded sailors any hope of more profitable employment on merchant vessels going up the river.[21] Patterson then got recruits. There were plenty of unemployed honest sailors who were not Baratarians. Patterson reported to the secretary of the navy on December 16 that he was paying a bonus of $30, plus $24 from the Louisiana legislature, and enlisting the men for three months only.[22]

On the morning of December 15, Claiborne informed the legislature of what had befallen Jones' squadron and asked for enlargement and completion of all defense measures. The news threw the legislature into a state verging on panic. The next day, Claiborne recommended that the legislature adjourn for fifteen or twenty days, while its members served the safety of the state, but the legislature refused to do so.[23]

Upon learning this, Jackson promptly proclaimed martial law and thereby positively established his supreme authority.[24] All persons entering the city would report immediately to the adjutant-general for examination. If they failed to do so, they were subject to arrest and detention. No one would leave the city's chain of sentinels without permission from the commanding general or one of his staff. No vessel or craft would move on the river or the lakes without a similar pass or one from the commander of the naval forces. Curfew was at 9 P.M.; persons found in the streets without authority after that hour were to be arrested as spies and detained. Jackson also ordered a *levée en masse*, since the militia was coming in so slowly. The imposition of martial law eliminated even the remotest possibility of a capitulation by the civil government of the city.

These drastic measures served their purpose. The threatened panic subsided and the city prepared itself for battle. The schemers, if any, were frustrated. Patriotic enthusiasm ran high, especially among the common people.[25] A portion of the legislature, of course, strongly resented Jackson's high-handedness, but they feared Jackson, too.[26] Jackson said later that he knew his actions were illegal constitutionally but that he was determined to stop at nothing to defeat the British.

Jackson scoured the city for supplies, particularly arms and ammunition, and the people volunteered large quantities of the needed stores. Naval records show that naval ammunition had been plentifully supplied in 1812–1813. Navy requisitions for replenishment of other supplies, but not for powder, are reiterated in later naval records. Patterson's raid on Barataria had captured thirteen vessels: brigantines, polaccas, small schooners, gunboats, and feluccas, all of them armed and ready for battle.[27] Patterson also must have obtained a considerable supply of powder and shot for the light guns there. He reported having taken twenty pieces of cannon; he said nothing of capturing powder or shells, but there must have been a supply of these things on hand that he certainly would not have left behind or destroyed. At Mobile earlier in the summer McRae had reported to Jackson a problem of guarding his large store of army artillery ammunition. However, a great deal of such ammunition would be needed in a siege.

It is known that no weapons or ammunition came down the Mississippi to Jackson until January 15, and that none reached him by sea. Still, no shortage of artillery ammunition is mentioned in any account at any time during the battle, and American expenditure was lavish and constant. The navy seems to have faced no ammunition problem either, according to naval records.

Bernard Marigny first told the story that answers how the shortage problem, if there actually was one, was solved. After the battle of Lake Borgne he went to Jackson with a committee of Creole gentlemen to urge again that the general use the Baratarians to help defend the city. The committee found Jackson, even in this extremity, adamant in his resolution not to employ the pirates. The committee then sought advice from Federal Judge Dominick Hall (later to be Jackson's bitter enemy).

All cases against the pirates and their associates in the city would come before Hall's court, and he well knew that those trials would be like the opening of Pandora's box. Therefore, he suggested to the committee that they obtain a resolution from the legislature to suspend proceedings against the buccaneers if they served the United States in this crisis. The legislature promptly passed the resolution on December 17, and Governor Claiborne issued a proclamation to that effect. How all this could have affected the proceedings of a federal court has no logical explanation, but logic evidently played little or no part in these events. Judge Hall could make the resolution work if he wanted to, and he did. He promptly released from jail all the Baratarians who would agree to enlist, and he gave Jean Laffite, who had been in hiding, a pass to enter the city.[28] This, too, seems to have been illogical if not illegal for a federal judge, but it was part of the act.

Laffite's situation was by then desperate. His pirate headquarters at Grand Terre had been raided and burned, and all his loot and ships were sequestered awaiting action in prize court in New Orleans. Most of his fortune was gone. His lawyers, John Grymes and Edward Livingston (well paid, in advance, before Patterson took Barataria), had advised Laffite not to resist forcibly, and they had prepared a suit against the United States for the restitution of this "personal property," but it was a most inopportune time to present it. If Louisiana fell to the British, Laffite and his men would be lucky to get away with their lives. If the Americans won, however, and if he and his men could contrive to play some dramatic part in the victory, his lawyers told him that he would get a pardon to cover his past crimes and that he would have a better chance in the admiralty court of getting his treasure back.[29]

On December 18, Jean Laffite called on Jackson. Latour mentions the interview, but says nothing of what passed between them. Latour should not be thought of as just another historian or hearsay reporter writing the story of the battle; he was a very active participant who played a major role in the drama. Latour, who had been a close associate of the Laffites, no doubt brought Jean to Jackson.[30] His account reads as if he might well have been present at the interview. All he says about it is: "Persuaded that the assistance of these men could not fail of being very useful, the general accepted their efforts."[31]

Laffite had a large cache of powder, ammunition, and flints for small arms at a place called "The Temple," as yet undiscovered by Patterson; and he had about 1,000 men ready to fight if the general would recommend clemency when the battle was won.[32] Never until this moment did Jackson act like a will o' the wisp. In his desperate situation he had come to realize that bravery was not enough: he had to have men and munitions. Even when Coffee and Carroll arrived he would still need powder and flints for muskets. Here they were. Angels appear in curious shapes, at times; perhaps this was an answer to prayer. Jackson accepted the offer and made a deal. He could again "walk with the devil as far as the bridge."

Judge Martin noted this phenomenon in amazement:

General Jackson had determined to have nothing to do with those he called "pirates and infamous bandits," unless it was to have them speedily hung [sic] . . . Notwithstanding all this, the two men met—Jackson and Lafitte—and General Jackson, fettered as he was by his own words and acts, revised his decision, changed his mind, and henceforth trusted to the utmost Lafitte and his bandits.[33]

Jackson did not, of course, trust them to the utmost. He organized them into three companies of "marines" and sent them out of the city to the forts at Petites Coquilles, St. Philip, and Bayou St. Jean. It is possible that some may have joined Patterson's ships' crews, but that is most unlikely because they hated Patterson and he distrusted them. Only two gun crews of Baratarians, under Dominique You (Jean Laffite's oldest brother) and Renato Beluché (his "Oncle"), were employed in Line Jackson on December 28 and January 1 and 8. These were the only Baratarians who saw any action. Jackson sent Laffite himself with Major Michael Reynolds to "The

Temple" on the west bank of the river to secure it. On December 25 Laffite came back in time to make a recommendation to Livingston about extending Line Jackson into the swamp,[34] but he took no other part until January 8, when Jackson sent him again to the west bank, to Morgan. But Laffite had served his purpose. The artillery ammunition shortage was no longer a problem.

On December 18, a Sunday, Jackson held a review of his troops in New Orleans to whip up public enthusiasm. It was very effective. According to Walker it was a great triumph for Jackson.[35] He appeared splendidly mounted and delivered a ringing speech (translated into French by Livingston) and issued a stirring proclamation. It was just what the people wanted. Their Latin blood warmed to the magic of Jackson's fiery leadership. Here was a man. So says Walker, the troubadour.

Two days later Coffee halted his advance guard of 800 men some 4 miles above the city.[36] Jackson ordered them to stay there, and kept secret all records of their strength. He was confounding British spies and keeping his unpopular "Kaintocks" away from the Louisianians at the same time.[37]

A few hours behind Coffee, Carroll's Tennessee division arrived, 3,000 strong, fairly well-disciplined men who were fairly well armed, since they had intercepted on the Mississippi a shipment of arms to Jackson from Pittsburgh.[38]

At this point Jackson could have thought he was reasonably well situated. Every approach to the city was either blocked or guarded—or at least so he believed; he had ordered it done. The Louisiana militia were scattered as covering forces or garrisons, under General Villeré or Morgan on assigned missions. Jackson himself held, in ready reserve, his two Tennessee divisions, his two regiments of regulars, the Mississippi Dragoons, the New Orleans uniformed companies of Major Jean Baptiste Plauché, and two battalions of men of color, ready to throw in whichever direction the British chose to show themselves. All the fortifications he had planned were being rapidly completed. He hoped, of course, to meet the enemy on some beach, probably near the Rigolets, and prevent a landing in force. He believed the route through the Plain of Gentilly would be the scene of conflict, but he held his striking forces back from there, too, until he was more certain where the landing would take place.

Nevertheless, on the very same day that he held his review, two British officers, guided by Spanish fishermen, found an open and quite unguarded approach within 9 miles of New Orleans. They reconnoitered the entire route as far as the left bank of the Mississippi itself, just south of the city.[39] The British army's plans for landing therefore were already made the day that Coffee and Carroll arrived at New Orleans.

The following day the next British blow fell, and it seemed to be another complete disaster for the American defenders. Actually, however, it was the very blunder that the Iron Duke had warned his compatriots not to make. Now the mistake was made, and it made eventual British defeat all but certain. But a great many men would die in battle before that conclusion would be reached.

6. THE BRITISH
LANDING

Immediately after the capture of the gunboat flotilla, Vice Admiral Sir Alexander Cochrane began the disembarkation of the British army from its transports to an assembly point on a desert island at the mouth of the Pearl River near the head of Lake Borgne, about 40 miles from the anchorage of the transport fleet.

The shortage of shallow-draft vessels restricted operations. Only about 2,200 men could be boated at one time, and there was need of all the light draft sailing boats, and especially the pulling boats, in the fleet; even the captains' gigs were used. The workload imposed on the sailors was stupendous, and both they and the army personnel suffered much from the extremely inclement weather, but the admiral was relentless; the men were further encouraged by the expectation that the prize money would be enormous.

Major General John Keane reviewed the army on December 21 and organized it for landing. He was nominally in command of troops but in fact he was merely a stooge for Cochrane, who had determined, about December 8, to attack New Orleans directly. Keane was then aboard Cochrane's flagship off Pensacola. Cochrane assembled the army at the aforementioned islet, variously called Pine Island, the Ile aux Poix, or Pea Island by different chroniclers of the battle.

Several gentlemen from Louisiana and West Florida joined the admiral—either at Jamaica, Pensacola, or Pea Island—and they probably brought the information about the passage through the swamp from Lake Borgne to a point 9 miles south of New Orleans, via the "Bayou Catalan," as the British called it. This waterway appears on old French maps as the River St. Francis, and was called "Bayou de Pescheurs" by people of the neighborhood, but it was generally known to Louisianians as the Bayou Bienvenue. Cochrane first makes mention of it officially in his operations report on the entire operations onshore at New Orleans.[1]

On the night of December 18, Captain Robert Spencer, R.N., and Quartermaster Lieutenant John Peddie, guided by some Spanish fishermen, had made a reconnaissance of the Bayou Bienvenue. They found it to be not only unobstructed, but completely unguarded. They reached General Jacques Villieré's plantation on the banks of the Mississippi, 9 miles below New Orleans, without being detected. On their return to Pea Island they reported that the city was guarded by fewer than 5,000 men, a correct estimate at that moment.[2]

This critical bayou emptied into the northwest corner of Lake Borgne, its mouth being about 30 miles due west of Pea Island. From its mouth to the Mississippi River was about 15 miles of very rugged travel for an army, or for supplying an army. It is amazing that trained, professional, battlewise veteran troops should have attempted to use it as their only avenue of advance and supply in an advanced landing operation. Used as a covered approach for a surprise attack, after Jackson had been made to commit his forces elsewhere, it could have been of great value, for such an attack could have been devastating, and quite probably decisive. Fortunately for Jackson it did not happen that way. Keane took command of the advance party himself, and everything that he did was wrong.

The failure by the Americans to obstruct or adequately guard this waterway is one of the most puzzling developments of the campaign; it has never been satisfactorily explained, and probably it never will be. All other routes of approach had been obstructed in accordance with Jackson's orders. The British themselves found La Coste's canal, which runs into the Bayou Bienvenue, completely blocked by felled trees.[3]

Jackson had ordered the closing of all approaches through the swamp.[4] However, as Gayarré naively comments:

> But, *for some unknown cause,* General Jackson's intentions were defeated, and be it from want of time, or of materials, or from negligence or oversight, it was very near producing the fall of New Orleans into the hands of the enemy.[5]

Jackson expected momentarily a report of a British landing reconnaissance *somewhere,* and he had ordered constant vigilance—videttes and patrols by small boats on the lakes. He hoped to meet a landing attempt at the water's edge, defeating it while the enemy was most vulnerable, before a beachhead could be gained.

Suspicions of treachery were entertained by Jackson and others at the time.[6] One biography of Jackson, written for Irish readers, called it the undoubted result of treachery.[7] However, the failure to close the bayou is now seen to have been caused, at the worst, by a very grave negligence of, or a delay in obeying, orders; at the least it was a grave error in judgment on the part of Major Gabriel Villeré.

The route through the bayous to the lake was commonly used by the people of the Villeré plantation. Had it been blocked in accordance with Jackson's orders, it would have been necessary to clear it again later, after the campaign, at the cost of much labor. (Gayarré says that fifty years after the battle the Bayou Manchac on the Iberville River, for example, was still blocked.) The younger Villeré may well have thought that the route was unknown to the British, but in any case, subsequent to the British reconnaissance of the 18th, the major did place a vidette at Fisherman's Village, and this would have been security enough against complete surprise—had not the vidette itself been surprised and captured. The most likely conclusion, surely the kindest, is that Major Villeré sought to avoid what he considered to be a useless expense and inconvenience to his father's property by deliberately overlooking the obstruction of this one bayou, or perhaps leaving it until the last in his obstructing operations. He had thoroughly obstructed the canal of his neighbor, La Coste, and evidence such as Gayarré's comment about the Bayou Manchac indicates that all the others were also blocked. Young Major Villeré took post at his plantation house with sufficient militia under his command to have guarded this approach efficiently, if he had been alerted in time by his outpost at the village. However, the negligence of the untrained militia was nearly disastrous. On the other hand, it seems likely that if Captain Robert Spencer's reconnaissance of December 18 had found the bayou on the Villeré plantation blocked or closely guarded, the British would not have risked forcing their way through the swamps by that route, and a different approach could well have been more successful for them.

It appears from the British accounts that Cochrane knew, through his collected intelligence, of the Bayou Bienvenue before he entered the lake, perhaps even before leaving Jamaica. When a reconnaissance on December 18 showed the Bayou Catalan or Bienvenue actually unguarded, the decision was made to use it.

The British had overestimated the strength of Jackson's forts at the Rigolets, too, because of the false information they received from the captured Thomas ap Catesby Jones and his sailors from the gunboats. Fisherman's Village, a settlement of Spanish and Italian fishermen about a mile and a half in from the mouth of the bayou, provided the necessary guides. When on December 21 a picket sent out by Major Villeré arrived at that village, all the fishermen had gone except one—and he was allegedly sick. But on the following night he was not too sick to shut up unobtrusively all the village's dogs so that their barking would not warn the picket.[8]

When the British troops were assembled at Pea Island, it was found that all the boats in the fleet together could not carry more than a third of the landing force at once.[9] This could have made it a hazardous undertaking except for the circumstances revealed by a British subaltern:

Several Americans had already deserted, who entertained us with accounts of the alarm experienced in New Orleans. They assured us that there were not present 5,000 soldiers in the State; that the principal inhabitants had long ago left the place; that such as remained were ready to join us as soon as we should appear among them; and that therefore, we might lay our account with a speedy and bloodless conquest. The same persons likewise dilated upon the wealth and importance of the town, on the large quantities of government stores there collected, and the rich booty that would reward the capture; subjects well calculated to tickle the fancy of invaders, and to make them unmindful of immediate afflictions, in the expectation of so great a recompense.[10]

Another controversy, which has raged for years, deals with the strength and composition of the British forces at various times during the battle. Some American chroniclers have striven to augment the British strength and minimize the American, while many British writers have done the exact opposite. Discrepancies are to be found even in the official records. The British returns of that day, unlike the French and American, counted only "sabres and bayonets," omitting officers, sergeants, drummers, artillerymen, engineers, sappers, miners, dragoons, and staff orderlies.[11] Even supposing there were no artillerymen or engineers present, it is necessary to add thirteen percent to the given numbers of the rank and file, for officers, sergeants, corporals and drummers. When supporting troops are present, as there always were throughout this campaign, the figures must be increased still further. (The authorized strength of the various regiments can be easily ascertained, but the information is of little value because few units, in either army, were ever up to strength.)

Units were increased by enlistments and decreased by desertions and casualties. In September, a total of only 270 replacements were sent to the 4th, 21st, and 44th British regiments. The 85th and the accompanying artillerymen, engineers, etc., who were with Ross in the Chesapeake area, received no replacements at all. Each unit was steadily weakened by battle casualties, sickness, and desertion. Chesapeake units apparently lost even more personnel before reaching Negril Bay. On November 25, 1814, when Keane assumed command of Colonel Arthur Brooke's contingent, which was previously General Ross' army, Keane's journal shows considerably fewer in Brooke's units than reported in September by Brooke when he succeeded Ross in command. Keane's journal and his D.A.Q.M. Records also vary. Colonel Alexander Dickson, the artillery commander, upon his arrival on December 25, submitted an artillery return of that date, but a few of the artillery could have come with Dickson himself on H.M.S. *Statira*.

Lord Bathurst wrote on September 29, 1814 that Ross had a total of 10,000 men for use against New Orleans, including the troops en route to join him.[12] Major Duncan MacDougall, the aide to Pakenham, stated that even after the loss of 2,036 men on January 8, the expedition still had an effective force of 6,400.[13] Therefore before the attack there were, by simple addition, 8,436 rank and file. By adding thirteen per cent for officers, sergeants, and drummers, the total would have been about 9,000 men.

So it can be concluded that before the battle the British government ordered about 10,000 troops to New Orleans. From that we can compute their approximate strength at any critical point during the battle by reinterpreting British records. This does not include troops ordered there later from Canada and Ireland.

Much has been said of the Duke of Wellington's veterans at the Battle of New Orleans. Only a few of them were Peninsular veterans. The advance force that moved out from Pea Island on December 22, under the command of Colonel William Thornton, consisted of Thornton's own regiment, the 85th or Bucks Volunteer Light Infantry, a battalion of the 95th Regiment (of the green-clad Rifle Brigade), and the 4th, or King's Own. At least one battery of artillery, a company of engineers, and a rocket battery accompanied the infantry ashore.

The 85th had been unfortunate during the Peninsular campaign and was looked down upon by veteran British regiments as "young hands" with "subaltern ideas."[14] Thornton was determined to prove himself and his regiment, and he had already accomplished a great deal toward that end in the Chesapeake campaign.

The 95th was a half-battalion from the elite and famous Rifle Brigade, which had always been in the forefront of any battle in which it participated. It was armed with British military rifles, which differed from those of the American frontiersmen in that they were shorter and lighter. This made them better suited for attaching a bayonet, with which the men of the 95th were very adept. Their rifles fired a heavier ball and had a much shorter range. The 95th were veterans of seven years on the Peninsula and in southern France, and were definitely crack troops, specialists.[15]

The 4th was another proud regiment, the King's Own. It had marched and fought under Wellington for five years, campaigned in India before that, and had taken the French islands in the Gulf of St. Lawrence in 1793. This regiment had been at the Battle of Bunker Hill in 1775 and had served throughout the American Revolution.[16]

The 21st, 44th, and 93rd were the other white British regiments; the 1st and 5th West India regiments were blacks. The 21st, or Royal North Britain Fusiliers, later known as the Royal Scots Fusiliers, was an ancient regiment with a history dating from 1678. The 21st had fought under Marlborough at Blenheim, but was surrendered at Saratoga in 1777. It was recruited again in 1781 and served in the West Indies during the 1790's. It was in Ireland during the insurrection and then served out the Napoleonic Wars in the Mediterranean. In spite of its hoary record, it was not one of the Iron Duke's regiments and Harry Smith belittled it for that reason. Nevertheless, at New Orleans the 21st did all that anyone had a right to expect of it—and more.[17]

The 93rd Highlanders had first been organized, principally of Scots as the name implies, in 1803. It had served since 1805 in the Cape of Good Hope. It had almost no battle experience, but it was a strong unit, numbering more than 1,000 men, a handsome group of soldiers who were trained to a high degree of precision and who were very proud of their organization.[18]

The 44th, or East Essex, was a newly recruited battalion of a famous regiment. This unit had served very briefly and without distinction in the Peninsular campaign, and now it was fated to be the scapegoat of the New Orleans expedition. The regiment and its commander, Lieutenant Colonel Thomas Mullins, had been praised at both Bladensburg and Baltimore, but it too, along with the 21st, drew criticism from Harry Smith, and for the same reason: limited or no service under the Iron Duke.

The 14th Light (Duchess of York) Dragoons was the only other named unit represented at New Orleans. At the outset it had only one dismounted squadron, but another later joined with General John Lambert's brigade. The dragoons were Peninsular heroes, but played no part of any significance at New Orleans, because they never obtained enough horses to become mounted. The dragoons were not sent ashore initially, nor were the two black regiments.

On the morning of December 22, an advance party of about 1,600 British troops, accompanied by a rocket battery and two pieces of 3-pounder field artillery, embarked in pulling boats. This echelon set out for the Bayou Bienvenue, followed by the next brigade in heavier craft, which were to go as far as they could. When the pulling boats became available, the men would be then ferried ashore from wherever their sailing vessels grounded. Heavy rain fell all during the day. When it ceased at nightfall, it was followed by a sharp frost. This and the crowded condition of the boats caused extreme discomfort among the men.

An advance detachment of three boats captured the American militia picket at Fisherman's Village. Four men escaped into the swamp, but only one of them reached Claiborne's headquarters—three days later. The others were recaptured. They were obviously neither alert nor properly trained.[19] Any outpost there should have had a man detailed to escape and report. Had just one man given an early warning, the British could have been stopped in a very awkward situation in the swamp, and Major Villeré might easily have emerged from it all a hero.

The boats of the main body entered the bayou at dawn, and by 9 A.M. the troops had gone ashore over a bridge of grounded boats on the edge of the bayou. The leaders then decided to advance immediately, and pushed on to the river. By noon they had overrun the Villeré plantation, where Major Villeré's entire company of militia was surprised and captured. Only one man escaped: Major Villeré himself.[20]

At noon the advance was halted. Reconnaissance in all directions found no enemy forces, and the troops were allowed to build cooking fires and make themselves comfortable. Keane thus threw away his last hope of surprise, and thereby vitiated the advantages which had been gained by the exhausting and unremitting labor of the British expedition up to that point. It was a colossal blunder.

In reviewing the foregoing, it is obvious that in this one instance, at least, Jackson was poorly served by his intelligence agencies. The absence of prepared fortifications south of the city was deemed shocking by Henry Adams, as it was by the ex-secretary of war, John Armstrong, another self-styled "military expert," who had the courtesy title of general but no military renown. Both critics chose to ignore the undeniable fact that Jackson *had* ordered the bayou closed, and the likelihood that, if it had been closed, or even well guarded, the British reconnaissance would have discovered the fact and sought another approach. The British landing seemed, of course, a crushing blow to all Jackson's hopes, efforts, plans, and future prospects. However, an unobserved movement of such a large force over such a distance could only have taken place in the seven-foot tall reed grass of the swamps and bayous of the Mississippi Delta.

Colonel Denis De La Ronde, who commanded the Louisiana regiment of which Major Villeré's detachment was a part, had sent a courier to Jackson on the evening of December 22 to apprise him of an intelligence report, just received, noting the appearance of several sails in the three bayous behind Terre aux Boeufs.[21] These were probably some of the heavier British light sailing craft that deliberately went aground as close to the entrance to Bayou Bienvenue as they could, in order to shorten the distance the pulling boats would have to travel when ferrying the remainder of Keane's advance ashore.

The next morning, Jackson sent his engineers, Majors Latour and Tatum, south of the city to investigate the sails. It was then that Latour met fugitives fleeing toward the city with the news of the British seizure of General Villeré's house and son. Latour continued the reconnaissance in order to confirm the news, while Tatum went back to relate it to Jackson. Some of the fugitives may have preceded Tatum with the report, but by only a few minutes if at all. In reporting the matter officially, Jackson said that he had learned of the British landing at about twelve noon, but he did not say from whom.[22] At all events, his decision to attack the British was taken the moment that he learned of their landing. An exploratory British landing attempt—or, at the very least, a reconnaissance in force—was the contingency

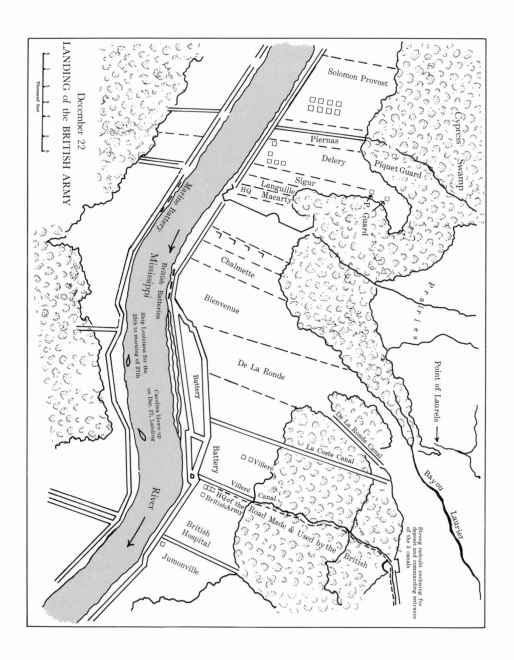

Map   8

that Jackson had expected and awaited. He had prepared to oppose the British by promptly engaging them—a fact that is proved by his readiness for an immediate counteroffensive. He waited just long enough to be sure that the British advance was not a feint and to be certain of their having landed and their dispositions. This is why Keane's decision to leave his stronghold in the tall reeds of the swamps so long before he was ready to attack seems incomprehensible. A noisy demonstration at Petites Coquilles would probably have pulled all Jackson's forces out to the east of the city, and a surprise from the swamp by even a small force would then have been catastrophic. As it was, Jackson moved to deal with the threat to his rear while he retained strong forces on the Plain of Gentilly. His plan of defense, shown by the distribution of his forces on the morning of December 23, was vindicated by the speed with which he moved to the attack. His defense was not by any means a haphazard affair.[23] By 2 P.M. he had Latour's report of his personal reconnaissance and his educated guess that the British strength amounted to 1,600 to 1,800 men.[24]

Jackson now sent forward a detachment of artillery with two field pieces, a detachment of marines, and the 7th Infantry under Major Henry B. Peire,[25] with orders to proceed as far as Mantreuil's plantation. He also sent for Coffee's brigade, which was then 4 miles above the city, and Carroll's brigade to the east of the city.

The Mississippi Dragoons, a well-trained "elite" unit led by Major Thomas Hinds, had arrived on the night of December 22. It was now hurried forward on a reconnaissance, assisted by Captain Thomas Beale's New Orleans Rifles and accompanied by Colonel Arthur P. Haynes, the inspector-general. They drove back the enemy pickets, forced the outposts to form a line of resistance, and enabled Haynes to get an estimate of their strength.[26] While this was happening, at about 3 P.M., the British were bathing, resting, or sunning themselves after dinner; the weather had been cold and wet (as it was to be again soon), but this particular afternoon was hot and without rain—a pleasant change. The outpost action was taken to be a rout of the American dragoons, and was imagined with amusement by the already overconfident British troops. "As the Americans had never dared to attack," they supposed, "there was no great probability of their doing so on the present occasion."[27]

By 4 P.M. Coffee was in position along the Rodriguez Canal. Daquin's battalion of men of color, the 44th Infantry, and Plauché's battalion of uniformed companies from New Orleans arrived during the next hour. With Claiborne in command, the 1st, 2nd, and 4th Regiments of Louisiana militia, plus a volunteer mounted company, took position on the Plain of Gentilly to cover the city in the event of another attack on the side of Chef Menteur, where Jackson still expected the main enemy effort to be made.[28] They were supported by Carroll's brigade of Tennesseans. In terms of the best estimate of the situation at the time, this was a sound and logical disposition of forces on Jackson's part.

Jackson had made up his mind at noon to attack that night, using about 2,000 men. The attack was to be made from three sides simultaneously—even in daylight a most difficult maneuver for highly trained modern troops, with their vastly superior means of communication among the several attacking echelons. Jackson was attempting it at night, using combined land and naval forces, many of which were as yet untried in battle. The *Carolina*, under Master Commandant Robert Henley, was to slip down the river, anchor opposite the British camp, and open fire at 7:30 P.M. Patterson, Henley's superior officer, went aboard for the battle but did not assume command of the ship. When they heard naval gunfire, Coffee's brigade, Hind's dragoons, and Beale's Orleans Rifles—about 600 men in all—were to attack from the edge of the swamp on the right of the British camp. Jackson would attack at the same time from the north, using his two regular infantry regiments, the New Orleans battalion of uniformed companies, and one battalion of men of color. He also had the artillery detachment with its two light fieldpieces, and the detachment of marines.

As so often happens when a time-schedule jumpoff is planned, especially at night, Coffee was unable to get into position until long after 7:30 P.M. He had to abandon his horses at De La Ronde's plantation, from where he proceeded on foot in the early darkness of an extremely short December day,[29] leaving Hinds and his Dragoons at De La Ronde's as a rallying point. They took no part in the night's action and were, therefore, available the next day and subsequently thereafter as a very efficient covering force. Coffee turned his horses loose—he did not wish to spare even a few horseholders—but most of the animals were recovered the next day (though the British did get a few strays).

Darkness fell soon after 5 P.M. The British camp was dotted with campfires, and the entire army was completely relaxed and unsuspecting. A picket challenged without receiving an answer as the *Carolina* anchored in the river near the eastern bank, opposite the point which she judged to be the center of the British camp. The British seem to have suspected nothing.

Thus, about twenty-four hours before the peace treaty was to be signed in Ghent, Belgium, the last battle of the War of 1812 was to be General Andrew Jackson's surprise night attack on the British invaders. It would decide the fate of New Orleans.

7. THE NIGHT ATTACK AND
ITS RESULTS
DECEMBER 23–31
1814

At 7:30 on that evening of December 23, 1814—right on schedule—the U.S.S. *Carolina*'s guns opened fire on the British camp. The surprise was complete, as "a deadly shower of grape swept down numbers in the Camp."[1]

Understandably in the circumstances, there was much panic and confusion at first. The alarm post was Major General John Keane's quarters in the Villeré house, which happened to be the central target of the American schooner's fire. The foremost picket of the 95th, under a very able officer, Captain William Hallen, stuck to its post throughout the battle; but a picket of the 85th, to Hallen's right rear, was driven from the field. Discipline soon reasserted itself, as officers and men in camp took shelter under the levee—or any other cover they could find—and sorted themselves into a semblance of order. However, the commanding officer of the 95th, Major Samuel Mitchell, was captured while taking reinforcements forward.[2]

Keane reported that there were three ships firing on him that night.[3] Gleig listened to the patter of grapeshot and the shrieks and groans of the wounded.[4]

General Jackson, on hearing the signal, moved forward immediately. His advance guard very quickly engaged Hallen and the 80 men of the 95th. These men held their position with tenacity and once even counterattacked vigorously, but Jackson's men extended to their left and took the position just evacuated by the picket of the 85th. Continuing to advance in that direction, the Americans now encountered more companies of the Rifles and the 85th, which were trying to come up on Jackson's left flank. There ensued a blind and confused struggle in the dark, with the British firing on British, Americans on Americans. In many places the fighting was savagely contested with bayonets, knives, and rifle butts. The Americans gained the road in the rear of Captain Hallen and captured 30 men on their way to him, but they were unable to carry his position, though the captain and 40 of his men fell, dead or wounded.

Colonel George T. Ross, commanding the New Orleans uniformed militia (who were brigaded with the 44th), would not let the uniformed companies charge with the bayonet, though they clamored to be led to the assault.[5] Gallant as those Creoles were, the bayonet was a weapon in whose use the Peninsular veterans of the 95th were thoroughly adept, and the Creoles could well have been overmatched. On the other hand, the picket might have been overwhelmed by weight of numbers, if nothing else, and this would have routed the British outposts. Hallen was the kingpin.

The British captain's riflemen made a determined effort to take Jackson's two artillery pieces, which were inflicting considerable damage, and the effort very nearly succeeded. Jackson himself rallied the marines, who were then faltering (as was a supporting company of the 7th Infantry), and the British charge was repulsed. During this stage of the action Jackson was within pistol shot of the enemy, seemingly fearless in the midst of a shower of bullets. His example inspired his men to heroic efforts and made his reputation for personal bravery as secure with the Louisianians under his command as it already was with his Tennesseans. This was attested years later by a participant in the action, one Vincent Nolte, a German merchant who fought as a volunteer with one of the uniformed companies. Nolte was no friend of the general, it seems, but he did admire the bravery and leadership exhibited by Jackson that night.[6]

Meanwhile, but somewhat later than Jackson had expected, Coffee fell on the outposts of the British right flank, driving them back until he faced the enemy drawn up in strength on La Coste's plantation. The British camp guards had stood their ground for a time, but the Tennesseans' murderous rifle fire finally drove them back behind an old levee, from which they could not be dislodged. Captain Thomas Beale's Orleans Rifles, a group of untrained American lawyers and businessmen, were supposed to be operating on Coffee's left, but they became separated from him and penetrated into Villeré's plantation, where they took a number of prisoners. However, many of the riflemen later fell among a strong body of British reinforcements just arrived from the lake and were themselves captured—an incident that afforded the British great amusement. Nevertheless, the rest of the company succeeded in reaching the American lines with several prisoners still in tow.[7]

Coffee, seeing that the British were being steadily reinforced, concluded that he could not carry the old levee without excessive losses, fell back in good order to consolidate his forces. Reporting his situation to Jackson, Coffee said that Beale's Orleans Rifles and 200 men of Coffee's own had been

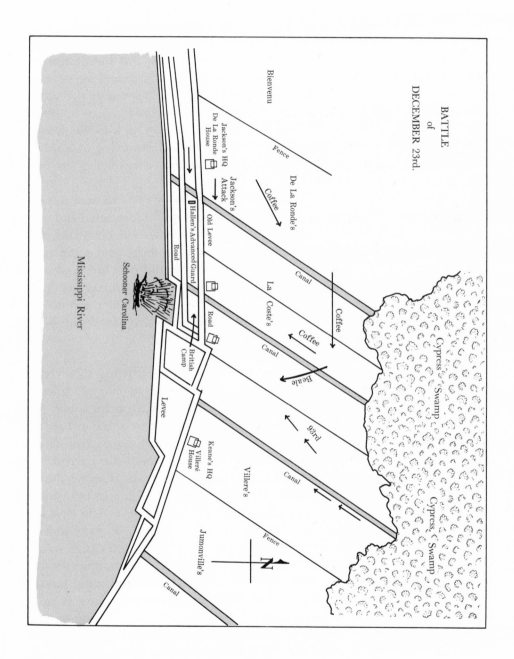

BATTLE
of
DECEMBER 23rd.

Bienvenu

De La Ronde's

Fence

Coffee

Jackson's HQ
De La Ronde
House

Jackson's
Attack

Hallen's Advanced Guard

Old Levee

La Coste's

Canal

Coffee

Road

Coffee

Canal

Beale

Schooner Carolina

Mississippi River

British
Camp

Road

93rd

Levee

Keane's HQ

Villeré
House

Villeré's

Canal

Jumonville's

Fence

Canal

Cypress Swamp

Cypress Swamp

Cypress Swamp

N

Map   9

lost on his left. He described the very strong position the British were then holding, the continual arrival of their reinforcements, and the danger of bringing his own forces under the fire of the *Carolina*'s guns if he were to close any further. Actually, though Coffee could not know it at the time, only 63 of the missing 200 men were lost (killed or captured); the rest, along with half of Beale's Rifles, successfully fought their way back to the American lines. When the *Carolina* heard the Tennessee rifles firing at a short enough distance to be within range of her guns, she ceased firing lest her projectiles hit Coffee's troops.

Jackson decided against taking further action that night. His own forces, ill disciplined and bewildered (no matter how brave), were scattered and out of efficient control. Beginning at 8 P.M. a thick fog had settled, obscuring the battlefield and making identification of friend or foe difficult and uncertain. Jackson believed that he had won an initial victory, and that he could improve upon it in the morning. With this in mind he broke contact with the enemy—though he remained on the field with his army during the remainder of the night—and sent word to Carroll's Tennessee Brigade to join him for a renewed assault on the morrow.

Jackson began to withdraw about 9:20 P.M., but according to several accounts a certain amount of desultory firing from "trigger happy" troops continued until well after midnight—an entirely normal phenomenon in any night action, even with seasoned troops. It was at best a drawn battle. The reported casualty figures favor the Americans, but in a very real sense Keane's report that the British had "won" the engagement was correct. A "loss" could have destroyed Keane's advance guard to a man. Hence, a draw was a victory of sorts for the British. The American official report of casualties shows 213 as the total loss: 24 KIA, 115 WIA, and 74 MIA. The British officially reported 213 dead and wounded alone: 46 KIA and 167 WIA. Added to that were 64 MIA who were prisoners of the Americans, making a total loss of 277.[8] It seems reasonable to suppose that only the most seriously wounded British personnel were reported as such. The additional naval strength on-shore and the number of naval personnel casualties is not known. It would also be interesting to know the number of non-battle casualties and the extent of British desertions; the latter were admitted by Gleig and Surtees to have become a grievous problem eventually.[9]

The strength of the forces engaged that night has been variously reported by historians. Keane was continuously reinforced during the battle. If he had only 1,600 (bayonets and sabres) to land with, as Gleig reports, he admitted in his official report to having 4,703 effectives on the field by the morning of December 24 (and this figure does not include staff and service personnel). British prisoners estimated his total strength that night at about 6,000. Opposed to them, on the morning of December 24, Jackson had under his command only 1,954 in action.[10]

Gleig says: "The victory was decidedly ours, for the Americans retreated in the greatest disorder."[11] This claim is clearly in error, since in point of fact Jackson was able to reform his forces not far from the battlefield, intending to renew the attack the next day. The comment of the official British Army historian, Fortescue, seems definitive on this point:

It is perhaps hardly too much to say that, if he [Jackson] had not encountered Hallen's handful of veterans from the Light Division upon the main road, he would have gone near to destroy one half, if not the whole, of Keane's detachment.[12]

Twelve hours after the advance guard had left Pea Island, part of the second British brigade followed in what were left of the fleet's light craft. Hearing the *Carolina*'s fire while still 20 miles away, they were rushed to the field by the pulling boats and arrived during the action. The boats of the first echelon, as they returned, were all hurried back, and by tremendous exertion the navy managed to get the entire landing force from Pea Island ashore before dark on December 24.[13]

Any idea of making a second landing at the Rigolets or the Bayou St. John was now almost impossible. The entire army had been committed into the cul-de-sac chosen by Vice-Admiral Sir Alexander Cochrane, and an attack on any new front would have to be preceded by a very difficult withdrawal, unless enough new troops arrived in Mississippi Sound to make a second landing in force. The precipitate action of the naval command in putting the entire landing force ashore through the Bayou Bienvenue was brought about by Jackson's night attack. Keane reported that he had been attacked by 5,000 men.[14] Gleig said:

Our loss . . . was enormous. Not less than 500 men had fallen, many of whom were our finest soldiers and best officers, and yet we could not but consider ourselves fortunate in escaping from the toils even at the expense of so great a sacrifice.[15]

For a moment, at least, the British high command feared being overwhelmed by Jackson. No further confidence was reposed in the tales of deserters whose every word had been so avidly listened to. Thereafter, indeed, they were treated by the British more like spies than deserters.[16]

The *Carolina* was joined by the *Louisiana* sometime after fire was opened, but at least a mile above her. The two ships continued to harass all British forces within range of their naval batteries and to interdict the road along the levee into New Orleans. It seems obvious from Keane's report that he was badly shaken by what had happened and by the situation confronting him. Any attempt on his part to advance, raked by flanking fire from the ships in the river, would be extremely costly, especially if he made the attempt without counter-battery artillery support. Before he would advance, therefore, he sent for heavier artillery on December 24 to drive the American ships from his flank.

With veteran troops like the Rifle Brigade present, it can be safely assumed that some sort of forward reconnaissance was made, if only by the junior commanders. However, "Subaltern" bewails the fact that none was made by *his* unit. Such a normal reconnaissance would have found that the plain in front of Jackson's lines was inundated by fully 30 inches of water, as a result of his having cut the levee below his lines.[17] But on December 27, unfortunately for the Americans and fortunately for the British in several ways, the river crest fell below the level of the levee.[18] As the water ran off the plain, Villeré Canal was filled with water for a time, greatly assisting the British in bringing up stores and naval artillery by boat. The inundation had, however, precluded any advance by the British in the period from December 25 to 27, during which interval Jackson was beginning to form his defensive position at Rodriguez Canal. If the river had continued to rise, the British would have had to retreat to their boats or else surrender. Thus, Jackson's cutting of the levee cannot properly be counted as an error on his part. It very definitely worked to his advantage for those critical three days, and it would have been still more advantageous but for circumstances wholly beyond his control.

Another break in the levee had been made, on Jackson's orders, by Brigadier General David B. Morgan's Louisiana militia, south of the British camp. This had been promptly repaired by the British, and the outpost commander in that area, a captain of the line, was put under arrest by Pakenham for not having prevented the break.[19] The fears of being flooded out by the Mississippi continued to preoccupy the British until their withdrawal, and such fears later influenced Lambert's decision to retreat.

By 4 A.M. on December 24 Jackson had withdrawn his army (except for Hinds' covering force) behind Rodriguez Canal, and early the next day he began on defensive fortifications there. Jackson had come to the conclusion that the British had been so heavily reinforced during the night that his earlier plan, to renew the attack at dawn, was no longer feasible. Accordingly, he elected to take the defensive. One American account of the battle gives partial credit for this decision to Edward Livingston by virtue of his having brought Jackson into contact with an officer who had served under Bonaparte, a Major Henri St. Gême, who commanded one of the uniformed Creole companies at New Orleans.[20] In any case, Jackson made the decision, and Jackson assumed responsibility for its consequences. The city and surrounding country were ransacked for entrenching tools, horses, vehicles, muskets, and men (slaves and conscript soldiers),[21] and the work of fortifying the line went on, night and day, Christmas included. Jackson, in the extant portions of his personal manuscript account of the battle (in the Library of Congress), discussed his decision to entrench, but there is no mention of his receiving any advice from St. Gême or anyone else. Jackson's manuscript tells of the reluctance of many of his troops—reluctance amounting almost to mutiny—to perform their fatigue duties. Many of the whites objected to doing manual labor, it seems, on the theory, widely held at the time, that such work was fit only for Negroes.

In New Orleans, meanwhile, martial law was tightened to such a degree that the mayor, Nicholas Girod, complained that the guardhouse was full.[22] Jackson's doubts about the loyalty of some of the Creole planters had been strengthened during the night of the battle, when one or more tried to ascertain from his provost marshal Jackson's plans about the city in case of defeat by the British.[23] They feared he would burn it before evacuating it, and in fact, he said afterwards, he had every intention of doing just that. This fear seems to have had no effect on the Creoles on Jackson's lines, those upon whose loyalty and valor he was depending, unless it was to make those fighting Louisianians all the more desirous of victory. But certainly the fear did play a part in the development of the animosity toward Jackson that was shown by some of the Creole gentry after the fighting was over.

To all intents and purposes, the Battle of New Orleans had been decided on December 23, 1814. In the fighting to come there was to be no repetition of Bladensburg, thanks in part to Jackson's leadership and acumen, but thanks also to the quality of the Americans under his command—Anglo-Saxon and Latin, militia, volunteers, and inhabitants of the western frontier in general. If the British had had an opportunity to win an easy victory on the afternoon of December 23—a very debatable point—they had forfeited it forever.

Christmas Day, 1814, was no holiday for either of the contending forces below New Orleans. The British troops had a very cheerless, frugal meal. Despite efforts on the part of some to be gay, the pall of their recent heavy casualties weighed upon them all. The long range harassing fire of the *Carolina* and the *Louisiana* was a constant reminder of losses already sustained, and occasionally inflicted new casualties. While Gleig was at dinner, one of his soldiers was cut in two just outside his hut. Surtees tells of a field hospital that was continually fired upon.[24]

Gleig and "Subaltern" also speak very resentfully of the "barbarous" lack of chivalry on the part of the Americans, who were constantly attacking the British pickets, "acting the part of assassins rather than soldiers."[25] On the Continent, it seems, armies led by "gentlemen" never molested each other's pickets or disturbed the sleep of the enemy by petty night attacks. But in their campaign for New Orleans, the British, after December 23, could not even have a campfire at night, lest it attract an artillery round.

Lord Macaulay, writing soon after the War of 1812, had no patience with his fellow countrymen's "chivalric" notions about war, as expressed by Gleig and other Britishers. Such a view, he believed, sprang from an utterly heartless idea of war as a mere game of chess, a game played for the love of it by gentlemen who think the world exists only for their use. War ought never to be undertaken, Macaulay declared, except under circumstances that render impossible any and all exchanges of courtesy between the combatants. For better or worse, Macaulay's idea seems to have outlived Gleig's in the conduct of modern war.

"Assassins" though they were in the opinion of "players" on the British side of the board, the defenders were working day and night—in defense of their country. While one rank slept on its arms, the other worked at fortifying its lines along Rodriguez Canal. Some there were who did not care for "Negro work," but they also worked, albeit reluctantly. Jackson, meanwhile, was alert to the possible threat of a second landing at Chef Menteur, and he answered several false alarms there.

Major Thomas Hinds' dragoons kept a constant watch to the front and bedevilled the British pickets throughout the day, while the Tennesseans and Captain Pierre Jugeant's Choctaw Indians "assassinated" them all night. Throughout the battle, the Mississippi Dragoons absolutely denied the British any reconnaissance of the American fortifications.[26] This allowed the idea to begin to grow in the mind of many a British enlisted man that the line might be so strong as to be impregnable.

One of Jackson's Choctaw Indians, who was known by the name of Poindexter, did a big business during the campaign by killing British sentries and selling their rifles to the American officers as souvenirs. These rifles were comparatively short, with round barrels only 30 inches long but quite thick and heavy, and fired a bullet weighing twenty-two to the pound (i.e. about three-fourths of an ounce). Such a blunderbuss made a terrible wound.[27]

A salvo of artillery from the British camp on Christmas Day caused momentary alarm, but Hinds reported that it was only a new general arriving.[28] It was not the Duke of Wellington, as was at first reported, but his wife's brother, Sir Edward Michael Pakenham, another North of Ireland Irishman, who had been born not far from the birthplace of Jackson's parents.

Pakenham's reaction to the situation to which Keane and Cochrane had committed him is best told by Fortescue, the British Army's official historian:

Sir Edward Pakenham . . . distrusted Cochrane and had been most anxious to take up his command before operations should have been begun.

When he realized the situation into which the Admiral had decoyed the army, he was with good reason furious. To all intents his force was cooped up on an isthmus three-quarters of a mile broad between the Mississippi and the swamp. In front was Jackson's fortified position; on the river were the enemy's armed vessels, flanking the only possible line of advance; and in rear was the lake and the sea. The only base of supply was eighty miles distant, and accessible only in open boats; and the last four miles of this waterway were so narrow that it could hardly admit two boats abreast. When water-carriage ceased, the track from the landing place to the camp—a distance of about four miles—was so bad after rains or high tides that provisions and stores could only be brought forward on men's backs. Moreover, victuals, with the exception of a few cattle, were unobtainable upon the spot, and the total quantity of supplies in the fleet did not exceed one month's store, which, taking the return voyage into account, was none too great. Again, the line of communication was insecure; for five miles north of New Orleans was Lake Pontchartrain, from which there was an outlet into Lake Borgne. The squadron could not provide guardboats to watch this and other channels, so that it was perfectly open to the Americans to send a force against the landing-place, destroy the depots there, and intercept all incoming barges. Lastly, Lambert's brigade had not yet appeared; and the force on the spot was reduced to fewer than five thousand effectives of all ranks. . . . The negroes of the West India Regiments, having been sent away without blankets or warm clothing, were so much numbed with cold that they were absolutely useless even for fatigue duties. . . .

In the depth of his disgust Pakenham used strong language, which was pardonable, but he used it without concealment, so that his opinions filtered down to the privates, which was inexcusable unless he had determined to abandon the enterprise altogether. . . . [But] he considered persistence in the undertaking, until he had at least dealt the Americans a severe blow, to be the only safe way of extricating his forces.[29]

Fortescue cites no primary authority in support of his statements concerning Pakenham's strong language or feelings. It is known that Pakenham had served before with Cochrane on amphibious operations in the West Indies. This may have been one reason why Sir Edward was selected to command this operation. Sir John Cooke hints at some sort of command disagreement, as hearsay. However, every official report consulted, army or navy, stresses interservice harmony. Even so, there is some evidence that Pakenham may have distrusted Cochrane.

The ever-imaginative Walker tells the story that Pakenham immediately wanted to withdraw and to effect a landing in another quarter. William James says that the possibility of an attack on the fort at Petites Coquilles was reconsidered (the fort's actual weakness then being known), but that the decision was reached that Americans could be defeated anywhere; this being so, it was obviously better to thrash them where they were rather than go to the trouble of a move.

According to Walker again, Cochrane shamed Pakenham out of a possible decision to withdraw by declaring that if the army shrank from the risk then his (Cochrane's) sailors would carry the "Dirty Shirt" lines alone and march victoriously into the city—and "the soldiers could then bring up the baggage."[30] This dramatic story, which many American historians and biographers of Jackson have quoted as authoritative—as "history"—is unquestionably a canard, whether told in the Walker version, as it usually is, or in a variant that has Cochrane "shaming" Pakenham in regard to the decision to make an assault on January 8. Such discrepancies aside, the idea that the old and courtly Cochrane would speak in this way to a young army lieutenant general—and especially to an Irish nobleman such as Sir Edward, who was related by marriage to the Iron Duke—is, to put it plainly, preposterous on its face. Furthermore, there is nowhere to be found even one British source that does so much as hint that any such incident took place on any occasion during the New Orleans campaign. More tellingly still, there is much evidence, apparently reliable, that indicates that the incident could not possibly have occurred. For example, Captain Edward Brenton, who had previously served under Cochrane in West Indian amphibious operations, states positively that Cochrane lived up to the letter of the tradition that prevents the naval commander of an amphibious operation from interfering in any manner with the landing force commander when the troops are on their beachhead.[31] Of course, Brenton presents the case for Sir Alexander Cochrane, his staff, and the navy, but Lambert's official report of the operation specifically states that the interservice cooperation was "excellent" throughout the campaign. Cochrane, in truth, was an old hand at amphibious operations, and he was one naval officer who had and continued to enjoy a fine reputation in army circles.[32] A British artillery junior officer who was at New Orleans recalled that Cochrane captivated those around him by his courtly and charming manner. After meeting Cochrane for the first time, another army officer reported that he "scarcely ever saw a finer old man than Sir Alexander, or one whose manners were more affable and winning."[33]

Sir Edward Pakenham, though younger than Cochrane, was a lieutenant general and thus held a parallel rank to the vice-admiral, and he was also experienced in amphibious operations and no stranger to large commands. Pakenham was personally known to Cochrane, and was known to both Cochrane and his staff as one of Wellington's favorite young commanders. That Wellington, as early as the previous June, had himself recommended against a direct attack against New Orleans was surely remembered by both

Pakenham and Cochrane. The admiral had been driven by circumstances, related above, into the rather precarious situation in which both officers now found themselves. Considering these circumstances, it is safe to assume, quite apart from the evidence cited above, that Vice-Admiral Cochrane would have been, and indeed was, prepared to abide willingly by almost *any* halfway plausible decision that Pakenham might have seen fit to make. In reaching his actual decision, Pakenham—who had never fought Americans before—was probably influenced to some extent by the contempt in which veterans of the Bladensburg campaign still held the "Dirty Shirts," as they had nicknamed the backwoodsmen. The decision was logical enough, considering most of the facts on which he had to base it. The first thing to be done, obviously, was to clear his left flank of the naval armament on the river—a task that Keane had already set about doing even before Pakenham's arrival on the scene.

On the day following Pakenham's assumption of command, a battery of nine fieldpieces—two 9-pounders firing hot shot, four 6-pounders firing shrapnel, two 5½-inch howitzers, and a 5½-inch mortar—was erected on the bank, with furnaces for heating shot,[34] and commenced firing. The *Carolina* was kindled (by the second shot fired) and burned soon after daylight on December 27. The *Louisiana*, anchored about a mile upstream from the *Carolina*, was towed out of range by her small boats.[35] Sir Harry Smith criticized the British artillery for not burning the *Louisiana* as well as the *Carolina*, and many American writers have made the same criticism. Dickson's account records that the *Louisiana* was out of his range. However, Pakenham had expressed doubts about the capabilities of fieldpieces for the purpose; he wanted to wait for four navy 18-pounders, which would definitely be capable of disposing of both vessels. Dickson admits to having persuaded Pakenham against such a delay. To a certain extent, therefore, Sir Harry's complaint seems to be warranted.[36]

As for the unfortunate *Carolina*, she might well have also escaped but for the fact that the second British hot shot lodged in an inaccessible spot where the fire could not be put out. Even so, Patterson or Henley could have saved the vessel. While it is true that an unusually strong current and adverse winds had frustrated all efforts to move her upstream, she could have been sent swiftly downstream.[37] Patterson admitted to the secretary of the navy that he was not insensible to the danger of her being burned, and that he was well aware of the vital importance of the naval enfilade fire to protect Jackson's position. He and his officers and men did well to save the *Louisiana*, the heavier and better armed of the two vessels. By his own account, Patterson considered the possibility of dropping the *Carolina* downstream, thereby saving her until the advent of winds and currents that would permit moving her upstream, but he continued to hope until it was too late that conditions would change. This is understandable, and the fact that the fire could not be extinguished was very "bad luck" indeed. Nevertheless, the loss must be scored as the result of another costly—indeed, disastrous—error of judgment on the part of the commander of the naval forces.

The *Louisiana* took station across the river from Line Jackson so as to be in position to enfilade his front. Most of the crew of the *Carolina* was saved (except for 1 KIA and 6 WIA) and was used, in part, to man artillery on Line Jackson. The crew might have been much better used to man a boat flotilla —to frustrate any British attempt to cross the Mississippi, or perhaps to attack their tenuous line of supply in Lake Borgne—but at the moment Jackson was desperate for trained gunners, and the well-trained crew of the *Carolina* had managed to land two of her guns before abandoning ship.[38]

At dawn on December 28 Pakenham advanced on Line Jackson in two columns—Major General Samuel Gibbs on the right with the 4th, 21st, 44th, and 5th W.I.R., Keane on the left with the 85th, 93rd, 95th, and the 1st W.I.R. The dragoons, still unmounted, were left to guard the camp and care for the wounded.[39]

It was a clear and frosty morning. On sighting the advancing columns, the American observation corps fell back, making no attempt to impede their progress. The British were in high spirits, despite their having been given a very bad night by the Choctaws, Mississippians, and Tennesseans— every one an "assassin," by Gleig's accounting. (Surtees was also to describe those same ungentlemanly harassing maneuvers, but this old soldier said only that he trusted that "Englishmen would be equally zealous and bitter to their enemies should our country be invaded."[40])

The British columns advanced 4 or 5 miles without encountering any check until, rather suddenly, they found themselves confronted by Jackson's fortifications. Several houses at a turn of the road on the British left had obstructed the view, making it impossible for them to see the American position until they had come quite close to it. At this point the artillery on

Line Jackson (only five pieces had yet been mounted) and the guns of the *Louisiana* in the river opened up with very telling effect on the British columns, which had been allowed to advance without hindrance until they were squarely in range. The British were later to admit that on no occasion did the Americans assert their claims as good artillerymen more effectively than they did on this occasion. Surtees called it "as destructive a fire of artillery as I ever witnessed."[41]

The British infantry were deployed and the field artillery went into action, but part of the latter was soon silenced by Jackson's artillery and the guns of the *Louisiana,* with a heavy loss of British cannoneers. The infantry halted on orders about 600 yards in front of the American line and took shelter in the wet ditches to escape the devastating American fire. Some of the infantry, those who were near the river, had to remain in the ditches until nightfall; the others withdrew as best they could, on orders, one or two at a time. Such a withdrawal did not appear to be in "good order." Thinking that the British were falling back in panic, the "Dirty Shirts" cheered them lustily—to the great mortification of the British soldiery.[42]

The British right column, near the swamp, was out of range of the *Louisiana,* and at this time Jackson had no artillery emplaced on that flank. Hence, the right column might well have had more success, but Pakenham, acting on the advice of his chief of engineers (Colonel John Fox Burgoyne), decided against making an impromptu frontal attack unsupported by artillery—an attack for which no plan or order had been made—and ordered a general withdrawal to a new position about two miles from the American lines. To protect the British line pending further operations, two detached advanced redoubts were erected during the next few days. Known as the "forward" and the "artillery" redoubts, they would become very important later.

Prior to the general withdrawal ordered by Pakenham, Brevet Lieutenant Colonel Robert Rennie of the 21st, the brilliant young officer who was leading the British advance on the extreme right (which had not been hit by American artillery fire), had become involved in—indeed, had initiated—a spirited engagement within the swamp. Carroll had sent out a detachment of 200 Tennesseans under Colonel James Henderson to drive off some British light troops (Rennie's) that had made a lodgment behind a fence and

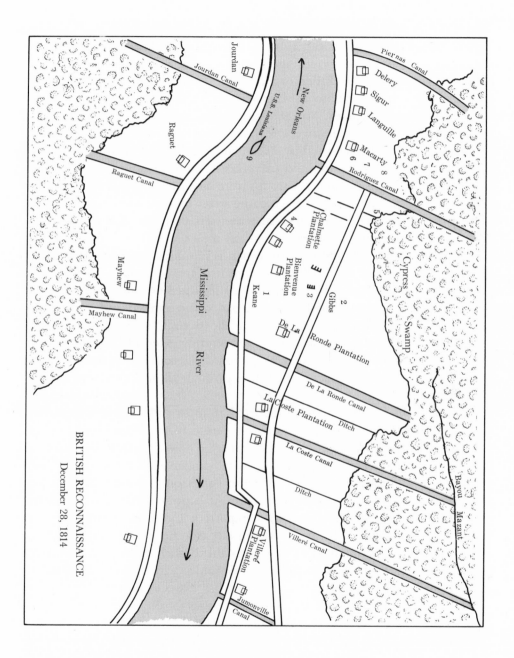

BRITISH RECONNAISSANCE
December 28, 1814

Map 10

ditch. Henderson's orders called for him to come up on their right, but he moved too far to his own right and in the ensuing action he was killed and six of his men were also killed or wounded. The American detachment retreated and a British follow-up was to be expected: the American left flank was then in acute danger. Much to the Americans' surprise, however, the British halted out of rifle range, and Jackson was able to strengthen his left.

The action had been halted by Pakenham's orders to withdraw—much to Rennie's disgust—issued to the entire army when the advance of the British left had stalled. Rennie and his troops were never to forgive Pakenham for not continuing, or promptly renewing, the attack on their flank; they claimed that they could have turned the American left that day, if they had been permitted to continue, or to resume, their attack.[43] Whether they actually could have done so is a moot point, but it is significant that in the interval between the withdrawal and the next British attack Jackson and Coffee's men went to great pains to extend the American line into the swamp—a herculean task in an area where earth had to be scraped and carried for miles—and to mount two cannon near the swamp. Livingston had previously quoted his client, Laffite, as recommending extension of the line into the cypress swamp, a recommendation based, of course, on expert smugglers' knowledge of the practicable routes through all of the swamps around New Orleans.[44]

British losses for the day were reported at 40 or 50 killed or wounded.[45] The official British return for the entire period from December 25 to December 31 listed 16 KIA, 42 WIA, and 2 MIA.[46] Those are army casualties reported by General Lambert a month later. Some of the artillery personnel were sailors and marines, and according to Patterson's personal observation their losses were rather heavy. Here again, it is quite likely that men who were only slightly wounded were not reported; Lambert's figures for the army may have been inaccurate, and in any case he would have reported only sabers and bayonets. The losses on the British right were reported unofficially to be one man in twelve of all ranks.[47] In this action, as in all others during the campaign, the actual British losses were undoubtedly far heavier than those they reported. American losses for the day were 9 KIA and 9 WIA, including a seaman on the *Louisiana*. On December 28 Jackson had 3,282 men on his lines. The best estimate of the British effective strength on the same day, based on careful analysis of all reports, is about 5,500 men.[48]

The gunfire of the *Louisiana* was the decisive factor in the December 28 action. Her crew, men of all nations (except England), had been recruited only two weeks before, but Patterson reported that they served their guns like veterans.[49] Great credit, he said, was due the commander, Lieutenant Charles C. B. Thompson, and his officers.

The accuracy of the naval gunfire is attested by the quick silencing of the British guns. One long British gun on the levee attempted to burn the *Louisiana* with hot shot, but this gun was quickly dismounted by counter-battery fire. However, this threat led Patterson to begin, the very next day, to mount his naval guns ashore on the right bank of the river—a sound idea if they could be protected there—and after December 28 the *Louisiana* was not used as a floating battery. Jackson approved landing the naval battery, and he sent orders to Morgan, in command of the Louisiana militia on the right bank, to move his line to protect them—an order that was to be of great significance later.[50]

Sir John Cooke, who did not arrive on the scene until much later (he did not see Jackson's lines until January 8), nevertheless sums up very graphically the operations up to this point:

General Jackson . . . had amused the British generals for the space of four days and nights with a blustering fire from the sloop, he had turned every moment to his own account, brought up cannon to the barricades, and caused planking to be laid down for heavy artillery behind the ditch. And though the profile of the crescent battery, and the long line of native barricade, and its rough exterior face, was not chiselled by the mason, and might have been laughed at by a Vauban, yet the sight of its smoking face caused the British general to halt.[51]

The Americans cannot be said to have effected, on December 28, a repulse of a British "assault," in the proper sense of this term. No formal orders for an assault had been prepared, and no reserves were committed by Pakenham, nor did he reform for a resumption of the advance after developing his enemy's flanks and fire power. What Pakenham had done was to make what is known, in more recent military parlance, as a "reconnaissance in force." From it, he learned for himself that the Americans to his front were not going to break and run at the sight of the British redcoats—no matter what certain other Americans had done on other fields. He learned that his Congreve rockets struck no terror in this enemy. He learned how good the American artillerymen were. But what he did not yet appreciate was the devastating fire power of the "Kentucky" rifle.

On the recommendations of his experienced senior engineer and artillery officers, Sir Edward now decided to treat American field works as regular fortifications, and to erect breaching batteries to silence their guns. Accordingly, the British spent the next three days and nights landing heavy naval cannon and bringing up ammunition. It was a backbreaking task for Cochrane's already overworked sailors, and for the soldiers also, but if it were successful it would greatly lessen casualties.

Pakenham remained in position, meanwhile, about 2 miles from Jackson and out of range of his artillery, but not entirely safe from Patterson's long range naval gunfire. The weather continued to be wet and cold, rations were poor and few, and the morale of the British army was suffering. Added to the naval cannonade were the constant petty attacks on the British outposts, to which Jackson "wisely never gave five minutes rest, caused not a few casualties, and contributed materially to wear down the strength and endurance of the invaders."[52] Moreover, according to one British participant, some light pieces of American field artillery were employed as roving guns by night so they could range more deeply into the British camp from unexpected firing positions.[53]

Pakenham sent a flag of truce to the American commander, explaining that the shooting of sentinels was barbaric, as compared with the way European warfare was usually conducted. Jackson replied that he saw nothing in the present hostilities but a cruel war of invasion. Eyewitnesses record that he told the British envoys that "sentinels of the opposing armies would be running great risks to drink out of the same stream."[54]

During the day of December 28 Jackson had been informed that a few of the Creole leaders in New Orleans were planning to surrender the city to the British in order to save it from destruction by one army or the other. Jackson sent word to Governor Claiborne to investigate, instructing him, if he found the information to be true, to "blow them up." Claiborne made no investigation whatsoever. He simply closed up the legislature's meeting hall, put a guard over it, and refused to let the legislature meet—an affront that was fiercely resented by its very sensitive members, most of whom were undoubtedly loyal. Indeed, the legislators immediately started an investigation of their own, and other, more detailed investigations were held after the battle. Ever since then, it seems, historians, politicians, and romanticists— not to mention the descendants of all members of that legislature and their friends—have wrestled with fact, allegation, fancy, and inference in an effort to assess the merits of Jackson's suspicions. The whole affair had no apparent effect on the military history of the battle, however, and it is mentioned here merely as an indication of the kind of trivial distractions with which Jackson had, or chose, to deal. The "smoke" suggested to Jackson that there must be some "fire"—and provided him with a further excuse to maintain martial law.[55]

Jackson took full advantage of the lull of the next three days and nights. New Orleans was searched from house to house for firearms and entrenching tools. A large number of Negro slaves were impressed to work on the fortifications and to serve the various units in their lines. The legislature resumed its sittings, and if some members were enraged at Jackson and Claiborne at least there was no recurrence of rumors of capitulation by civil authority.

The number of guns on Line Jackson was increased from five to twelve, with most of the increase on the left. Emplacement of the additional guns called for considerable ingenuity and labor. Cotton bales were sunk into the yielding soil and wooden platforms built on them. In some places the cheeks of embrasures in the ramparts were faced with cotton bales plastered with mud, but within a few days later these were found to be inadequate and were replaced prior to the Grand Assault. Legends to the contrary notwithstanding,[56] it is as certain as can be that "only a few hundred bales were used . . . mostly as platforms to place cannon on." Vincent Nolte's reminiscences on this subject are of special interest, since some of the cotton was his—commandeered by Jackson and never paid for.[57]

Patterson had sent two naval gun crews to serve on Jackson's lines. Lieutenants Ortho Norris and Charles E. Crawley of the late schooner *Carolina*, with part of her crew, "cool New England seamen," served heavy naval guns in a battery on the right of the line.[58] The other naval contingent was a company of 66 marines under Lieutenant Francis B. de Bellevue. Major Daniel Carmack, u.s.m.c., served with Plauché's battalion.[59] He was wounded in the action of December 28 and died soon after the battle.

On the right bank, Master Commandant Henley, of the late *Carolina*, took command of the square redoubt, formed by a brick kiln, opposite the city, on the very bank of the river. The redoubt was furnished with a small powder magazine, and its battery of two 24-pounders commanded the road and the river.

On December 29 Patterson placed two 12-pounders in a battery on the right bank behind the levee, in front of the Jourdan plantation.[60] On the following night he added a 24-pounder to this battery. On December 31 he began to emplace two more 12-pounders on the levee, the better to harass the British camp. However, only the 24 and two of the 12's were ready for action on January 1.

Finally, brief mention should be made here of a fateful project that had been started on December 26, when Morgan of the Louisiana militia and his forces, which had been stationed in Fort St. Leon at English Turn, were transferred to the right bank opposite Line Jackson, where a strong fortification had been ordered built. A complete description and discussion of that project and its fateful progress will be given in a later chapter.

Pakenham, meanwhile, had elected not to wait for the arrival of his siege train of field artillery—it was somewhere at sea, and who could know when the convoy would arrive. He would use heavy naval guns and ammunition instead. Cochrane did not seem to be at all reluctant to send naval armament ashore, though doing so would be an extraordinarily difficult task, the description of which is a rarely told epic in itself. As it happened, the siege train did not reach Mississippi Sound until January 11.[61]

So ended the month of December, and with it the year 1814. Ironically enough, the Treaty of Ghent, or the "Peace of Christmas Eve," had been signed the evening that Sir Edward Pakenham had reached the fleet anchorage in Mississippi Sound. But it was not to be effective until it was ratified, and in Louisiana it was not to be effective until Pakenham received confirmation from the prince regent.

8. THE ARTILLERY DUEL
AND ITS RESULTS
JANUARY 1–7
1815

By General Pakenham's estimate of the situation, if his men were to advance, they would have to do so on a narrow front, their way barred by a strongly entrenched line studded with emplaced and well-manned heavy artillery. They would also be subjected to fire from a powerfully armed ship, anchored just across the river in good position to enfilade Line Jackson. Such an advance would certainly result in a great number of British casualties, and victory, though probable, would be costly indeed. On the other hand, for Pakenham's renowned veterans to retire before raw militia —in order to open a new front at the Rigolets or for any other reason— would be degrading—and might also involve many casualties. In the end, Pakenham decided to deal with the Americans' still-slight fieldworks as he had dealt with the heavy fortifications that he had encountered in Spain— that is, to breach them with heavy cannon fire before attempting an assault.[1] An examination of the merits of this decision, which was to be much criticized, would seem to be in order here.

Before leaving England, Pakenham had received voluminous instructions, copies of all pertinent documents that had been sent to Major Generals Robert Ross, John Keane, and John Lambert, and to Vice-Admiral Sir Alexander Cochrane, and one special secret order of his own.[2] As we have seen, this order, contained in a letter from Bathurst, specified that Pakenham was not to suspend hostilities on account of any report of a peace treaty until he had received positive verification of its having been ratified, such verification to come to him only through a special emissary of the prince regent himself. Bathurst's letter made it very clear that he did not expect any treaty to be ratified soon, and that he did not want the conquest of Louisiana and Florida to be interrupted by any premature rumor of peace. Pakenham knew, therefore, that he and his army would have much still to do after he took the City of New Orleans.

Upon assuming command, however, Pakenham had found that his army had already suffered much heavier losses (from battle casualties, sickness, and desertion) than had been anticipated. Reinforcements had been promised and could be expected to be available eventually, but Pakenham had no way of knowing just when that might be.[3] All things considered, then, the general must have concluded that he was in no position on December 28 to accept heavy casualties if there were any possible way of avoiding them.

Pakenham's decision was approved by, and partly based on the advice of, two of the best specialists from the Iron Duke's magnificent army: Colonel John Fox Burgoyne, one of the Royal Engineers, who served as his commanding engineer in the New Orleans campaign, and Colonel Alexander Dickson, of the Royal Artillery. Dickson, one of those many men whose latent talents had been discerned and nurtured by the Iron Duke,[4] was an officer whose recommendations in artillery matters carried a great weight of authority, and earlier that day he had given a practical demonstration of his competence. The few British light artillery pieces had suffered severe damage on December 28, but Dickson had been able to keep some of them in action throughout the day. Burgoyne was also highly regarded by Wellington, and of course Pakenham was, too.[5]

When the British advance was halted by the American artillery, both Burgoyne and Dickson accompanied Pakenham on his reconnaissance, and both of them shared their commander's belief that to attempt a simple frontal assault against superiority in artillery fire would be prohibitively costly. Moreover, no objections to this view were raised by the regimental commanders or by the naval support commander. Thus, Pakenham's decision, supported by so many experienced military men who were actually on the scene, seems on balance to have been a wise one—notwithstanding the contrary opinions of such later critics as that arrogant young captain of foot troops, Sir John Henry Cooke, writing in the 1830's, or that very young subaltern in the Light Regiment, Gleig, writing in 1847, or those assorted armchair strategists, British and American, who have fancied themselves as military experts.

Colonel Dickson, with his talent for keeping notes of record, has preserved for historians a great amount of graphic detail concerning the trials and tribulations of getting the British artillery ready for its duels on January 1 and 8, 1815. Without good draft animals, proper transport facilities, or even lifting gear (e.g., there was no gyn, an artillery tripod instrument for lifting heavy weights), the task was herculean in magnitude. The 18's and 24's were very heavy indeed, and to mount them, when they finally did reach their battery, the gun carriage was placed upside down over the gun, the cap squares were keyed upon the trunnions, and the gun was then righted on its trucks by sheer manpower—a procedure that strained the carriages even more than it did the men. Transporting the heavy naval guns from the fleet to their final positions was even more arduous. They were brought by the sailors in their pulling boats as far as they could go. At the bayou, they were loaded into native canoes—one to a canoe—and dragged to the end of the canal, about half a mile from the road, from where they had to be hauled over the mud to the road and loaded into the wagons that would carry them up to the camp. There were no sling or carriage platforms at hand; they were to come with the siege artillery, but there could be no waiting for their arrival; the Americans were known to be steadily strengthening their positions, and it was obvious that more and more of them were arriving every day. The British commander set a deadline, Sunday morning, January 1, 1815, and all hands—infantrymen and artillerymen, sailors and marines—worked around the clock to meet it. Dickson himself supervised the construction of sling carts, using the high, strong, spoked wheels and iron axles (designed for moving sugar hogsheads) of country bullock carts.

A powder laboratory was set up near the head of the canal and cartridges were made up there for the heavy guns. At least 420 men were so employed throughout the daylight hours. Powder was no great problem, but many of the empty paper cartridges from the fleet were found to be very bad.—for reasons not given in Dickson's report. Window curtains, bed curtains, sheeting, etc. were commandeered from all the Creole houses in the British area and were used in place of the defective cartridge cases.

Heavy caliber ammunition came up very slowly; it was heavy and hard to handle, and there was a definite limit to what the ship's boats could carry. Many items, such as food for the troops, had to be brought ashore every day. The amount of ammunition available by the evening of December 31 represented a very small proportion of the number of rounds experienced artillerymen knew to be necessary in a counterbattery operation such as they were undertaking, but the general decided that the bombardment could not be delayed beyond the first hour of visibility on the first day of 1815.

Not until the afternoon of December 31 did the four 24-pound carronades arrive, and they had to be dragged on their own low wooden trucks. This caused so much friction that it was only with the greatest difficulty, and the use of nearly two kegs of grease, that they could be brought to their destination without burning out the axles.

Burgoyne and Dickson were ordered to construct and arm the batteries that night, but the American pickets had to be driven back before the main battery of heavy ordnance could be emplaced according to plan. The batteries had then to be laid out in the darkness, their epaulements completed, platforms laid and leveled (as well as they could be), guns mounted, and the ammunition brought up to the guns—all before daylight. Dickson personally took charge of the job at the main battery, and kept the infantry working parties up until 2 A.M. The bulwarks, or epaulements, which were constructed of sugar hogsheads filled with earth, could be neither high nor thick; the British were rather forced into this expedient, when they found that when digging on the banks of the Mississippi one hit water at a depth of only a few inches. By 5:45 A.M. five artillery and two rocket batteries were emplaced, with their crews waiting for daylight (as shown on the sketch map preceding this chapter.)

The left battery on the levee, which consisted of two 18-pounders with 110 rounds per gun and a furnace for heating shot, was to deal with the *Louisiana*. That vessel did not appear, however, because a British deserter had warned Patterson of the British plan. The second battery, from the British left to right, comprised two additional 18-pounders, both of them situated on the road near the house that had been burned by the American artillery on December 28. To the right of the house was the third battery, three 5½-inch mortars with thirty shells each, manned by a detachment of Royal Marine Artillery. In front of them was one of the two Congreve rocket batteries, and a little to the right of the rockets was a seven-gun battery of field artillery: two 9-pounders, three 6-pounders, one heavy and one light 5½-inch howitzer. This battery, which was to engage the American guns in the center of Jackson's lines, was amply supplied with ammunition.

The main battery of six 18-pounders and four 24-pound carronades, constructed under the eye of Dickson himself, was the farthest to the right. It was situated on the center road of the area, about 800 yards from the American lines, almost out of the range of Patterson's guns. The second rocket battery was to the right of this. The 18-pounders had only sixty

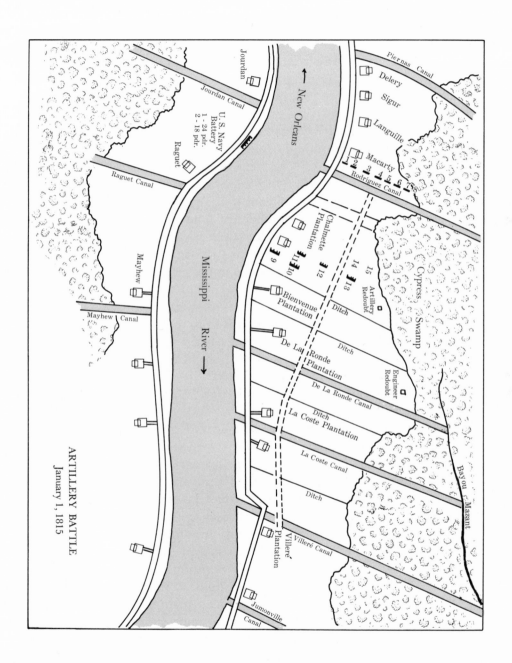

ARTILLERY BATTLE
January 1, 1815

Map 11

rounds per gun, and the carronades only forty apiece. Their fire was to be used, first, to silence the American artillery from the center to the American left, and then to breach the entrenchment a little left of center. The Royal Artillery were handling the 18's, but navy gunners were serving the carronades.[6]

By December 31 the British preparations were complete for the siege bombardment. On the morning of January 1, 1815, Jackson had a total of sixteen guns ready for action.[7] One long 32, three long 24's, one long 18, three long 12's, three long 6's, a 6-inch howitzer, and a small carronade. In addition to these guns, Patterson had one long 24 and two long 12's in action on the west bank. The *Louisiana* did not fire. The entire American artillery threw a total salvo weight of two hundred twenty-four pounds. By the lowest British estimate, their heavy batteries that morning threw two hundred twenty-eight pounds per salvo; by their highest, two hundred fifty-eight pounds.[8] The latter estimate was probably the correct one.

The British army was moved forward on the night of December 31 and took cover as well as it could about 500 yards from the American lines, ready to launch an assault when the artillery breached the American works. Detailed orders for the storming of Jackson's lines had been issued.[9] One column was to attempt to turn the American left, the weakness of which had been reported from the action of December 28.

On that New Year's morning there was a heavy fog that lasted until quite late. About 10 A.M. the massed British guns opened fire.[10] As the fog dissipated, the British could see the American troops, and there might have been considerable loss to the Americans had the British anticipated such an excellent personnel target. But they had not heard of Jackson's plan for a Sunday morning parade in celebration of the New Year, and orders had been given to use demolition ammunition instead of anti-personnel ammunition. Their first fire was directed at Jackson's headquarters in the McCartney House, and "in less than ten minutes upward of one hundred balls, rockets, and shells struck the house."[11] Jackson was in the house at the time, but—surprisingly—the Americans experienced no personnel casualties whatsoever.

The few cotton bales used in the American rampart were torn apart and set on fire; the carriage of one 24-pounder was broken; the 32-pounder and a 12-pounder were silenced; and a rocket blew up a caisson of American ammunition, whereupon the British infantry sent up a cheer, thinking the signal to storm the lines was about to come. They were quickly convinced to the contrary, however, by redoubled firing from the remaining American guns.

These guns had been somewhat slow to reply, but when they did their fire was rapid and precise.[12] The British were soon overmatched: by noon their fire began to slacken, by 1 P.M. the batteries on their right and center had ceased to fire, and at 3 P.M. the guns on the levee ceased firing. Dickson reported that the great battery ran out of ammunition, but it had been forced from the start to fire too slowly to deliver effective counterbattery fire. Army field artillery siege guns would have been successful, he said, but the naval artillery recoiled off their inadequate platforms with every shot. The seven-gun field artillery battery was demolished, but the heavy naval ordnance was not hard hit.

The American artillery's counterbattery fire had been surprisingly effective, especially on those targets within Patterson's range. The sugar cask ramparts were soon demolished and several fieldpieces disabled. Some of the casks were full of molasses, and this "Battle of the Bales and Hogsheads," as it has been called, represented the British army's first encounter with that substance in battle.[13] The British gunners were driven from their guns with heavy casualties, reported to be 32 KIA, 42 WIA, and 2 MIA between January 1 and 5.[14] Again, these were army infantry casualties only, but even so they seem surprisingly low. In addition, artillery losses amounted to 1 officer and 12 men KIA and 13 men WIA in the Royal Artillery. Royal Marine and navy gunners losses were not included here and apparently have not been published (at least this writer has never been able to locate them).

Codrington, ashore in charge of commissary stores for the landing force, said the result was a big disappointment and deplored the "blot on the artillery escutcheon."[15] The outcome of the action was certainly a bitter disappointment to Pakenham, who had expected the American artillery to be speedily silenced and had optimistically issued detailed orders for a general advance. Having insisted on beginning the action before sufficient ammunition was prepared, he was now forced to retire his army again and to abandon the guns. The Americans made no attempt to capture them, however, and that night, despite a heavy rainfall, the British were able to recover or disable the guns that had not been destroyed in the day's action. Sir Harry Smith tells the story of his own failure to bring back the guns when he was sent with a working party to do so; he was very ashamed to report that the men would not obey him. Pakenham then called out the entire army and personally saw to the retirement of the guns that night.[16]

The British had attacked the American left at the edge of the swamp that morning as planned, but Coffee's riflemen had quickly repulsed that effort. The British opportunity to turn that flank was gone by then, thanks to the prodigious efforts of Coffee's men to extend the lines into the swamp and to strengthen them.

The British had suffered the greatest fatigue. The troops were baffled, disappointed, and discontented. The harassing tactics of the American sharpshooters and the American artillery's day and night bombardment were taking their tolls. The troops' complaints were not all defeatist, of course, and one British officer thought "they resembled the growling of a chained dog when he sees the adversary but cannot reach him."[17] Nevertheless, the rate of British desertions increased.

Quartermaster William Surtees, the old soldier, thought that the British should have made an assault on January 1 as soon as the barrage began. He thought it could have succeeded while the Americans were still surprised.[18] He may well have been correct in this supposition, but none of the British leaders ever recorded that opinion.

Jackson complimented his troops that night. Nevertheless, on the following day he continued to strengthen his fortifications, correcting weaknesses that had shown up in the artillery duel. His casualties were 11 KIA and 23 WIA.[19] He hastened work on two new lines in rear of his first, too, and prepared himself to meet whatever new plan the British could contrive. The third round of the fight for New Orleans had been won, and this time the American artillery and naval gunfire had made the advantage positive and unequivocal.

The next week passed in disturbing quiet for Jackson. Hinds and his dragoons by day, and the backwoods riflemen and Indians by night, continued to harass the British outposts and to deny the British any reconnaissance, while Patterson's gunners kept an unremitting watch for possible targets in the British camp by day and let loose harassing fires by night. The weather remained cold and wet, and constant American artillery fire and sniping raids denied the British even the small comfort of a campfire. Desertion became a serious concern to the British commanders.

As the supply of cattle within foraging distance as far south as English Turn had been exhausted, all provisions had to be obtained from the fleet, and they were scanty and coarse.[20] As the campaign continued, Cochrane's early fears about his short supply of commissary stores were being increasingly realized.

Battle and non-battle casualties now made it essential for Pakenham to await the reinforcements of Lambert's brigade before resuming the offensive. The brigade had arrived in Mississippi Sound on December 31, 1814, but the last of them did not reach the British camp on the Mississippi until January 6.[21] Another dismounted squadron of the 14th Dragoons—160 men —and 40 staff personnel were added to 2,000 foot troops in two crack regiments, the 7th and 43rd.[22]

While waiting for Lambert and his men to be brought ashore, the British had not been idle. Cochrane had proposed a very ingenious plan for passing troops over to the right bank, seizing Patterson's batteries, and turning them on Jackson's lines. The admiral's idea was no less than to widen and deepen Villeré's Canal, extending it through the levee into the Mississippi, thereby securing a waterway from the advanced base into the river.[23] An amphibious force would then secure the right bank of the Mississippi and establish British batteries there. This would involve placing batteries along the eastern shore of the river for the purpose of destroying any American ships that might be sent to contest the river crossing.[24]

In his autobiography, Sir Harry Smith recalled that the plan was scoffed at, but it should be noted that in all references to Smith on this matter Fortescue makes no secret of his doubts as to Smith's veracity. Deliberate falsification cannot be charged to such a sterling character as Sir Harry; however, his editor's introduction shows that the autobiography was begun in 1824 but carried only as far as the Corunna campaign. Sir Harry resumed writing in 1844, when he was an adjutant general in India, but he quit work on it again in 1846. The editor, a great nephew, G. C. Moore Smith, used "other material" to finish the book. The story of the New Orleans campaign was therefore written no earlier than 1844, and by that time Sir Harry's recollection of events could well have been inaccurate. They are very interesting, however, and cannot be ignored. Neither Smith nor Dickson nor Wrottesley say anything of Sir Edward's reaction to the idea of improving and extending Villeré's Canal, either when it was first suggested or while the work was underway, but Codrington thought that he put no confidence in it. It is significant, perhaps, that its engineering was left entirely to Cochrane's naval officers, though army work parties were employed. Burgoyne, the chief army engineer, had nothing to do with the project, so far as is known.

Surtees said that nothing could exceed the grandness of the conception, but that it was a most laborious and dirty undertaking. The troops were divided into four watches, one of which was working every hour of the day and night. The West Indian Negro regiments were almost worked to death on the project. The troops experienced severe fatigue in the arduous task, but they were obedient, even though the entire idea was considered unsound by many of them.

Since the troops had dragged the 24-pounder naval guns overland from the head of the creek to their present position, it seemed obvious to the soldiers that the boats could have been moved to the Mississippi in the same manner. They also surmised that the operation would have been much easier, and might even have been accomplished without the Americans realizing what was projected, if rollers had been used to move the boats.[25] No naval opinion of this idea is recorded, but a man-o'-war man's horror at such a suggestion can be readily imagined. Pulling boats were in very short supply, and besides that they were not constructed to withstand such rough treatment; no doubt many of them would have had their bottoms stove in if they had been moved on rollers.

An arresting idea concerning the canal is submitted by Sir John H. Cooke and supported by the mysterious "R.S.": that the troops, toiling knee deep in, and covered with, mud for nearly a week, were held to their prodigious effort by the idea that this was the only possible solution to their problem— that their leaders after two attempts to storm the American lines had decided they were too strong to be taken by frontal attack. Thus the troops may have been psychologically well-prepared to accept defeat when called upon to assault on January 8.[26] This seems a valid conclusion.

On the night of January 6, the naval officers in charge of construction reported that everything had been completed to their satisfaction. The next day fifty boats of all sizes were brought into the new canal and dragged to within a short distance of the Mississippi.[27]

While the canal was being dug, some British artillery was emplaced with a double mission: to prevent any American naval forces coming down the river to interfere with the canal project, and to support by fire from those positions the British attack on the American right. Four batteries were emplaced behind the levee, so distributed as to keep under continuous fire any vessels coming down the river, but also prepared to turn their guns to Jackson's line. The southernmost battery was two 24-pound carronades, emplaced where the battery that had destroyed the *Carolina* had been. This one could not have been used against Line Jackson without displacing. The battery of four 18-pounders, nearest the American line, was still waiting with a heated furnace to burn the *Louisiana,* or any other American vessel in range, with hot shot.[28]

Nevertheless Pakenham seems to have placed very little reliance on the canal in his plans. He believed that the Americans would certainly learn of the scheme and have guns emplaced across the river to take the boats under fire if they reached the river. The defenders did in fact become aware of the British intentions but did not emplace guns across the river—though Patterson mentioned the possibility of doing so.

The entire success of the canal project depended upon a dam that would have to hold the water of the canal under the boats. The level of the Mississippi then was higher than that of the water in the canal. When the levee was cut into the river (the last operation before launching the boats into the river) this dam, built behind the boats, would have to resist the flow from the river. When Pakenham inspected the project on January 7, he questioned the naval officers in charge and remarked to them that there should be a second dam behind the first, in case the weight of the river's water should carry away the first. The naval officers insisted that this precaution was unnecessary. As it happened, the British general's surmise was correct. The dam did give way, and the delay that resulted was fatal to the success of the endeavor.[29]

Even if British boats were moved into the river, the British commander had every reason to expect them to be attacked not only by American artillery but by a far bigger American flotilla than the British could spare the boats to launch, especially since Cochrane had been forced to begin the operation with fewer than half the boats that he believed necessary. Jackson did suggest this flotilla to Patterson, as we will see, but Patterson did not act on the suggestion.

Complete plans were laid for an all-out assault on the American lines on the left bank as soon as reinforcements were ready. The 7th Royal Fusiliers and the 43rd Light Infantry, two of the best regiments in the Peninsular

War, were in camp on January 6. Every man in each of those regiments, much to his discomfort and disgust, had been required to bring one artillery round with him in his knapsack from the fleet anchorage. Clearly no effort was spared to have plentiful ammunition on hand at the cannon for the Grand Assault.[30]

As already noted, the British had begun constructing a redoubt near the woods on their right, even before the first artillery duel, and this was strengthened during the lull. The Americans believed its purpose would be to guard against another American night attack from that direction and to serve as a reserve base for British pickets. It was at this redoubt that fascines and scaling ladders were gathered by the engineers for use in the coming assault. As it happened, however, another, smaller redoubt (it was called an artillery redoubt, and in modern parlance would probably be termed an artillery forward observation station) had already been built in advance of this one, and it was at that smaller redoubt that the carrying party looked for the engineers.[31]

The scaling ladders were made of green wood that was available in the cypress forest edging the swamp, and they were heavy and cumbersome. The fascines were made of sugar cane and were also heavy. Some of these had been prepared for the planned assault of January 1, but additional ones were prepared thereafter.

The artillery technicians, aided by ships' carpenters from the fleet, had worked wonders in repairing the damage done to gun mounts in the artillery duel and in preparing better platforms. Before daybreak on the day of the assault, a battery of four 18-pounders and four 24-pound carronades was constructed on the ground occupied by the seven-gun field artillery battery on New Year's Day. Much more care was taken with the platforms and palisade, and this time there was no shortage of ammunition. Just before daylight, the field artillery batteries were also moved from the river into a forward position from where they could continue to support the attack after the first line was carried.[32]

While all this was going on, the Americans on the left bank were far from being idle. Damage done to Line Jackson by the British bombardment was repaired and the fortifications were strengthened throughout. Work on two rear lines was continued. Near the river an advanced redoubt was begun, with a view to mounting two 6-pounders in enfilade of the line. (Jackson approved this step reluctantly and, just as he had feared would be the case, the redoubt was still incomplete at the time of the assault.)

The Rodriguez Canal had been widened, deepened, and filled with water, and the earth that was removed from the canal was used to help construct the parapet; however, much more dirt had to be carried to the lines from some distance. To prevent the earth of the parapet from sliding into the canal, the banks were revetted with fence rails collected from miles around. Since all work had been done by successive working parties in an almost incessant rain, little regularity and system prevailed. For miles around slaves had scraped up earth and carried it back to the lines for use in the parapet. The British, without slaves, could not do this for their epaulements as well as the Americans could. The American parapet was thicker and higher in some places than at others: at some points it was twenty feet thick at the top but only five feet high, at others the base was so narrow that it could be easily perforated by the enemy's artillery. Weak spots noticed during the New Year's Day bombardment were strengthened.

The length of the line was something over a half-mile, extending into the swamp for some distance and then turning at a right angle in the direction of the city. The breastwork in the woods and swamp was thick enough to withstand musketry but not much more. It was formed by a double row of logs, each row laid one over the other, with the space between the rows (about two feet) laboriously filled with earth. A *banquette* extended along one part of the line, but in some places the height of the breastwork above the soil was hardly sufficient to cover the men. At the left extremity of the lines, near and in the swamp, were Coffee's Tennesseans, wading knee-deep in mud during the day and sleeping at night as best they could, usually on rafts of logs tied together. The rain and cold plagued them constantly, and they were very short of tents. Their hardships were extreme, and their fortitude was most commendable. As a result of all this exposure many of them died of sickness after the British retreat.[33]

On January 4 the men of the Kentucky militia under Major General John Thomas began to arrive, but to Jackson's consternation they were for the most part unarmed, poorly equipped otherwise (they were not even adequately clothed), and had received no training. They had only seven hundred firearms of various descriptions, some of which were not even serviceable, for 2,368 men.[34] The rifles from Pittsburgh, requisitioned by Jackson in August, had finally been sent by the Ordnance Department in November —by flatboat in order to save the cost of shipping by steamboat. They arrived on January 15. Carroll had encountered a portion of that shipment on the river, however, and had brought it with him, but this was the only part of the critical requisition to arrive on time.[35]

It is proper to mention here the name of the ordnance supply officer responsible for this dismal logistical failure, since history so often unjustly damns the generals whose failures are caused by the lack of supplies. He was Captain Abram R. Wooley, officer in charge of the army ordnance plant in Pittsburgh.[36] It was some satisfaction to this writer to learn from Old Army Records that Wooley was eventually dismissed from the army for cause, though not until many years after the Battle of New Orleans.

The women of New Orleans, by prodigious effort and generous sacrifices, set about providing blankets and clothing for the shivering Kentuckians, but nothing could be done about supplying firearms in sufficient number. About five hundred ill-assorted small arms, held by the mayor of New Orleans as a reserve in case of a slave revolt, were surreptitiously made available to Jackson, but that was all.

General Thomas, in poor health at the time of his arrival, soon became too ill to exercise command of his Kentuckians, whereupon the responsibility devolved upon his senior subordinate, the capable Brigadier General John Adair. This led to an unfortunate complication later. Early on January 7, with commendable initiative, Adair secured from Mayor Girod the most serviceable of the small arms mentioned above for his Kentuckians on the east bank. For some reason this was never reported to Jackson. Later on the same day, Jackson ordered that 500 Kentuckians obtain those same weapons from the mayor and then proceed to reinforce Morgan on the right bank. To make matters worse, Jackson's orders were delivered to the sick Thomas, who did not tell Adair.[37] As a result, only about 170 of the men that Jackson had ordered to reinforce Morgan obtained arms in New Orleans (i.e., the ones that Adair had not acquired earlier).[38]

The main body of the Kentuckians had gone into bivouac in the rear of Jackson's line as part of the reserve. Only every second Kentuckian there possessed a fowling piece, or Spanish *escopeta,* of some kind. About 500 of the well-armed, or at least better-armed, Kentuckians, some of whom had brought their own trusty rifles, were placed in the line under Adair to reinforce Carroll's Tennesseans. After conferring with Adair and Carroll, Jackson guessed, correctly, that the main British assault would be delivered here, since it was beyond the range of Patterson's guns.[39] The location and disposition of all American units and batteries, with their commanders, are shown in the accompanying map ("Battle of New Orleans, January 8, 1815") and caption.[40]

Jackson had not ignored the possibility of a British river-crossing operation against the American position on the western bank of the river in extension of and reinforcing his own line by artillery fire. However, he considered it a remote threat. He obviously overestimated the capabilities of his army and navy components there, as well as the capabilities of his subordinate commanders, and he underestimated the British. Such an attack, he felt sure, would not be made in force. His military intelligence convinced him—correctly, as it happened—that the main effort would be made on the east bank.

The situation on the right (i.e., the western) bank requires considerable discussion, nevertheless, because the controversy over what happened there on January 7–8 became a *cause célèbre* in contemporary and later accounts of the battle, both British and American.

On December 24, Jackson had ordered Brigadier General David Morgan of the Louisiana militia to abandon his post at English Turn and take up a position on the right bank of the Mississippi in line with his own on the left bank. Latour, Jackson's fortifications engineer, was sent to lay out a fortified line for Morgan. Latour chose one at Boisgervais Canal, 3 miles below the city. In six days Latour's assistant engineer, working 150 Negroes, built a parapet along the entire canal and formed a glacis on the opposite side. Time did not permit the completion of the bastions and redoubts designed by Latour, but it was at this line that Morgan would eventually rally his men, in part at least, after their flight on January 8. The entire project had Jackson's approval.[41]

Later Latour was again sent across the river by Jackson to locate a forward position.[42] At a place halfway between Raguet's and Jourdan's canals, he chose one from the river to the swamp that was only 900 yards long (about the length of Line Jackson). Latour made a sketch and plan for the position and left overseers to build it, using Negro labor. Jackson also approved this plan, but Morgan countermanded Latour's orders and began to prepare a position farther forward on Raguet's Canal, where the swamp and the river

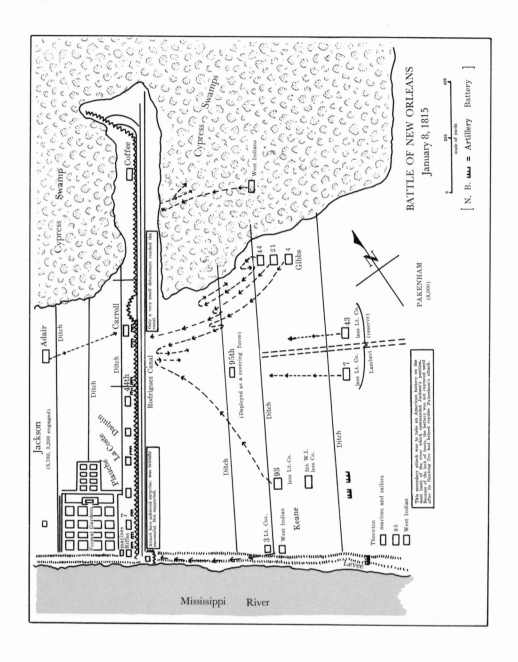

BATTLE OF NEW ORLEANS
January 8, 1815

[N. B. ▬ = Artillery Battery]

0   200   400
scale of yards

Units	Leaders	Strength	Approximate Location	Artillery Pieces
New Orleans Rifles	Captain Thomas Beale	39		
U.S. Marine Detachment	Lieutenant Francis Bellevue	56		
BATTERY #1	Captain Enoch Humphrey		75 yards from river	Two 12 pounders / One 6" howitzer
	(Major Henri H. Gême)			
7th Infantry	Colonel George T. Ross	422		
BATTERY #2	Lieutenant Ortho Norris, USN		100 yards from #1	One 24 pounder
	(Dominique You)			
BATTERY #3			50 yards from #2	Two 24 pounders
(Baratarians)	(Renato Beluche)			
Uniformed Companies	Major Jean B. Plauché	369		
BATTERY #4	Lieutenant C. E. Crawley, USN		25 yards from #3	One 32 pounder
Men of Color	Major Louis Daquin	171		
	Major Pierre La Coste	286		
BATTERY #5	Colonel William D. Perry, USA (Ret)		200 yards from #4	Two 6 pounders
	(Lieutenant John Ker)			
44th Infantry	Major Henri Peire	289		
BATTERY #6	General G. Flaugiac		50 yards from #5	One 12 pounder
BATTERY #7	Lieutenant Samuel Spotts		200 yards from #6	Two 18 pounders
	(unknown corporal)			
BATTERY #8	Lieutenant Colonel William McRae		50 yards from #7	One carronade
Artillerymen		112		
Tennessee Militia	Major General William Carroll	1,562		
Kentucky Militia	Brigadier General John Adair			
Tennessee Mounted Volunteers	Major General John Coffee	1,218		
Reserves				
Mississippi Dragoons	Lieutenant Colonel Thomas Hinds	230		
Louisiana Militia	Major General Jacques Villeré	446		
		5,200		

Map 12

were so far apart—nearly a mile—that he did not have enough men to cover it, even had he been able to fortify it. He built a strong earthwork that stretched only 200 yards from the river into the plain, and mounted two fieldpieces therein. His line of defense was extended for about a quarter of a mile farther from there by a dry ditch. From the ditch to the swamp, a distance of a half-mile, there were no defensive works at all, nor men to man them had there been any. That half-mile was unoccupied. This was an impossible position to hold, since one flank was completely vulnerable to being turned. It was not even bent back at an angle, as was Coffee's line within the swamp on the east bank.

It has to be admitted, in Morgan's defense, that his choice of position, however unsound militarily, was partly dictated by the position chosen by Patterson for some of his water batteries. On January 2–3 Patterson had landed and mounted four more 12-pounders at a point below his original water battery. He erected a furnace there for heating shot with which to destroy a number of buildings between Jackson's lines and the British camp that were occupied by the enemy. He accomplished this destruction on the evening of January 4. On January 6 and 7 he erected another furnace and mounted two more 24-pounders on the bank of the river. He also mounted, on Morgan's entrenchments, one 12-pounder to augment Morgan's two brass 6-pounder fieldpieces. All of Patterson's guns were sited with a view to enfilading the right of Jackson's lines on the opposite shore, of course, but more especially to harass the British camp and to keep the enemy from erecting batteries on the levee road or using that road in any other way.[43] Patterson could not reach the British batteries behind the levee.

All of that was very laudable and helpful to Jackson, but the defense of these batteries devolved upon Morgan, a militia general in command of very small force of poorly armed and poorly trained militia, who was himself lacking in both military education and experience. After the battle, Morgan said that he "had" to move from the second line of 900 yards selected by Latour to the line of 1,700 yards about half a mile below Patterson's newest water battery, and Patterson said that he had planned to use some of his guns by turning them at least ninety degrees (a most difficult maneuver) in order to defend the exposed flank by artillery fire alone, if necessary. Such a defense would be impossible against a quick attack by light forces. In retrospect, the abandonment of a short fortified line of defense, as planned by Latour, in favor of an almost open field in which poorly armed militia would be subject to flanking maneuvers by veteran British troops, seems utterly fantastic. However, by placing a new water battery south of the defensible short line determined by Jackson's military engineers, Patterson practically forced Morgan to make *some* sort of change in plan, if he were to attempt any defense of that battery. The change he decided upon was made before January 8, and so presumably it was presented to Jackson for approval. Jackson never criticized the move later, and he seems to have held both Patterson and Morgan in high personal esteem during and after the battle. He must have concurred in the change, then, but if so he should certainly have reinforced Morgan very heavily.[44]

Morgan had available 546 Louisiana militia: 260 of the 1st Regiment, 176 of the 2nd, and 110 of the 6th.[45] The 2nd arrived on January 4, the 1st on January 6. These men were all very indifferently armed and trained. They were dissatisfied with their arms and the position, and they distrusted Morgan.[46] Jackson ordered only 500 Kentuckians to reinforce Morgan, and those not until January 7. Only 400 of the Kentuckians started, under command of Colonel John Davis. About 180 of them got arms in New Orleans, while 70 more received arms from the naval arsenal. Thus, only about 250 armed men were eventually added to Morgan's strength, and they were also poorly armed, undisciplined militia, worn out with fatigue.[47]

Patterson personally reconnoitered the river bank opposite Villeré Canal on January 6 and ascertained the enemy's intention to land on his side of the river, with the objective of capturing or destroying his guns. But all he did was tell Morgan about it and write to Jackson twice, sending the second letter that night by his volunteer aide and friend, Richard S. Shepperd. Both letters asked for more troops.[48] The aide reached Jackson about 1 A.M. on January 8, by which time there was nothing further that Jackson could do except to try to send word back to Morgan "to maintain his position at all hazards."[49] Jackson was betting everything on his own estimate of the situation. He told Shepperd that the main attack would take place on the east bank. Fortunately for him and for the United States his estimate proved to be correct.

There was one other factor in the struggle for New Orleans that Pakenham may have failed to consider on the eve of the final assault—the "Kentucky" rifles of the backwoodsmen. There is evidence that the British rank and file had begun to appreciate and fear this weapon, for its continued use against their outposts had proved that it could be fired with deadly accuracy from far beyond the return range of their own muskets (or even their rifles), and they had also tasted that bitter fire in action. At least some of the junior officers were also becoming a bit apprehensive concerning this heretofore unappreciated weapon. Cooke recounts that when he asked his old friend, Major Thomas Wilkinson, what had been holding the British up, he was told, "Bullets stopped us—bullets, that's all."[50] Wilkinson was killed on the barricade on January 8; in a letter home that was found on his body, the major had written that he hoped the assault would be delayed until the British could get supporting fire from across the river.[51]

Under cover of the rifled small-arms fire of parties of the 95th, and the gunfire of artillery emplaced during the night, the main attack was to be delivered against the American left by the 21st and the 4th under Major General Samuel Gibbs. Pakenham chose that point, close to the edge of the swamp, for his main assault in column of companies because there he would only have to contend with the artillery in Jackson's lines, and not with Patterson's across the river. The attack at dawn would also obviate any observed artillery fire. The light companies of Gibbs' brigade and some Negro soldiers were thrown out into the swamp to protect the right flank.

The second column, on the British left, was commanded by Keane and subdivided into two sections whose movements would be guided by events. Rennie, commanding the light companies of the 7th, 43rd, and 93rd (together with a hundred men of the 1st w.i.r.), was to advance quickly along the road and break into the new American unfinished advance redoubt, in which two guns enfiladed Line Jackson. Long range observation and study of the American position by spyglasses made the British aware of the new fortification. However, they did not know the dimensions or the strength and weaknesses of the American line as a whole. Had that line been built before the British landing, their intelligence operatives would have known all about it. The very fact of its newness, and of its being built behind the screening operations of Hinds and his dragoons, was the reason for the British ignorance about the fortification and their troops' growing fear of it.

One British officer, writing in a British periodical years later under the *nom de plume* of "R.S.," who was wounded and captured in the American lines on January 8, said that he found it possible to cross the ditch in places without scaling ladders or fascines. Indeed, some of the British did this. But the Americans had prevented the British from making any reconnaissance, and the rank and file, having little or no knowledge of what faced them, were reluctant to attempt the assault. If the British soldiers had known beforehand the diminutive dimensions of the ditch and parapet, they would never have hesitated, surely, for these were men who had triumphed over obstacles ten times more difficult at Badajoz and San Sebastian. At New Orleans, however, they convinced themselves in advance that they would have to have fascines and scaling ladders.[52]

The bulk of Keane's brigade (the 93rd and the remainder of the 1st W.I.R.) was to advance on the right of Rennie, parallel to him, and attack to reinforce either Rennie or Gibbs, according to circumstances. The rest of the 95th Rifles, only a few score who were not used to cover the front of Gibbs' column, would provide cover for Keane. The main bodies of the 7th and 43rd, under Lambert, were held in reserve. It was a well-planned assault, all in all, particularly Rennie's surprise maneuver.[53]

Preparations for the assault on the east bank went on throughout the night of January 7. British working parties went forward under cover of darkness to prepare artillery emplacements—and no sugar hogsheads would be used *that* night! Instead earth was obtained by paring the soil for a long distance around. The work was slowly and imperfectly done, however, and the epaulements were still not shot-proof when, shortly before dawn, four 18-pounder guns and four 24-pound carronades were laboriously installed in position.[54]

The ground across which the British had to advance was very muddy, owing to the almost incessant rain and to Jackson's having cut the levee. The ground was traversed at intervals by shallow drainage ditches from the river to the swamp.

Pakenham's plans were excellent. Over 300 of the 95th Rifles and about 120 of the 44th (those who had not been assigned to carry fascines or ladders) were pushed forward very early in the morning to cover the emplacements that had been built during the night. These men were then, on rocket signal, to precede the assaulting columns, taking firing positions within musketry range and beating down the American small-arms fire, while the main columns closed to assault distance.

Lieutenant Colonel Thomas Mullins, commanding the 44th, had been instructed to have 300 of his men carry forward sixteen ladders to be used in scaling Jackson's line and the fascines to fill the ditch. His orders called for

Mullins to ascertain, before the assault, where the fascines and ladders could be obtained and to bring them with him to the front well before daylight. Instead of going himself, Mullins sent his operations officer for the information, and confusion between the two forward redoubts resulted.

The British troops fell in at 4 A.M. and moved up to their appointed places. The skirmishers closed quietly to within perhaps 200 yards of the American lines, and the assault troops to within less than a half-mile from them.[55] Lieutenant General Sir Edward Pakenham's veteran British army, comprising about 9,600 men supported by Colonel Dickson's guns, was poised for the Grand Assault. Ready to receive them, in a mud rampart, was a motley American army of about 5,200 men and Major General Andrew Jackson, whose life 'til now had been but a preface to this morning.[56]

9. THE GRAND ASSAULT AND
ITS AFTERMATH
JANUARY 8 TO MARCH 13
1815

There was no hope of a surprise. The Americans had the British camp under constant observation, and the many British deserters had much interesting information to relate. Colonel Reuben Kemper had just returned from a reconnaissance through the swamp to the Bayou Bienvenue. A British sloop was captured in Lake Borgne by Sailing Master William Johnson on January 6, and the prisoners gave the British plan away. In Jackson's mind there was no doubt that Sunday, January 8, 1815, would be the day.[1]

Patterson's aide awakened the general at 1 A.M., hours before daybreak at 6:57 A.M., and he did not go back to sleep but called for his staff to accompany him to the lines.[2] Jackson trooped his line from the river to the woods, cheering up his men and alerting them. They could hear the sounds of the British guns being mounted, and other noises confirming the British intentions, about which they had already been alerted.

Jackson's strength on his lines that morning had been estimated variously by Latour, Marquis James, Fortescue, and others. There were in all probability about 5,200 men, including reserves, but no more than 2,000 were to see any action. The uniformed companies of New Orleans, the two battalions of men of color, and the 44th American Infantry would not fire a shot. About 6 A.M. first light began to appear, but there was mist and fog; some hoped that it would clear in an hour, but it remained rainy and overcast all day. The returning outposts reported the British to be less than half a mile away. Actually, they were even closer than that.

To the front of where Jackson stood near the woods a rocket rose and burst with bluish silver shower. Another answered from the river bank. Jackson remarked, "That is their signal to advance, I believe."[3]

The time fixed for the crossing of the river by Colonel William Thornton's 85th (reinforced by a naval brigade of sailors and marines to a total of about 1,200 officers and men) was 9 P.M. on January 7. But there were no boats. The dam that Pakenham had distrusted had given way, and the canal collapsed upon itself, blocking all the boats a quarter of a mile from the outlet to the river. Only with tremendous effort, and after a long delay, were a few boats dragged forward.[4]

For some reason nobody told Pakenham about this until shortly before sunrise. He was then about to cancel the river-crossing operation, but when he learned that the 85th and a few marines and sailors were already boated, he decided to let Thornton make a diversionary attack with the forces that were available, without waiting for more boats. It was by Pakenham's order, then, that about 560 soldiers, sailors, and marines were launched on the venture, well after 5 A.M.[5] Fortescue claims that Thornton took the gallant decision to make the try on his own initiative; that was not the fact, of course. Dickson was having breakfast with Pakenham when he heard the bad news, and he stayed with him until the decision was taken. Some light field artillery was supposed to accompany Thornton, but that was now canceled by the general on his artillery chief's recommendation. Dickson finished breakfast with Sir Edward shortly after five and never saw him again.[6]

The young British general's troubles were far from being over. The assault units had moved out under cover of darkness, but Lieutenant Colonel Thomas Mullins led the 44th to its position without bringing the ladders and fascines. He waited for ten minutes by the redoubt where he expected to find them, and where they actually were, but the responsible engineer officer did not show up there to give them to him, and Mullins continued without them to the forward artillery emplacement, where he then supposed they had been taken. In fact, however, the "missing" engineer, Captain Henry Tapp, had been dozing in the first redoubt, waiting for Mullins to come to him. By British tradition, in a storm attempt the engineers had always taken responsibility from the unit commanders for leading the men with fascines and ladders, but for some reason only Mullins was held to blame in this instance. With dawn fast approaching, the 44th were hurried back from the forward redoubt to get the ladders and fascines.[7]

This peculiar sequence of events had been discovered by Major General Sir Samuel Gibbs, who took steps to rectify matters, and so reported to Pakenham. It was not yet 5 A.M., but Pakenham sent one of his own staff to check the report. The staff officer, Major Sir John Tylden (who had relieved Harry Smith, just two days earlier, as Pakenham's assistant adjutant general by virtue of his seniority), found the 44th belatedly straggling up to the front,

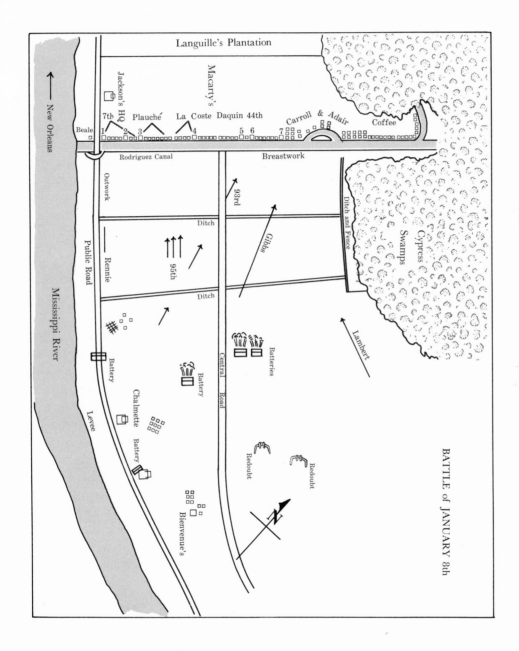

Map 13

carrying the fascines and ladders in a disorderly fashion. The men were out of breath and in poor temper from being hurried forward, then back, and now forward again, and their loads were heavy. Tylden reported to Pakenham that the battalion would regain its place in time, and the general rode off, reassured.[8]

As it happened, the 44th did not all get back to their position in time, and the entire failure of the Grand Assault was finally blamed upon that circumstance by the British. But Surtees, the old soldier from the ranks, who had seen a score of such assaults, said: "It would not have availed much if they had been there in time because the right column never reached the point to which it was directed."[9] The reason was, of course, the dreadful fire of artillery and small arms that was poured into them long before they reached the ditch.

There had to be a scapegoat, of course, and poor Mullins was chosen for the role. The evidence given at his court-martial shows that Mullins decided that the fascines and ladders were in the forward artillery redoubt after he failed to meet an engineer at the first one. His executive officer or his operations officer might have told him the truth, but neither of them did so, and swore, for reasons that the testimony fails to make clear, that the fault was Mullins'. Obviously the command relationships in the unit were not happy. One of Mullins' junior officers, whom he had recently disciplined, flirted with perjury in an effort to get him shot or hanged for cowardice; but the testimony of his senior and junior noncommissioned officers proved that Mullins had gone forward to the edge of Jackson's ditch, even after he was wounded, and with no other officer in sight—not even the staff officers who testified *they* had not seen him there and who intimated broadly that he had fled. The enlisted men's evidence proved not only that Mullins had been there, but also that many of the prosecution's witnesses were not. However, there had to be *someone* upon whom to place the blame for the British defeat (rather than admit the Americans had been the cause of it) and so Mullins, though fully acquitted of two charges (one of cowardice, the other of "predicting defeat"), was cashiered from the army for "neglect of duty." He had been commended both at Bladensburg and Baltimore for bravery and leadership. Even the hard-boiled Sir Harry Smith said that Mullins was victimized.[10]

Smith gives an account, very difficult to believe, of the firing of the rocket that Jackson saw. According to Smith, Pakenham complained bitterly to him that morning about his difficulties. After being relieved by Tylden, Smith had been sent to Major General John Lambert, whom he served as military secretary for the rest of the campaign. Nevertheless, according to Smith, he was sent for by Pakenham, whom he found greatly concerned over Thornton's delay. It was still not quite daylight then, and the ground was covered with a thick mist. This would have been after Pakenham had parted from Dickson. Where Tylden and MacDougall were at that moment Sir Harry did not say.

Smith claimed that he counseled Pakenham to call off the attack immediately and to fall back before daylight disclosed his troops to the American fire. Pakenham replied that he had twice put off assaulting those lines and would not do so again. He then peremptorily ended further remonstrance from Smith and directed the signal rocket to be fired.[11]

Major Duncan MacDougall, the general's aide, was supposed to be with Pakenham constantly that morning—as a good aide would be—and said later that he had been with him until the moment Pakenham died in his arms. The major testified most positively during Mullins' court-martial that Pakenham had placed no reliance in Thornton, and that he was anxious to begin the assault before daylight in order to escape Patterson's observed fire from across the river. MacDougall was interviewed at length about the battle later, in another connection, and again said nothing to substantiate Smith's self-serving story. Smith wrote this part of his *Autobiography* in 1844 or thereabouts (see chapter 8, p. 129) when he was a justly famous general in his own right, and it is possible that by then he had come to believe sincerely that he had dared counsel his general that morning. However, Pakenham was not a man to taken counsel of his fears, certainly not with a junior officer, and Smith, still in his early twenties at the time, was very "junior" indeed. Pakenham, it is true, might have had a momentary premonition of disaster, but if he did, neither MacDougall nor Tylden saw any sign of it. When the rocket was fired, the assault plan was operating on schedule (except for delay in the diversionary action across the river). Pakenham knew that the plan was a good one, and he believed that his troops would be able to execute it, provided it were launched before daylight.

When the rocket roared into the air, the British right, Gibbs' brigade, moved forward in column of companies to the assault. The 21st was leading, the 4th was in support, and those men of the 44th with ladders and fascines were dispersed around, trying to keep up, but still breathless from all their earlier exertions.[12]

To the left Brevet Lieutenant Colonel Robert Rennie's three light companies moved out at their best speed toward the open redoubt that had so worried Jackson. They encountered a very heavy fire, which brought down two out of every three of the attackers. Their purpose was to draw the fire of the redoubt away from the main attack, which the redoubt guns could take in enfilade. The naval guns across the river could see nothing at the moment, owing to the fog that clung to the river and to the left bank for some distance inland. Rennie's gallant group not only reached the advance redoubt but entered and took it. As the British broke in, however, Rennie himself was killed by one of Captain Thomas Beale's riflemen. The fascines and scaling ladders for this column had been entrusted to the company of West Indians accompanying them, but none of them arrived at the ditch. Nevertheless, the ditch was crossed and the redoubt taken. The British still would have had to cross over Rodriguez Canal on some planks to get into the right of the American line. Their numbers were too few for this without reinforcement, which they never received. In the end, when they realized no support was coming to them, the remnant of this column retired from the redoubt as best they could. The light company of the 7th Fusiliers went into this action with 64 officers and men; only 16 returned, all of them wounded.[13]

Keane was commanding this left column and was originally supposed to have directed the 93rd Highlanders to go to the support of Rennie's men if he saw them succeeding, but he did not do so. Very early that morning when Pakenham gave up hope of any help from Thornton's mission, he rode to Keane and gave him direct orders to close in on Gibbs' column and forget Rennie. He let Rennie go ahead, hoping he could stop the enfilade fire from the outwork, which he did.[14] Dickson sent several artillerymen with Rennie to spike the guns that had been captured. In retrospect, this must be judged another poor decision on Pakenham's part, for had the 93rd come to the support of Rennie, the right of the line might very well have been entered.

The rocket signal was not intended to be a signal for opening fire by the British artillery, which had been ordered to open fire only when they heard the musketry begin to fire, and to be careful not to fire into their own columns. Their targets were to be the artillery on Jackson's lines until such time as those guns were silenced.[15]

The Americans first saw the British when they were about 500 yards away, with fascines and scaling ladders carried ahead of them. The Kentucky rifles could range effectively no more than 400 yards, but Battery #6, General Garriques Flaugiac's brass 12-pounder, fired the first round shortly after he saw the British rocket. All of the American artillery then opened up, and the British replied instantly. "R.S." says the American artillery opened first when the rocket flared and the British artillery replied. This almost concurs with the statement of Butler, Jackson's adjutant general, and is believed by this writer to be correct, because of corroborating details in other accounts.[16]

Tapp, the British Royal Engineer responsible for advancing the fascines and ladders, eventually did go forward with them and the 44th, and at least half of them were ahead of the 21st when the rocket was fired. More may have caught up later, but a number of fascines never did reach the ditch.[17] Some of the men carrying them were casualties; others threw the heavy and unwieldy fascines aside and retired to the woods on their right in hopes of escaping the American fire.

When the American artillery opened on the main attack of the British, it was quite effective, even though some pieces were fired blind through the fog that still obscured the vision of their gunners. Indeed, Patterson's guns were firing blind at British gun flashes throughout the action. Artillery fire was nothing new to the British veterans, however, and they continued their steady advance. The fire of the American naval 32-pounder, loaded with musket balls and laid to the nicest accuracy, was murderous: one single discharge swept the entire center of the attacking force into eternity.[18]

As Jackson expected, the main attack was delivered against the part of the American line that was held by Carroll's Tennesseans, with Adair's Kentuckians in support. To escape the artillery smoke obscuring his target, Adair asked very early that Batteries #7 and #8 cease fire.

When the British were within 350 yards, the first Kentucky rifle cracked, fired by Ensign Ballard of Adair's command. The target, selected by Adair, was a mounted officer in front of the British line—later ascertained to be Brigade-Major Anthony Whittaker, of the 21st Foot—who fell dead on the spot. The order to fire then ran the length of the American line.[19] Fire was delivered by three ranks. The first rank to fire stepped back to reload while the second one fired, and so on; thus each rank was ready with another volley when its turn came.

The American rifle fire was so heavy that an eyewitness thought it "not easy to conceive of its power."[20] From the dreadful fire of every kind poured into them, the battalions began to waver, to halt, and to fire back, and then they completely broke. The casualty rate was horrendous.[21]

Gibbs tried to rally the fleeing troops but could not, and so reported to Pakenham, who then rode forward, hat in hand, accompanied by his aide MacDougall, and succeeded in rallying the troops for a second advance. Gibbs was by then mortally wounded.

Meanwhile, the Highlanders, who had obliqued their march to the right, went forward past their commanding general (Pakenham) at this moment, to his great satisfaction. He cheered them on—and a moment later was dead, and the attack soon collapsed completely.[22]

Major Harry Smith, with his new chief, Lambert, had seen Pakenham gallop past on his way to the front. Pakenham said then, "That is a terrific fire, Lambert."[23] Smith considered it the most murderous and destructive fire, of all arms, ever poured upon a column. In another part of the field, with his unit of the 43rd, Cooke also thought it the most terrific fire he ever faced.[24]

The British rallied for the second attack. Some 20 or 30 men of the 21st, led by Major Thomas Wilkinson and Lieutenant John Leavock, actually entered the American lines, but they were all killed or captured. Some of the 4th did as well. "Subaltern" said that he was wounded at the ditch but that his men carried him back.[25]

The 93rd Highlanders lost their colonel early in the advance, but they continued forward into the hail of lead until they were all but annihilated.[26] The fire was heavier than any troops could face, and their lieutenant colonel finally led what few were left in retrograde.[27]

With the fall of Pakenham and Gibbs, Lambert found himself in command. He had arrived on the scene only a few days before (January 5) and knew almost nothing of his predecessor's orders, plans, or expectations. He did know that two more defensive lines, perhaps as tough or tougher than the one he now faced, would also have to be passed. He still had his own brigade—the two superb regiments that he had brought with him—and on seeing that Gibbs' brigade and the 93rd were irrevocably demoralized for the time being, he brought forward his own brigade to meet the expected American counterattack and to cover the retirement of the rest of the troops. He called a council of war soon afterwards.[28]

At 8:30 A.M. the American infantry ceased firing—for lack of targets. Their artillery ceased at 2 P.M. About the time that the last British attack failed, the sun shone as brightly as it would that day; but, as the testimony of the soldiers of both armies proves, for the most part it was a gray, rainy day with poor visibility.[29]

Later American writers' descriptions of the advance of the British in the bright sunlight in serried rows of colored uniforms are sheer imaginative fiction. A breath of wind blew the mist away long enough for Jackson, who was then on the American left, to see his enemy's advance, but only momentary glimpses like that could have come to anyone.

The redcoat-carpeted stubble in front of the American lines was clearly visible when the firing ceased. Some of the Americans came out of their lines to attend the British wounded, and some of them were fired upon. The British probably thought this was the expected counterattack, but Jackson did not permit one, even to Hinds and his dragoons who pleaded to be allowed to go. About 500 redcoats arose from the stricken field and came in to surrender. Another 400 wounded Britishers were later taken to hospitals in New Orleans. By British accounts their army casualties on January 8 totaled 2,036.[30]

Jackson was later to offer high-sounding reasons for his decision not to take the offensive. Among other things, he claimed, he was reluctant to risk any of his citizen soldiers. The cynical historian is at liberty to doubt that this was the compelling reason. In fact, or at least beyond any reasonable doubt, the reason was a disaster that had befallen his defenses on the right bank shortly after the apparently decisive victory on the left. By Jackson's own testimony, this disaster could well have deprived him of any victory on either bank.

The story of events in that quarter reflect little credit, and no glory, upon any American. Only a chain of circumstances, lucky from the American viewpoint, kept the action there from being the most decisive of the entire campaign. Despite the misfortunes and delays that had initially beset Thornton, he and his men were able to execute their mission, gallantly and brilliantly, but by the time it was accomplished the campaign had been ended by the bloody repulse on the left bank. Cochrane's harebrained idea succeeded almost to the admiral's highest expectations—thanks to Thornton's brilliance and Jackson's, Patterson's, and Morgan's mistakes.

Thornton's composite brigade had made ready to embark at nightfall on January 7.[31] His orders were to land before midnight on the opposite shore, to storm Morgan's and Patterson's battery during the night, to train the captured guns on the flank of Jackson's lines, and finally, when he saw Pakenham's rocket, to open fire. As it happened, by the time a third of the requisite number of boats had reached him, Thornton was already behind schedule by seven or eight hours, owing to the collapse of the canal. Just before daylight Pakenham let him proceed with what troops he had boated up to that time, and Thornton shoved off into the stream with his own regiment plus a few seamen and marines—a total strength of about 560 men.[32] Thornton and Pakenham actually accepted a great risk, and the British historians give the former the high praise he fully deserves. Had Patterson provided only one or two gunboats or similar craft anchored along the opposite shore, as Jackson had suggested he do,[33] Thornton's venture might have ended in disaster before it was well begun; or if only some artillery and a few determined riflemen had held the western levee against Thornton's landing, he would probably have failed at the outset—just as Pakenham had expected from the first.

After the battle Jackson said, "The unerring hand of providence shielded my men."[34] There is no better explanation of the American escape from complete disaster during the attack on the west bank on January 8.

The mighty current of the river carried Thornton's boats a considerable distance downstream from the landing point he had selected. Just as he was finally getting ashore, quite unopposed in the embarkation, the crossing, and the landing, he saw the signal rocket. He then pushed on his troops in furious haste along the shore, with three pulling boats carrying carronades keeping abreast of him in the stream. After a half-hour's progress he encountered an advance party of Americans.

Morgan had a total strength of about 888 men on the west bank, including the 250 Kentuckians under Colonel John Davis, who had joined him during the previous night. Morgan had sent about 120 Louisiana militia forward during the afternoon of the 7th, under Major Jean Arnaud, to prevent any British landing. Of these, 15 were unarmed and the rest had only fowl-

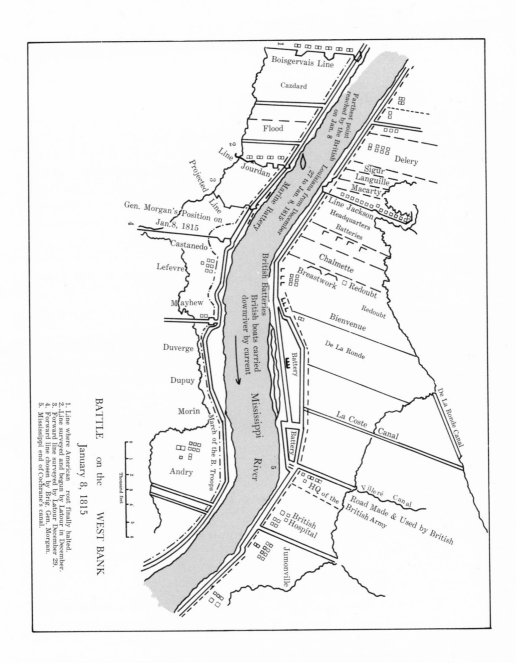

BATTLE on the WEST BANK
January 8, 1815

1. Line where American rout finally halted.
2. Line surveyed and begun by Latour in December.
3. Forward line surveyed by Latour December 29.
4. Forward line chosen by Brig. Gen. Morgan.
5. Mississippi end of Cochrane's canal.

Map 14

ing pieces.[35] They took up a line along a canal some 3 miles below Morgan's main position.

Only about 250 of the 500 Kentuckians ordered across to reinforce Morgan actually arrived. The others, being unarmed, had fallen out before leaving the east bank or during the long march from the ferry. Those who did arrive were almost exhausted from their night march, but Morgan nevertheless ordered them on to reinforce Arnaud immediately. That they went on without protest weighs heavily in their favor, but not in Morgan's. In any case, they met Arnaud's men, who were already retreating (even before the arrival of the British), and the two detachments took up a new outpost position along a canal, or drainage ditch, with the Kentuckians on the left toward the river.

There was a language barrier between the two groups. There was no mutual understanding or confidence. There was no joint command. And neither group had had enough military training to give it any sense of morale or confidence in itself. Nevertheless, on the arrival of the British, the Kentuckians opened fire and delivered several effective volleys. At that moment, however, one of Morgan's staff officers arrived and ordered a retreat to the main line of defense. Why—not even Morgan knew! The order was given in English to the Kentuckians, and was translated for the Creoles, according to Gayarré, as: "*Sauve qui peut.*"[36] At that, quite understandably, Arnaud's detachment disappeared from the battlefield completely. Morgan said that the only man from that battalion whom he ever saw again was its executive officer, who did put in an appearance late that afternoon.

The Kentuckians fell back as ordered—in great confusion, according to Morgan—and were posted in the open, some 200 yards to the right of the Louisiana regiments. They were deployed at intervals of 2 yards, but even then their right flank was exposed because there were not enough men to extend the line into the woods and swamp, while Morgan, with some 350 men, was holding the breastwork covering the road on a front of about 300 yards.

Upon the arrival of the British on his front, Morgan's two fieldpieces and one naval gun that was emplaced in his lines opened effective fire on the enemy, but none of Patterson's other guns were brought to bear as planned. Thornton had brought no artillery except rockets, and it was clearly a case for an immediate assault without preparation (such as he had led against Barney's naval brigade at Bladensburg). To such an experienced soldier, it was obvious that the American right was completely vulnerable, and Thornton quickly deployed his 85th as skirmishers and sent them on the double, with fixed bayonets, against the exposed flank of the line held by the few exhausted Kentuckians. Simultaneously, the naval battalion charged Morgan's breastworks, while the marines were held in reserve. The British did not even stop to return the American small arms fire—which accounts for the very few American casualties[37]—but moved straight ahead, rapidly, with the bayonet and cutlass. The rockets caused terror (but no casualties) among all of the militia, just as they had at Bladensburg.

It is doubtful that any American regulars of that day could have stood their ground in such a situation, with almost no fortifications; that the worn out and untrained Kentucky and Louisiana militia could do so was too much to hope. The Kentuckians broke and fled before the British regulars had closed to within 100 yards of them. The Louisiana militia, who were posted in the open on the Kentuckians' left, followed them almost at once. Those behind the breastwork made a better show of resistance, but shortly afterwards, when their flank became exposed and no fire came from Patterson's guns, they also departed.

Thornton's casualties, by British accounts, were 33 killed and wounded, not including navy and marine casualties. Thornton himself was wounded, as he had been at Bladensburg, and so was the naval battalion commander, but the mission was almost accomplished.

Patterson, a half mile away, had time to order all his guns to be spiked before his naval gunners went aboard the *Louisiana,* which then escaped into the river. It seems obvious from the speed with which Patterson withdrew that he had expected to have to retreat. Very few, if any, of his guns can have been well spiked, because the British accounts claim that at least half of those captured were quickly restored to action by them. (They themselves spiked them all before retiring.)

The British pursued the fleeing Americans for 2 miles but were ordered to halt when word reached them of the British disaster on the left bank. Some of the Americans, including 90 of the Kentuckians and a number of the Louisianians, were rallied by Morgan on the line of the Boisgervais Canal.

Jackson promptly sent the French general Jean Humbert across the river to assume command and made tremendous efforts to provide reinforcements to retake the lost position, but the Louisianians on the west bank, from Morgan down, refused to accept a foreigner in command. When Humbert reported this, Jackson sent Governor Claiborne himself, with orders to dislodge the British at all costs. The governor had steadily insisted upon taking the field in command of his state's militia, and had been importunate about getting an opportunity to gain battle honors. But on crossing the river, he soon reported to Jackson, Claiborne found his troops so demoralized that he could not even attempt an offensive.[38]

Meanwhile, a British reconnaissance by Dickson reported that 2,000 men, and continued naval control of the river, would be needed to hold the position taken. Dickson also learned that General Lambert, as soon as he found himself in command, had sent orders by Major Harry Smith to recall Thornton, for at that moment Lambert had every reason to expect an immediate counterattack in strength, and he needed every man he could get. Gibbs' brigade and the 93rd no longer existed tactically, and an American advance might have overrun all the remnants of those units in the woods on the British right and made prisoners of them.

Dickson saw no evidence of a counterattack, however, and he asked to be allowed to countermand the orders for the withdrawal until he could learn whether Thornton's success could be exploited. Lambert agreed and sent Dickson and Burgoyne to reconnoiter. Burgoyne did not cross the river at that time, and Dickson, who lost time waiting for him, finally crossed alone.

When Dickson did arrive on the west bank, he found that both Thornton and the naval captain commanding the naval contingent were casualties, and that the 85th was now reduced to about 270 effectives. In accordance with the orders to retreat that Smith had delivered, all the guns taken had been spiked, either by the Americans or by the British, before Dickson's arrival. The sailors and marines were in great disorder and, in Dickson's estimation, could not be counted upon in event of attack. Dickson surveyed the terrain, with the help of Quartermaster Lieutenant John Peddie, the path finder of the landing, and found that any position could be turned through the swamp, which was not as impenetrable on the western side of the river as it was on the east.

Dickson ordered the troops to retire to their boats while he himself returned to General Lambert to recommend a withdrawal. After conferring with Admiral Cochrane, Dickson said later, Lambert ordered the withdrawal. The British recovered all their boats from the river and carried their wounded back to the fleet without hindrance.

The Americans were able to reoccupy their old positions that night, and within a few days Patterson was able to unspike his guns and resume his bombardment of the British.[39] American defenses on that bank were now made as impregnable as possible, to guard against another British attack in that quarter.

The entire episode was a brilliant exploit by the British, and a disgraceful exhibition by the Americans, but obviously it had no effect on the outcome of the battle or the campaign. It did, however, give rise to a deplorable and persistent controversy among the Americans themselves—a controversy in which military and civil officials took part for years. The papers of the Adair family say that it went so far as to bring Jackson and Adair face to face on a dueling ground in 1818, but friends dissuaded them from the encounter. The British commentators (and some Americans, too) also did much second-guessing about the wisdom of Lambert's withdrawal.[40]

In their official reports, Jackson and Patterson incontinently placed all blame on Davis' unhappy Kentucky detachment and stoutly upheld Morgan. But a court of inquiry held soon after the battle, over which Carroll presided, absolved Davis and his men of sole blame, and found that Davis' own conduct and that of several Louisiana militia leaders was not at all reprehensible in the circumstances. The court did condemn Arnaud's flight, however, and severely criticized Morgan's choice of position, though Morgan's zeal and gallantry were not impugned. Morgan, it was shown, had done all he could to rally his men by personal example. Jackson approved the proceedings and dissolved the court, but he would never alter his official report. A very bitter and public altercation ensued. The Kentuckians' bitterness against Jackson endured for the rest of his life. Kentucky editors' vilification of Louisianians' conduct in the battle made for additional bad feeling. Morgan was never called to testify in his own defense at the court of inquiry, an omission that angered the Louisianians and rather vitiated the appearance of credibility and judicial validity of its proceedings.[41]

In retrospect it is obvious that neither of the opposing generals considered operations on the right bank to be especially important. Both Jackson and Pakenham prepared for and sought a final decision on the left bank. This turned out well for Jackson, disastrously for Pakenham. Jackson knew of the projected attack on the right bank, but he thought it would be diversionary and concluded, considering the limited resources at his command, that he could not afford to divide his forces. As it turned out, he might well have sent one of his regular regiments, as Patterson had requested him to do more than once. However, preparations for a major assault against his own front were clearly in evidence, and British deserters constantly warned him of it. He undoubtedly supposed that Morgan's forces were in better shape than they were. Jackson's decision, based on his estimate of the situation, was to put his best effort into stopping the main assault. It was the fateful decision of a gambler—as was Pakenham's "fatal, ever fatal rocket"[42]—and Jackson won.

At the British council of war on January 8, only a few officers, one of whom was Colonel Burgoyne, were in favor of renewing the attack. For many years thereafter, Burgoyne kept the secret of his having taken this position, and because it was he who had carried the final order for the retirement across the river, he "laid for many years under the imputation of having counselled relinquishment of the undertaking."[43] Codrington, who was in charge of provisions for the joint force, urged shortage of food as an incentive for another immediate attack to capture New Orleans, presumably to replenish his supplies. Smith states that he answered Codrington, saying, "Kill plenty more, Admiral, so fewer rations will be required." He must have been a very obstreperous young officer, if he said that; perhaps in later life he came to believe he had said what he was then merely thinking. Mac-Dougall, the late Pakenham's aide, expressed the only other recorded opinion then in favor of another attack. Dickson was not present. Harry Smith was definitely opposed. Cochrane's opinion was not recorded, and in his official letters he carefully refrained from expressing anything except concurrence with Lambert. The latter did not vacillate, but decided to retreat as soon as he could extricate the remnants of his army. Gleig, though by no means a military genius, does make a very pertinent observation that the British had to retreat in force; had they been repulsed a second time with heavy losses, the remainder of the army would have had to surrender. Lambert, whose military record, discussed above, shows him to have been a very able soldier, must have recognized that danger himself.[44]

Lambert feared that Thornton's detachment would be cut off by the American naval forces and that his own badly battered army would suffer another night attack. Early in the afternoon of the 8th he sent a flag of truce, which was fired on at first, asking that hostilities be suspended while the wounded were collected and the dead buried. As a subterfuge to allow time for his own reinforcements to cross the river, Jackson refused to receive a message from Lambert until it could be proved that Lambert was in command. Lambert, for his part, was of course trying to avoid reporting Pakenham's death. Finally, Jackson said he would agree to a truce only if both sides would agree not to send reinforcements across the river. By that time, he felt sure, the troops that he had already ordered across under Humbert were there. Lambert asked for twenty-four hours to consider the proposal; but he decided almost immediately after receiving Dickson's report of his reconnaissance (which fortified his own earlier conviction) to bring Thornton back. Under cover of darkness, Lambert destroyed his own heavy guns on the east bank and withdrew his troops to their old position. A truce went into effect until noon of January 9, and Lambert immediately began preparations for a retreat.[45]

Not having counterattacked on January 8, even with his eager Mississippi Dragoons, Jackson did not take the offensive at all—a decision that appears to have represented excellent judgment on his part. There is some question whether or not Jackson knew very much British military history. If he did, Poitiers, Agincourt, and Crecy would have been reminders of what could happen when a British army that wanted to retreat was forced into battle. Notwithstanding their many casualties, the British still had over 6,000 effectives on shore, and the 40th Foot arrived on January 11, followed soon afterwards by a brigade from Canada. Nevertheless many military reviews of the campaign, both American and British, have severely criticized Jackson for not attacking. Obviously, the British reviewers wish that he had given them an opportunity to recover lost British military prestige, whereas most American criticism is clearly intended to belittle Jackson. At the time, however, all of Jackson's militia generals counseled against taking the offensive.

However, as soon as all Patterson's guns were back in operation, Jackson did resume his incessant cannonade by day and night. The defenses on the right bank were strengthened greatly. The Americans also began tempting the British soldiers to desert. Both measures were very effective. Patterson, at long last, began sending armed boats (but not many of them) through Lake Pontchartrain to intercept British supply and evacuation operations in Lake Borgne.[46] These were merely harassing tactics, however, and no determined American attempt to prevent the retreat was made by either the navy or the army.

Cochrane made a belated effort to have the fleet force its way past Fort St. Philip—a project that he had considered before the operation began but had discarded as impracticable. A bombardment by two ships, two bomb ketches, and two sloops, from outside the range of the fort's battery, was maintained for several days, from January 9 to 12. One of the companies of Baratarian "marines" came under fire here (the only one). But the bombardment only succeeded in killing 1 American and wounding 3. It was a desperate gesture, and one can only wonder why it was not attempted, if it were to be done at all, earlier in the operation—if for no other reason than to add to Jackson's worries and to alarm the already jittery Louisianians. At length the British vessels withdrew when a heavy mortar capable of reaching them was brought from the New Orleans Navy Yard and emplaced in the fort by its commander, Major William Overton.[47]

Though Lambert had decided to retreat, accomplishing the withdrawal

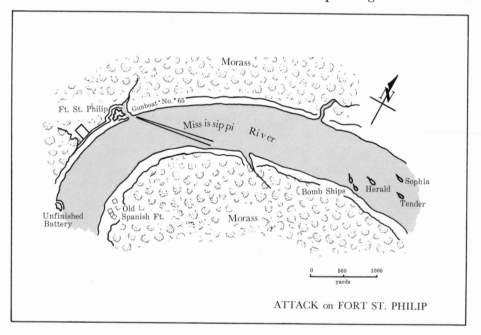

ATTACK on FORT ST. PHILIP

Map   15

was no easy matter. There were not enough boats to embark more than half of his army at a time; thus, one half might then be intercepted on its way to the fleet, while the other half might be overwhelmed by Jackson. In order to retire the entire army at once, the British had to make a road to Fisherman's Village on the shores of Lake Borgne. This required nine days of very arduous labor, and even then the "road" was only a trail covered with faggots of reeds and brush brought from a distance. Finally, on the night of January 18, the British army moved off in dead silence, leaving behind details to keep bivouac fires alight to mislead the Americans. The retreat was somewhat hazardous, and several men either deserted en route or were lost in the swamp, but by the end of the month the remnants of the army were back aboard their transports.[48]

Jackson made no vigorous attempt at pursuit. Hinds took a force into the field but accomplished nothing, and his supporting battalion of Kentuckians ran away.[49] Several of Patterson's small boats in the lake did take a few additional prisoners, but such efforts were not pressed and in sum amounted to very little.

Weather delayed departure of the fleet until January 25. The amphibious force then moved on to attack Mobile, an operation Jackson had been predicting since midsummer. Fort Bowyer had no chance against a large and competent landing force, of course, and it was entirely invested by the morning of February 11. On the following day Major Lawrence very wisely surrendered his 400 men. Jackson was furious with him, but the major had held out as long as would have done any good, and further resistance under the circumstances would have been sheer suicide. And the fort had held out long enough to keep the British from arriving in Mobile before official news of the ratification of peace at Washington reached the armies. Jackson's displeasure with Lawrence was unwarranted and ungracious, and a court of inquiry held in March, 1815 after Jackson had turned over command in New Orleans to General Edmund P. Gaines, absolved the major of all blame. General Gaines approved the court's findings.[50]

On February 14 a sloop of war brought the news to the British that the peace had been signed, and no further hostilities were conducted against Mobile. The British remained at Dauphin Island until the middle of March, when they finally sailed for England.

At Jackson's suggestion to the Abbé Dubourg, the head of the Catholic clergy of Louisiana, a *Te Deum* was celebrated in New Orleans on January

21. At that time the city gave Jackson a Latin welcome and celebration.

The story of events from that date until March 13, 1815, when Jackson finally received official notice of the ratification of the peace, is an unhappy one. Jackson did not revoke martial law until that moment, and his popularity in New Orleans vanished for the next twenty years. The legislature would not even pass a resolution thanking him for defending the city and would not agree to give him the commemorative sword that had been suggested earlier. After martial law was rescinded, finally, Federal Judge Dominick Hall hailed Jackson into his court for "contempt" and fined him $1,000. Jackson paid the fine in order to end the controversy, but it was refunded to him many years later.[51]

Lambert had left 80 of his most severely wounded men under the care of a surgeon. These received the same attention as was given the American wounded. Prisoners had been exchanged with the British and all negotiations had been meticulously courteous. The final comment of the British Army's official historian, Fortescue, about the Battle of New Orleans merits quotation here:

Jackson proved himself to be not only brave and able as a commander, but courteous in negotiation, modest in reporting his own achievements, and kind and considerate to the British wounded who fell into his hands. His countrymen in New Orleans emulated his example in the matter of the wounded with a generosity that did them infinite honour: and thus the repulse at the Mississippi, though the most crushing blow that was sustained by the British in the course of the war, left behind it less bitterness than any other . . . The war . . . revealed to both nations their strength and their weakness, and did more than is suspected to preserve peace inviolate between them for a hundred years.[52]

10. SUMMARY AND CONCLUSIONS

The international struggle for the northern coast of the Gulf of Mexico and the mouth of the Mississippi River persisted actually from about 1698 to 1815. There would be some adjustments after the Battle of New Orleans and the Treaty of Ghent, such as the British-American Conventions under the provisions of the treaty, and the Adams-Onis Treaty with Spain concerning Florida, Texas, and the Spanish-American boundary of the Louisiana Purchase. They would be taken in stride. As the full import of Jackson's victories in the Creek War and in the New Orleans campaign became apparent to Ferdinand VII and his ministers, the Spanish monarch began to see that further efforts to keep the Floridas out of American hands would be futile.

The race of Creole settlers that the French had left in America in 1763 played a very conspicuous part in the entire history of Louisiana. Without their loyal help and courageous fighting, the Spaniards under Don Bernardo de Galvez could never have retaken the Floridas for Spain in the American Revolution; instead, Spain could easily have lost New Orleans to the British during that war. But the same French Creoles gave Louisiana such a non-Spanish character, and made it such an expensive drain on the Spanish treasury, that the Spaniards were eventually glad to turn it over to Napoleon in 1803. For several reasons, Bonaparte then sold the vast territory included in the Louisiana Purchase to the United States (with a most imperfect title under international law).

Had those Gallic gentlemen of Louisiana decided during the War of 1812 that they would rather live under the British crown than the American Constitution, they undoubtedly could have effected the change. But they did not desire this. They supported Jackson and their support was of decisive importance. Perhaps some of them chose what they considered the lesser of two evils—and did so with scant enthusiasm—but the fact remains: their swords were drawn on the side of the United States.

Thus for a second time in history the Creoles contributed very decisively to a British defeat at New Orleans. Official American accounts of the battle, and many later histories of the New Orleans campaign, have failed to do full justice to the participation of those Americans of Latin descent—Spanish as well as French, women as well as men. Louisiana historians and their friends and sympathizers have railed at the injustice of the Anglo-Saxons' claim to all credit for the victory at New Orleans. The Louisianians have had good grounds for complaint against the conceits of some Tennesseans and Kentuckians. On the other hand, the fact is inescapable that if the Westerners had not come so stoutly to the defense of New Orleans and the Gulf Coast, the whole area might well have been irretrievably lost by the United States, for the Creoles alone certainly could not have thwarted the British designs.

When the credit is divided fairly among those who contributed to the final decision in this struggle, fought out over a century and a half ago, the largest share surely must go to Major General Andrew Jackson and to the state of Tennessee, which sent him and his men into the Creek War and into all of the subsequent operations on the Gulf Coast from 1813 to 1815.

Not only have some American and British historians cheated Americans of Latin descent of their share of the glory of the victory at New Orleans, but some of them have also striven mightily to prove that there was no victory for which credit might be shared.

When the War of 1812 came, it afforded the American West the opportunity for the destruction of the confederation of Tecumseh in the Northwest, the elimination of British and Spanish support to the western Indians, and the incidental destruction of the powerful Creek Confederacy in the Southwest. The Creek War, instigated in part by British and Spanish agents, was definitely part of the War of 1812 and of the struggle for the Gulf Coast.[1]

When in the summer of 1814 British amphibious forces arrived on the scene to champion further resistance by the Indians and to strengthen the enfeebled Spaniards, the West prepared to do battle again. Andrew Jackson, the hero of the Creek War, and his Tennesseans, supported by Mississippians, Louisianians, and Kentuckians, threw themselves against the British invaders. This wrote *finis* in letters of blood to the long international struggle for the Gulf Coast and the Mississippi Valley. Of what import was that stirring and epic final struggle? Was the battle but a useless blood-letting of no

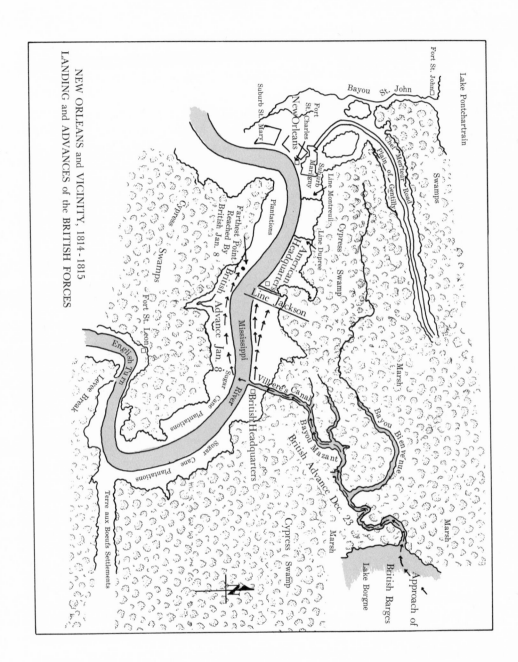

Map 16

moment to the conditions of peace, and of no importance in the history of the world, or even in the history of the United States? Many historians, American as well as British, have answered this question in the affirmative. Pointing to the fact that the Treaty of Ghent was signed December 24, 1814, two weeks before the final British defeat on January 8, 1815, they conclude that the battle was fought in vain. The fact is persistently overlooked, or perhaps deliberately ignored, that by its terms the treaty could not go into effect until ratification was exchanged by both nations—and that did not happen until February 16, 1815. And the British treaty right to navigate the Mississippi River was not relinquished by them until the Convention of 1818 was signed.

A study of (1) the British government's plans, operations, and orders, before and during the New Orleans campaign, (2) the negotiations at Ghent, and (3) the correspondence of the Spanish and British governments (before and during those negotiations) concerning their territorial claims on the Gulf of Mexico and the Mississippi Valley does not appear to support the notion that the Battle of New Orleans was "fought for nothing." And yet this viewpoint still has its adherents. Only recently, for example, the American historian Fred L. Engelman, on the basis of his study of the Ghent negotiations, concluded: "It is a figment of historical imagination to imply that the British cabinet still clung to any plans as to the future of New Orleans in the first months of 1815."[2]

The superabundance of Admiralty and War Office letters to and from the British amphibious forces of Vice-Admiral Cochrane concerning British operations in the Gulf has been discussed above in some detail. Pakenham's already sizable command was heavily reinforced from Canada and Great Britain between January 9 and 11. On January 9, five more regiments were ordered from Cork, fully seven days after the new chargé d'affaires to the United States had sailed for New York with the copy of the Treaty of Ghent that bore the prince regent's ratification. The chargé had detailed instructions as to when and under what circumstances he was to exchange ratifications. Just what these instructions were has not yet been made public, but it is known that as late as February 28, 1815, more than two months *after* the signing of the treaty, the British prime minister wrote to Wellington that he was hoping "momentarily" to receive news of a great victory by the duke's kinsman (Pakenham), towards which victory, he said, the British government had done everything possible.[3]

Why? Was all this terrific expenditure of blood and treasure by a war weary British government, harassed by niggardly parliamentary appropriations of funds, all for nothing—or perhaps to stimulate the fevered "imaginations" of future historians to the invention of "figments"?

The documentary evidence is not "imaginary," and all of it that bears on the British government's intentions toward New Orleans and Louisiana, as adduced in the present work, serves to support the thesis: "The Battle of New Orleans is second in importance only to Washington's victory at Yorktown."[4]

But whatever the British plans for the Gulf Coast may have been, Jackson's victory put an end to them. Anthony St. John Baker, the newly appointed British chargé d'affaires in the United States, who had been secretary of the British commission at Ghent, reached New York on Saturday, February 11, with the British ratification of the treaty of peace in his possession. The news of Jackson's victory greeted him in New York. It was a complete disaster to British plans.

Before the war, Baker had served as attaché to the British legation in Washington, where he had been very cordially detested, and his journey overland by coach from New York to Washington must have been a sore trial. He arrived in the capital on Friday, February 16, to find that Christopher Hughes, secretary of the American commission at Ghent, who had left England after Baker, had come via Annapolis, Maryland with his copy of the treaty and had preceded Baker to Washington by three days. The British chargé then learned that the United States Senate had unanimously recommended ratification of the treaty to the President on the very day of Baker's arrival in Washington.[5]

The British government had hoped to conclude a separate treaty of peace with the New England states,[6] and this hope might well have been realized if Jackson had not won so handsomely at New Orleans. Pakenham was under orders to continue his operations until a special emissary from the prince regent reached him.[7] However, with Pakenham dead and his expedition a failure, there was nothing else for Baker to do on February 16 but to exchange ratifications—and it was that exchange which ended the war. Whatever Baker may have been instructed to do under different circumstances, the compelling fact of the American victory at New Orleans decided the matter for him. On February 16, just four hours after the Senate voted its ratification unanimously, Baker exchanged ratifications.[8]

The first news of Pakenham's defeat and death reached London on March

9, the same day that Napoleon's escape from Elba became known. News of the American ratification of the Treaty of Ghent came four days later. In the new Napoleonic crisis, peace with the United States was a boon that the British gratefully accepted. Major General George Johnson's corps at Cork was ordered to Belgium (instead of to New Orleans) and became the nucleus of the army with which the Iron Duke was to win at Waterloo, restoring the British army's *amour propre,* which had been so badly shaken at New Orleans. The 4th, 7th, 40th, and 43rd of Lambert's army, plus Sir Manley Power's brigade (the 27th Eniskillen, the 89th Dublin Foot, the 41st Welsh, and the 1st Royal Foot), returned in time for that battle, too. The 21st, 44th, 85th, and 93rd were unable to fight so soon after their heavy losses at New Orleans, but they relieved other units in Ireland for service in Belgium.[9] The 95th reached Belgium too late for Waterloo.

Jackson's victory at New Orleans was a major factor in a resurgence of American nationalism. As they bragged about New Orleans, Americans conveniently forgot their dismal record of defeats by the British earlier in the War of 1812. But even so, the revival was preeminently in the West and South and developed rather slowly in the Northeast.[10]

Major William Lawrence's successful defense of Fort Bowyer in September, 1814 kept Mobile out of British hands then, and his delaying action in February, 1815 again prevented their winning that prize until news of the ratification of the Treaty of Ghent put an end to British designs on Mobile and West Florida. The value of the major's achievements is too often overlooked.

It is impossible to see on what grounds, under terms of the Treaty of Ghent (or any other treaty), the United States could have expected Mobile or any part of West Florida to have been returned to her, had the British and Spaniards actually been in possession when the treaty was ratified. The American title rested entirely on the right of possession by forcible occupation in 1810 and 1813.[11] By 1815, only Jackson and his subordinate, Lawrence, retained a vestige of title for the United States—but that was enough.

The British campaign plans for New Orleans and the Gulf Coast were sound, both politically and strategically. Politically, the British had condemned the Treaty of San Ildefonso and the American seizure of West Florida. That made a good case for them in international law if they championed Spanish rights, as they had promised to do.[12] It could be claimed that a later provision of the Treaty of San Ildefonso denied the right of the deposed Napoleon to dispose of Louisiana to any state other than Spain, even if the United States argued her rights by purchase. As the great American historian Edward A. Channing put it, the United States was "the purchaser of stolen goods from a known highwayman."[13] Strategically, British possession of the mouth of the Mississippi might well have confined the United States economically and commercially to the Atlantic seaboard. Produce from New Orleans and the upper river would have solved the supply and marketing problems of the British West Indies.

Considered from an operational point of view, the original plans of the Admiralty, insofar as they are revealed by documents available in the Public Record Office and reported by the contemporary British naval historians, seem to have been very sound indeed. The amphibious striking force for use against Louisiana was to have been assembled secretly at either Bermuda or Barbados. Cochrane had asked for and been promised light-draft Dutch vessels for navigation of the shallow coastal waters of Louisiana and West Florida. Provisions and supplies in ample quantities were to have been forwarded from Europe to the base selected. Secrecy was to have been maintained. A cover operation of an attack on the Georgia coast was intended to divert the main effort of the American defense forces.[14]

This excellent plan was later modified and changed beyond all recognition for a variety of reasons. For one thing, because of Parliament's parsimony the British cabinet failed to support all the original plans for the New Orleans amphibious offensive. The cabinet notified the Admiralty, and also Cochrane in America, that Lord Hill's big expedition would be replaced by the reinforcement of Ross's smaller command, which was already in America. Because of the easy British victory at Bladensburg the cabinet grew more and more contemptuous of the ability of the United States to resist even a reduced British effort.[15] Undoubtedly Parliament's announced intention of ending the collection of war taxes influenced the cabinet to begin to economize in their preparations. In any case, only about half of the number of troops originally planned for were sent in time to participate in the landing. Later, however, the government ordered more and more reinforcements, finally exceeding the total planned for originally. The very tardy departure of Lambert's brigade, a month after he received orders from Lord Bathurst in the War Office, and the even more tardy sailing of the 40th

Foot, were probably due to the Admiralty's delays.[16] The Admiralty had been told by Bathurst on August 17 that the big show under Lord Hill was off, and the navy lords seem to have lost any sense of urgency. The 40th Foot, a later reinforcement, did not arrive until January 11, after the decision to retreat from New Orleans had been taken, but orders to the 40th and the artillery siege train were issued before those to Lambert. More troops, four regiments under Major General Sir Manley Powers, arrived from Canada shortly after the 40th Foot.

Secrecy was compromised almost from the first.[17] The press in both England and France discussed the expedition openly. Castlereagh himself was said to have boasted of it at Ghent, when he stopped by there to confer with the British peace commissioners on his way to Vienna. Discussion of an attack on New Orleans, however, had been carried on all through the war by the British press, and such talk in itself would not have alarmed or alerted the Americans. Nobody but Jackson and the westerners ever did show concern.

The worst British mistake was changing the advance base to Jamaica and thus removing all doubt as to what the objective was to be. After the preparations in Jamaica were reported to Jackson, no cover operation in Georgia would ever have drawn him away from the Gulf Coast. A letter to Rear Admiral William Brown, commandant of the naval station at Jamaica, arrived shortly after his sudden death, and the officer in temporary command opened the dispatch in the presence of a merchant who had American friends and business connections, and the latter promptly passed the word on.[18]

Perhaps an even more damaging blunder than that was the Admiralty decision to rent shallow-draft vessels for Cochrane in the West Indies, and also to purchase provisions there for the men of the fleet and army. Cochrane's hiring cargo ships to bring back the loot was his own amazing contribution. Flatboats that the Admiralty had promised to send with each transport were forgotten. All these changes of plan were most unwise militarily and did not even effect a saving of money—on the contrary, prices skyrocketed. The available West Indian vessels were not of shallow enough draft for use on the inland waters of the Gulf Coast; and at the best of times food was always in short supply and expensive in the West Indies. Possession of New Orleans was coveted by the British West Indies planters largely on that account—as a cheap source of food from the American West. In addition to widely advertising the size of the expedition, the best British efforts could not obtain sufficient food, as the Admiralty surely should have known in advance. Not only did this add greatly to the privations of the men engaged in the campaign, lowering their morale, but it also, as Cochrane pointed out, put the expedition under tremendous pressure to secure an early and speedy victory, if success were to be achieved at all.[19]

The inability of the small vessels to navigate the lakes threw the entire transportation, supply, and evacuation problem on the navy's pulling boats, of which there were not nearly enough to meet the requirements. This shortage was also due to the failure of the Admiralty lords to heed Cochrane's counsel. The stupendous work load was handled very creditably by Cochrane's sailors, but its existence points up Cochrane's intransigence in persisting in an attack on New Orleans by way of Lake Borgne and Bayou Bienvenue.

Of course, one can appreciate Cochrane's dilemma. His stores and provisions would not sustain a long campaign, and he decided to try for the quick victory that Bladensburg had led him to expect would be possible. And he would have succeeded if Jackson had been another Winder, or if the westerners had been no more interested in victory than were the troops called up for Winder to lead.

The failure of the diversionary effort in Georgia was complete. Cockburn was driven off the coast by a storm. He had asked Cochrane for army troops, but the latter could not spare him any. He had to depend on sailors and marines. The operation against St. Mary's, Georgia was not begun until January, 1815, too late to have any influence on the expedition against New Orleans. As a cover plan it was an utter fiasco, though the navy finally did win some booty.

Cochrane's decision to strike directly at New Orleans seems to have been made after he received Captain Sir William H. Percy's report of Jackson's attack on Pensacola. Cochrane may have concluded that Jackson was too far from New Orleans to defend it and that he was concentrating on repelling an attack on Mobile. In fact, however, Jackson arrived at New Orleans two weeks before the British. Cochrane's intelligence reports that New Orleans was very weakly defended were correct. But he was also told that the Creole inhabitants were thoroughly disaffected, and this was not true. Perhaps some of them who might have been inclined to support the British did not do so for fear of what Jackson might do to them, but most of the Creoles, if not enthusiastically pro-American, were valiantly and effectively anti-British.

If Cochrane knew about the Villeré Canal approach before he reached the Mississippi Sound, he did not mention it to his chief of staff, Codrington, who as late as December 16 expected to attack the fort at Petites Coquilles. The interesting thesis has been advanced that Cochrane was tricked into this landing by the Baratarians, who deliberately fed him misinformation about the terrain and extravagant stories of Jackson's weakness and his unpopularity with the Creoles.[20] Nothing has been found to substantiate this conjecture—though Gleig says that he suspected treachery, on December 24—but it is undeniably arresting.

Cochrane was much interested in prize money, and so was the British cabinet. There was a huge fortune in cotton at New Orleans, not to mention other wealth, and it is possible that the British expected the campaign to pay for itself in loot from the Crescent City. Cochrane brought along cargo ships in ballast to secure that loot, and Wellington later criticized Cochrane harshly for doing so, on the ground that it further compromised the secrecy of the expedition.[21] The Iron Duke's antipathy to Cochrane was unjust, but it colored many British accounts of the operation afterwards.

The admiral's quick organization and dispatch of Captain Nicholas Lockyer's British boat flotilla to cope with the American gunboats did him credit. Lockyer also deserved credit for his dashing attack and capture of the gunboats. The capture of five large shallow-draft sailing vessels was alone well worth the casualties expended, and at the same time Jackson was deprived of naval gunfire defenses at the Rigolets and of his lookouts on Lakes Borgne and Pontchartrain.

Why Patterson did not replace his scouting gunboats with other small craft on the lake, and why he did not order Jones to burn his gunboats rather than lose them intact to the British, remain unsolved mysteries. Of course, it was sheer bad luck that most unusual conditions of wind and current prevented Jones from taking his miniature fleet back to the Rigolets, as Patterson had ordered him to do. Some naval historians try to give Jones and Patterson credit for gaining the nine days delay that allowed Jackson to collect his forces for the defense of New Orleans. But that is a gross exaggeration. The gunboat battle may have delayed Cochrane by two days at most, and the main reason for this delay was a lack of shallow-draft sailing ships, a lack that the capture of the gunboats alleviated somewhat.

The Dutch *schuyts* would have moved the army up the bay. The rented West Indian small craft all went aground near the entrance to the lake. The army had to be moved and supplied thereafter by pulling boats over a very long distance. The logistic problem of the British was prodigious from the very start.

Jackson seems to have been wholly unaware of the British move to Pea Island. If his intelligence agencies were organized by that time, they were certainly not yet operating effectively. Patterson was woefully short of sailors at this point, since the navy could not enlist any men until the legis- lature of Louisiana embargoed all ships in port and appropriated money to be used as bonuses for short navy enlistments—things the federal govern- ment had never allowed Patterson to do. Soon after that the Baratarians were promised a pardon and four companies were formed and used in garrisoning forts. Only a handful, those in two gun crews on Jackson's line, saw any real action, but another company of Baratarians did come under fire at Fort St. Philip.

Jackson himself cannot escape all blame for his lack of intelligence con- cerning the enemy's movements. Every commander, in every echelon, is responsible for his own security, and he can never transfer the blame for a security failure to anybody else. The British surprise landing was apparently another disaster for Jackson, but as events proved, it was a blessing in dis- guise. British penetration of Lake Pontchartrain and a landing on the Plain of Gentilly would have given Jackson a harder problem of defense, while simultaneously giving the British more freedom to maneuver and a far easier problem of logistic support. The use of boats across Lake Pontchar- train from a supply base on the Mississippi coast west of Pascagoula (Coch- rane's earlier plan) would have greatly reduced the time and space factors of supply and evacuation. Cochrane already knew, from Captain Hugh Pigot's investigation, that plenty of animal transport was available in the Floridas. That was the approach that Jackson dreaded most. Even after the British were in front of him at Villeré's plantation, the American general was still wary of an attack from the Rigolets or the Chef Menteur—and with very good reason, for he did not have a force large enough to be divided efficiently. It has been said that if Jackson himself had been granted the privilege of selecting his enemy's approach, the Bayou Bienvenue would have been his choice.[22]

A great deal has been written by both British and American historians and experts in armchair strategy about Keane's failure to push on with his advance guard to capture the city on December 23. William James, writing soon after the battle, effectively answered such criticism of Keane's decision.[23] The testimony of Jones and his officers and men who were taken on the gunboats was deliberately misleading as to Jackson's strength. The testimony of the Fisherman's Village outpost, which was captured that morning, confirmed Jones. From those two supporting elements of information British intelligence officers concluded that the city was defended by 15,000 men, with more arriving hourly. The British troops were thought to be near the limit of their endurance as a result of the privations that they had suffered for many days, and the rigors of their final trip from Pea Island under the grim conditions described by Gleig. If the British were reluctantly accepting the risk of being destroyed, why should Keane ever have been expected to rush into action and thus make such a grim outcome a virtual certainty?

The official British army historian, Sir John Fortescue, writing many years later, when Jackson's actual unreadiness for immediate battle was known, concluded that Keane, with very good fortune, might have succeeded. Fortescue notes, however, that the approach would have been through a long straggling suburb where riflemen could have wrought great havoc among Keane's scanty troops. It is certainly true that house to house fighting through a long suburb of a city or town is very slow and exhausting work even for fresh troops who are mentally prepared and trained for it— and it can be very costly in casualties. Such an operation requires special training and physical conditioning. Every minute that the British would have had to use in attacking the first houses would have given the defenders time to garrison other houses farther along the road—and good sharpshooters, firing from upstairs windows, can do terrific damage in this type of operation.

Fortescue's final comment on Keane's decision is definitive: Jackson was a man who would have fought to the very last, a man who would certainly have burned New Orleans if he found he could not hold it.[24] However, it seems to the present writer that once Keane abandoned all secrecy and moved out of the swamp, he should then have moved on to the attack as Colonel Thornton urged him to do. The limit of the disciplined veteran soldiers' endurance had not been reached; the limit of Keane's daring had been.

The most caustic criticism of Jackson, and one very widely quoted by American historians, comes of course from Henry Adams, a grandson of Jackson's bitter political foe of later years, John Quincy Adams.[25] The military opacity of Henry Adams in this matter is phenomenal, and his criticism of Jackson is utterly fatuous. According to Adams, Jackson should have been in New Orleans all summer, fortifying that city and paying no attention at all to Mobile or Pensacola. This bizarre thesis has no validity whatsoever.

It has been concluded repeatedly by many critics of the campaign that if the British had moved with greater dispatch after their arrival on the Gulf Coast they could have gained a victory—that only the incredible blunders of the British "brass" prevented such a triumph. The record shows, however, that no time was wasted after the British fleet's arrival. The time and space factors that were encountered were very formidable but they were attacked with a maximum effort and fortitude by both army and navy. Considering the available transport equipment, it is difficult to see how the British forces could have moved any faster. That equipment could easily have been better except for unwise economies on the part of the Admiralty, and these cannot be held against Cochrane.

Of course, if the British expedition had reached the Gulf Coast two weeks or even ten days earlier, before Jackson had had time to organize or plan in any way for its reception, a British victory would have been all but certain. Jackson's expedition against Pensacola cut his time of preparation very precariously short, it is true, and without him there would have been no defense of New Orleans.

There can be no doubt that Jackson's prompt and violent reaction to the British landing of December 23 was the most decisive single factor in the campaign. The night attack inflicted heavy and completely unexpected casualties on the British, and threw them into a state of uncertainty from which they never quite recovered. Jackson's troop dispositions, which permitted such prompt action, were remarkably efficient. Patterson's subsequent steady cannonading of the shaken British, night and day, until the loss of the *Carolina,* was also most effective.

The night action is accounted a drawn battle, but in effect it was a decisive American victory. The British veterans, badly hurt by casualties, were somewhat shaken. Conversely, the Americans' morale was lifted to the skies, and they never lost heart again. That was an imponderable, but tremendously important, result of the action. Another, more tangible result was the British admiral's haste to throw the last reserve of the Joint Force into the cul-de-sac on the bank of the Mississippi, thus depriving the commander of troops on shore of maneuverability. By the extraordinary efforts of the British sailors, the last element of the original British landing force, including the naval brigade, was put ashore before nightfall of December 24, and the British were committed to attack the city from the south and from no other direction.

One oft-repeated criticism of Jackson is that he should have attacked at daybreak instead of in the darkness of early evening, or that he should have renewed his offensive at daybreak on December 24.[26] This criticism is not valid. A daylight attack would not have been the complete surprise to the British that the night attack was. Hand to hand fighting in the darkness makes for an even match, whereas daylight gives well-trained troops a decided advantage. Moreover, it was, and still is, standard practice in all professional armies to stand-to for a possible attack at daylight, even when none is really expected. There could not have been the necessary deployment in the darkness to make the attack without alerting the British veteran soldiers. To have waited for daylight would have been to lose the effect of surprise—the only advantage Jackson had.

Jackson was wise, then, to follow the Shakespearean advice: "If 'twere well 'twere done, 'twere well 'twere done quickly." Jackson whipped up his own and his raw troops' enthusiasm and courage and struck before those emotions cooled. In a log wait for H-hour, even the best of troops begin to waver in their resolution. If Jackson had waited, even his regulars, largely untried, might well have "melted away" during the night. On this night, one suspects, Jackson may have steeled himself to imitate the legendary Swiss hero, Arnold von Winkelried. Any criticism of Andrew Jackson for launching his attack when he did is mere carping.

It is not in the least surprising that the attack was uncoordinated. Veteran troops are very apt to make the same mistake, and they have frequently done so on countless fields. A commander can do no more than set up a plan (on the basis of his knowledge of the time and space factors involved) designed to put the various elements in position to strike at a prescribed or signaled time. The unit commanders have to take it from there. During the Creek War, Jackson himself once wrote to his chief, Major General Thomas Pinckney: "A general cannot guarantee success, he can only conduct himself and his affairs so as to deserve it." In this instance, Jackson deserved success, and he received a good measure of it.

By far the wisest of Jackson's decisions at New Orleans seems to have been his choosing to move from the offensive to the defensive along Rodriguez Canal in the early morning hours of December 24. Considering his impetuous nature, it must have been a hard decision for him, but it was the correct one. Any renewal of the attack against the irate, alert, vengeful, and very heavily reinforced British veterans would have been disastrous.

When Pakenham arrived on Christmas Day, he found himself deprived of all freedom of maneuver, committed to a frontal assault against successive lines of unknown strength (which apparently had both flanks secure), and opposed by an enemy of unknown numbers. Throughout the battle Jackson kept him from learning those essential items of information. The counter-intelligence work of Hinds and his Mississippi Dragoons was superb. As late as January 7, Pakenham told Lambert that before he reached the city he expected to find two or more defensive lines beyond Line Jackson as strong or stronger than the first. Jackson even kept the various elements among his forces separated so that very few persons in his own army could know his actual strength.

It is hard to understand why Patterson made no attempt to interfere with the British lines of communications through the lakes. They were most vulnerable, as the British admiral and general were well aware. The landing force had a very difficult problem of supply and evacuation, and it could have been made far worse by the Americans, but they scarcely molested the British on that score.

Pakenham did everything a resourceful commander could do. His destruction of the *Carolina* with hot shot was a very cheering success for the British and another severe blow to the Americans. Her captain ought to have stood her downstream with the wind and current and saved her for later use, but he failed to do so. Patterson was fortunate to save the *Louisiana*. Had Dickson listened to Pakenham and waited for a naval 18-pounder, both ships might have been destroyed on the same day. The *Carolina*'s veteran crew was saved, and part of it later became of great value to Jackson on his lines. However, those officers and men were lost to Patterson when he needed them to prevent the river crossing—a naval responsibility that he never accepted. There were plenty of suitable vessels for an armed boat flotilla in the navy's possession. The small, fast, armed sailing craft that

Patterson had captured from the Baratarians in October were at the New Orleans Navy Yard awaiting disposition by the admiralty court, but they were certainly available for use in the emergency, and Baratarian crews were also available to man them.

Jackson's cutting of the levee worked to the British advantage after the river fell on December 27; but when he cut it initially on the early morning of December 24, releasing 30 inches of water, it served to screen the frantic beginning of his construction of the line along Rodriguez Canal. Hinds' Mississippi Dragoons could patrol the front on their horses in that depth of water, but his mounted troops and the inundation itself combined to prevent foot-troop reconnaissance by the British. The British would have been forced to withdraw had the river continued to rise, so it was well worth the effort. The cut made by Morgan below the British camp upset Pakenham very much. The river did begin to rise again soon after the British had started preparations for their withdrawal, and it "hastened" their departure. Fear that it would continue to rise worried Cochrane from the moment it was cut the first time.

It was perhaps fortunate for Jackson that Pakenham's December 28 reconnaissance in force was no more than that, but it is to be remembered that it was Jackson's counterintelligence activities that forced the British general to resort to such a major reconnaissance. If the British intelligence agencies had been able to plan for an assault on December 28, Rennie might very well have turned the left flank of Line Jackson. Pakenham accompanied his own left flank column. The punishing fire of the *Louisiana* and of Jackson's artillery kept Pakenham from knowing that fortune was favoring his right. He made a personal reconnaissance, but he did not go all the way to his right flank. On advice of his veteran staff, he then ordered a withdrawal. Dickson's field artillery was greatly overmatched, his light pieces useless, and his heavier pieces too few and short of ammunition. Jackson and Coffee saw to it that by January 1 no further opportunity was afforded to the British on the American left.

Why Pakenham decided to wait for the heavy naval artillery before making any new attempt has been a subject of considerable speculation among historians, but no trained artilleryman would question his decision. It appears to some critics that when Pakenham received Colonel Robert Rennie's report on the weakness of Jackson's left on December 28, he might well have ordered a prompt assault that night or the following day, making his main effort on his own right, with perhaps a noisy demonstration of some sort on the American right. Since Jackson had only five guns mounted on his lines and none of them on his left, it seems quite probable that such a British assault might have been successful on December 29, whereas by January 1 the weakness of Jackson's left had been corrected.

Pakenham was clearly reluctant to accept the heavy casualties of a storming operation, if he could avoid having to do so. The British naval artillery was available and his highly experienced staff officers had great faith in its effectiveness; thus, he chose to listen to counsels of caution. His staff officers had seen Marshal Massena's tragic failure to break a British line, with both its flanks secure, at Busaco. Napoleon had censured Massena severely for trying it without waiting for adequate artillery preparation. Here, however, in contrast with Busaco, it was far from being certain that the American left flank was secure, and some of Pakenham's best young line officers contended that it was not. Nevertheless, it is hard to see why some historians insist that the general should have taken their advice instead of that of his more experienced staff members.

Sir Edward's dwindling numbers must have also concerned him. Battle casualties—including those from Patterson's harassing fires, the steady drain on the picket lines from the Tennesseans' "hunting parties," and Choctaw Indian raids—must have been, in the aggregate, much heavier than those indicated by British returns now available. And the rate of desertions was another constantly worsening problem. In view of the inclement weather and the very poor food, it is probable that the number of non-battle casualties, which were never reported, was also quite high. Contemporary American newspaper reports tell of much dysentery in the British camp—a disorder probably caused by the raw sugar that the British were reduced to eating. Many American troops fell sick from cold and exposure, and it is likely that many British soldiers did so as well. Both of the West Indian regiments, which were not properly clothed or equipped, were utterly ineffective.

Against a foe of unknown strength, holding successive fortified lines with secure flanks, a storm attempt was injudicious until the 40th Foot and Lambert's brigade arrived, and both were expected on the scene momentarily. If the American lines could be swept away by heavy naval gunfire even before the army siege train arrived, a sanguinary storm would not be necessary. It is very likely that Pakenham reasoned along such lines, and properly so. He had seen Major General John Lambert's transports at

Jamaica, and he had been informed that the 40th Foot and his siege artillery had been ordered to him before Lambert's brigade had been ordered to join his forces.

It is surprising that the artillery duel was such a total failure from the British standpoint. The first British concentration on Jackson's headquarters miraculously caused no casualties at all. If it had killed Jackson, or wounded him seriously, the battle probably would have been won at that point, since there was no recognized second-in-command to replace Jackson. After a slow start, the American artillery, though outweighed and outnumbered and heterogeniously manned, outshot the enemy. The British reliance on sugar hogsheads as epaulements for their gun emplacements proved to be a serious mistake. Jackson's use of cotton bales in places was also ill-advised, but was not quite so costly. American gunnery clearly demonstrated its superiority. An attack on the American left that day, under cover of the artillery duel, showed that that approach was now closed for good.

This being so, Pakenham's only remaining alternative was to order a direct assault, and he forthwith prepared to launch a storm, to begin as soon as Lambert arrived. This he did, with the fatal results already recorded. But he *almost* won. William James said, "the death of a British general saved an American city." That might perhaps be true. After Pakenham's death the will to take the offensive went out of the British leaders, if not the entire army. But that will had already been steadily sapped by the series of events that preceded Pakenham's demise, and it is probable that there was a growing suspicion among the greatly put-upon British soldiers that their officers were convinced that the American line was nearly impregnable. If they were not so convinced, a foot soldier might well wonder, then why dig that monstrous canal? Such a thing had certainly never been asked of the British troops before.

The fiasco on the west bank is an ineradicable blot on the Americans' otherwise glorious victory. There is no excuse for the Americans—for neither Jackson nor Patterson, but especially not for Patterson. Cochrane's contempt for American militia was, in that action, abundantly confirmed. Fortunately for the Americans, the British general did not share his naval opposite number's confidence in that maneuver. It is most difficult to understand why the British were permitted to pass a single man across the river, or how, after the defeat on the left bank, a single man of the British detachment was ever allowed to rejoin the main body. Lambert deserves credit for ordering them back so quickly, since the British detachment could not possibly have been reinforced then or for several days, and Jackson was forcing him to decide immediately. Isolated, they surely would have been lost, and the few British pulling boats could not have kept control of the Mississippi River below New Orleans against an American flotilla.

The entire affair should have put a brake on American claims of invincible bravery and made them thank heaven for the collapse of the walls of Cochrane's canal, as the Hebrews thanked God for the miraculous fall of the walls of Jericho in biblical history.

Morgan chose his position unwisely and constructed it poorly, but he was not given sufficient troops, not even enough militia, to defend it, if the right bank were to be purely a military defense problem. Jackson sent him no regulars at all, though he could have done so. His best move might have been to send the 44th, which had been recuited in Louisiana. The militia reinforcements he finally did send were Kentuckians, and this introduced a language problem that could have been easily avoided, since there were many unemployed Louisiana militia on the left bank. On January 6, it is true, Jackson had written Patterson to suggest that he anchor armed ships or boats below Morgan's lines in order to control the river, and he might well have sent a Baratarian company from Fort St. John or brought one from the Temple to man such vessels. Patterson's reply, on January 7, stated that he dared not employ the *Louisiana* in such a way, and explaining why; but he said nothing of using other craft. He could only think of securing reinforcements from Jackson.[27]

It must be concluded that in the matter of the defense of the river and the right bank Jackson did not show the strategic acumen that he displayed elsewhere. It is to be deplored, too, that Jackson did not have the magnanimity and greatness of character to accept the blame that he most certainly deserved—at least in part. His unqualified condemnation of the Kentucky battalion of Colonel John Davis was certainly most unjust, and his unflagging championship of Morgan and Patterson is very difficult to understand. Fortescue's comment—and he is on the whole quite kind to Jackson—is very pungent: "The American general . . . appears to have taken no notice of . . . his warning. . . . The event was to prove that this neglect might have cost him very dear."[28]

Jackson has been criticized frequently for entrusting Morgan with the command responsibility on the west bank, but it is difficult to see why. Poor Morgan did, it is true, make almost every military mistake possible in the circumstances, but no man is born knowing the military art and science. It has to be learned. And throughout this affair, to Morgan's credit, he showed no lack of personal courage.

Traditionally, the senior commander is held responsible for the failures of his juniors. Any military field commander has the problem of having to accept the junior commanders that are assigned to his command by higher authority, both military and political, and many promising military careers have been wrecked by mistakes of incompetent subordinate officers that have been laid at the door of the unwitting but still responsible senior commander. At times the military higher command has supported such an incompetent over his senior in command in the field; at other times, political influence has brought about the same result. To cite specific examples would prolong this discussion needlessly; their name is legion.

One function of command, in all echelons, is the careful selection of able subordinates and the weeding out of the "others." This takes time for adequate observation, and it also requires an ability on the part of the responsible commander to make accurate estimates of his subordinates' capabilities. The commander may have no opportunity to recognize the incompetence of a subordinate until the acid trial of battle. That may have been the case here. Battle is always the supreme test, and many apparently promising prospective leaders have failed that test on many fields, in many climes.

One of Jackson's problems in New Orleans, from the moment of his arrival, was that of command relationships. The State of Louisiana would not send her militia outside the state to fight the Indians, either in 1813 or in 1814. In Louisiana resentment of command by regular army officers over the state's militia went back to the Creoles' justified hatred of General James Wilkinson. This resentment was by no means peculiar to Louisiana, however, in the War of 1812.[29]

With the enemy at the gates, actually ashore, Louisiana militia began to come forward, but the great majority of them refused to serve except under their own state officers. Governor Claiborne took to the field personally and claimed a command authority subordinate only to Jackson's. He wanted direct command of all his state's militia, and he even wrote vainly to the secretary of war asking for a confirmation of such a peculiar chain of command.[30] Jackson showed sagacity, some tact, and great leadership by not directly challenging Claiborne's claim. He simply put the governor in command of the troops on the Plain of Gentilly—and left him there. Claiborne was very dissatisfied by this state of affairs; he had hoped to win military honors; but on January 8, when he was given a chance to garner them on the right bank of the river, he was unequal to that opportunity.

To revert to Morgan: he was one of the few Louisiana senior militiamen in the field when Jackson arrived at New Orleans, and he was then working hard to prepare the defenses of Fort St. Leon, the critical point at English Turn. This must have made a good impression on Jackson, who inspected those defenses during his trip down the river with Patterson. Jackson seems to have formed a high opinion of Morgan, since he defended him so warmly later and commended him in his official report of the battle. Jackson's ability to select competent assistants was of a high order, but, as his biography proves, he was not infallible. Once he had given his approval or disapproval of anyone, he was adamant—a not uncommon failing in men of great strength. It was a trait that worked both for and against him at times during his career. In this case, he must have also received good opinions of Morgan from both Governor Claiborne and General Villeré. In any case, he *had* to put a Louisianian in command across the river. Generals Coffee, Carroll, and Adair were undoubtedly better and battle-tested leaders, but so were Humbert and Flaugiac, the Napoleonic generals who volunteered to serve under Jackson. Jackson could not have separated any of the first three from their own state commands, and when he finally did send Humbert, Morgan refused to surrender the command and the Louisianians refused to serve under a foreigner. All in all it was most fortunate for General Jackson that General Pakenham agreed with him that the right bank operation was of no great importance!

It is also very significant that Jackson never designated a second-in-command at New Orleans. Selecting a second-in-command from the militia generals present, with Governor Claiborne also making claims to a military command status, would have been diplomatically hazardous. Jackson asked the War Department to supply one, and Brigadier General Edmund P. Gaines was ordered to serve in that capacity, but he did not arrive until after the battle.[31] As matters stood, an injury to Jackson on the night of December 23 or the morning of January 1—to cite two occasions when he narrowly escaped injury or death—would have meant complete disaster for the United States. The risk he took is hard to justify, but it is not at all clear now what else he could have done, after he decided to leave Winchester in Mobile, except to wait for Gaines.

Jackson has been criticized for not taking the offensive after January 8 and for not capturing or destroying the British army, but both criticisms seem completely untenable, for reasons previously given. With the number and caliber of troops that he had, Jackson could very easily have thrown away all his gains had he been so reckless. Moreover, his own confidence may well have been shaken by the reverse on the right bank (his first report of the battle to the secretary of war shows how aghast he was at the time). Adair, Coffee, and Carroll all counseled against an offensive, and they were right to have done so. After his own battle experience with the British on the night of December 23, Jackson himself may not have really wanted a rematch. It is significant that every British commentator present at New Orleans earnestly desired another American attack on any day after January 8.

Lambert has been criticized by some for retreating after the repulse on January 8. Knowing all of Jackson's precarious circumstances at that time, it can easily be argued that Lambert might well have been successful, especially after Thornton's unbelievable success on the west bank. Several British commentators, writing about the battle some years afterwards, agree that many officers present thought likewise at the time, but these were second guesses, made long afterwards. That view certainly did not appear in Lambert's council of war on January 8. Even many years later, Sir Harry Smith, by then a combat-wise, much-decorated lieutenant general himself, and one given to taking long chances, stoutly defended Lambert's decision. Sir Harry's expert opinion, backed by his proven military knowledge and ability, should outweigh completely that of any of his young contemporaries at New Orleans, or that of any armchair strategist since that time.

Lambert had lost a large number of his regimental commanders, as well as many of his junior officers and men. He was the only general left, and he had been on the ground only two days. Pakenham had said that he expected to encounter a series of positions that would have to be stormed successively. British estimates of American strength were agreed upon to be at least 24,000 men, who were now presumably flushed with victory and constantly increasing in numbers. To Lambert the chances of a successful renewal of the offensive seemed very doubtful. Codrington had told him that supplies for both the army and navy stood at a dangerously low level. Lambert very wisely determined on retreat. And Jackson very wisely decided to let him go, if he would.

The British naval personnel, who would lose whatever remaining chances there were for prize money, could have been expected to be indignant over this ignominious end to all their own casualties and back-breaking labor. However, the senior naval officer present, Vice-Admiral Sir Alexander Cochrane, fully concurred in Lambert's decision. Rear Admiral Sir Pulteney Malcolm and Captain Nicholas Lockyer of the Royal Navy, both staff officers ashore with Cochrane at New Orleans, informed Brenton later that there was no naval disagreement whatever with Lambert's decision.[32] Cochrane concluded to his own satisfaction (as shown by his letters to the Admiralty) that the expedition had failed because of the cabinet's deviation from his recommended plans, and that he could wash his hands and conscience of all responsibility.

On May 22, 1815, the Duke of Wellington wrote a letter of condolence to Lord Longford, the head of Pakenham's family. The Iron Duke regretted that Pakenham had been handicapped by such a colleague as Cochrane, and he blamed Cochrane for having originated the expedition against New Orleans solely for purpose of plunder. The duke said that he himself had advised that transports could not go within ten leagues of New Orleans, unless special craft were provided to land their troops, supply them, and maintain communications with them. He blamed Cochrane's use of the "Sharks" (who accompanied the fleet "to carry off from a place at which he [Cochrane] well knew he could not remain") for having betrayed the secret of the expedition to the Americans.

This is no fairer to Cochrane than Fortescue's judgment a century later. As a good Scot, the admiral was surely not indifferent to prize money, but the project of taking New Orleans originated with the cabinet, not with Cochrane alone. The Iron Duke apparently forgot that he, too, expected New Orleans to be taken easily, and that he himself had recommended to the prime minister that Louisiana and West Florida become the subject of a separate treaty. He said nothing in that letter of November 9 about any British inability to hold New Orleans.[33]

On the whole, the Duke of Wellington, and most later British writers on the subject of the Battle of New Orleans, remind one of Aesop's fable about the fox and grapes. In later years, the Iron Duke said that he resented and expected nothing from battles that were fought on Sundays.[34] It is true that January 1 and January 8, 1815 were Sundays, but so was October 21, 1805, when Nelson won at Trafalgar.

Whether the death of Sir Edward Pakenham saved New Orleans from capture by the British has been argued pro and con. On the other hand, there has never been room for doubt or argument that without Andrew Jackson, New Orleans could not have been, and would not have been, saved for the United States.

From a tactical standpoint, Jackson's generalship can be challenged in certain particulars. Neither he nor Patterson showed to advantage in their intemperate condemnation of the Kentucky detachment, which, after all, had put up all the fight that was made on the right side of the river on January 8. If it was not entitled to praise for uncommon gallantry, that detachment of Kentuckians certainly did all that could have been expected from brave but untrained and exhausted men. Too much was asked of them. Of course, the second failure by another battalion of Kentuckians, during the attempted pursuit of Lambert, very probably helped to convince Jackson that he was right in the first instance.

Aside from that, Jackson cannot be condemned for any other bad strategic or tactical decision in the entire compaign. He took quite a number of risks, especially in his dash to Pensacola when time was running out on him. But generals must take such risks, as one of the hazards of their profession. When they are successful they are good generals; when they fail they are poor ones. Jackson, like every successful general, was lucky at times, but it should be remembered that his resolution and quick performance helped that luck to break for him. His march on Pensacola, his assault without a long parley, and his prompt return to Mobile constituted masterly movement and handling of an army, especially of an army that was short of transport and not highly trained. Several historians, following the lead of Henry Adams, claim that Jackson should have ignored the British in Florida and betaken himself to New Orleans in August. Nonsense! To defend New Orleans, Jackson *had* to take Pensacola. And he had to promise action against Pensacola to get troops from Tennessee in the first place.

Jackson's luck against the British at New Orleans was far from being consistently good. The loss of the gunboats, the failure of his intelligence agencies, the failure of Major Gabriel Villeré to block or guard the Bayou Bienvenue adequately, the landing of the British at that one unguarded spot, and the loss of the *Carolina* were all bad breaks. Jackson was poorly served in each of those instances, so what blame there is has to be shared. The fall of the river, instead of the rise that was expected to submerge the British camp, was not foreseeable, and it must have been another blow to him.

On the other hand, the Americans were lucky that the British government initially sent only 10,000 men instead of the 20,000 originally intended, and that the British fleet was delayed in Negril Bay and did not strike two weeks sooner than it did. They were also lucky that the *Louisiana* was saved, that Pakenham called off Rennie's attack on Jackson's left on December 28 and did not renew it that day or the next, that Jackson escaped death during the night battle and again when the British guns concentrated on his headquarters on January 1, that Cochrane's canal collapsed on the night of January 7, that the river current carried Thornton a couple of miles downstream to delay him further, that Keane led the Highlanders to the assistance of Gibbs instead of Rennie on January 8, and finally that Pakenham and Gibbs were killed and Keane wounded early that fateful day.

In considering such "fortunes of war," one must not overlook or discount Jackson's inspiring personal leadership. That is beyond doubt and above criticism. He had many men under him who were brave individuals, but it was Jackson who created an *army* that not only stood its ground against some of the best and proudest troops the British could muster, but carried the fight to them most gallantly and effectively on December 23 and never flinched after that. Jackson's conduct of operations on the left bank was brilliant, and his leadership there was superb. Without Jackson, the motley array that was the American army might well have been as ineffective as Morgan's force on the west bank or Winder's in front of Washington.

The effect of the battle in cementing American nationalism has been conceded by almost every historian. That it also secured for the United States positive title to the Louisiana Purchase, the Gulf Coast, and the mouth of the Mississippi is equally certain. Without Jackson's victory the subsequent history of the United States might have been vastly different. With that victory the international rivalry for that area was ended in favor of the United States, as Great Britain conceded when by the Convention of

1818 she relinquished her claim to navigation rights on the Mississippi River.

After long analytical study of this campaign, and after giving General Andrew Jackson all the great credit due him and his men, one nevertheless comes back to the inescapable conclusion that the American victory was fully as astounding as historians originally accounted it.

The legislature of Massachusetts passed a resolution in 1818 giving all credit for the victory to the Lord in heaven. They would not even credit Jackson with an assist. The resolutions of thanks to the defenders of the state from the Louisiana legislature did not even mention that Jackson was there. Many statements of Jackson himself, as well as his request for a *Te Deum* in the cathedral of New Orleans after the British retreat, show that he was very much of the same opinion as the legislators of Massachusetts —at the time of the British withdrawal, anyway. He may have grown less humble in later life. Pakenham's brother-in-law, the Duke of Wellington, referring to the British defeat, also declared that "Providence willed it." Thus it would appear that at the time there was no question on this score, on either side of the Atlantic. Certainly there should be no question raised about it now. Nevertheless, it seems to this writer that the instrument chosen by the Lord to get His will done, as Gideon was chosen in Biblical times, was General Andrew Jackson.

NOTES

The following abbreviations are used throughout the notes.

A.H.R. . . . . *American Historical Review*
Captains' Ltrs. . . . . . Captains' Letters in Naval Records in National Archives, Washington, D.C. (U.S. Navy)
D.A.B. . . . . *Dictionary of American Biography*
D.N.B. . . . . *Dictionary of National Biography*
D.O.W. Died of Wounds
D.P.M. . . . . District Paymaster
D.Q.M. . . . . District Quartermaster
F.R.S. . . . . Fellow of Royal Society
J.S.A.H.R. . . . . *Journal of the Society for Army Historical Research* (British Army)
KIA . . . . Killed in Action
L.C. . . . . Library of Congress
L.H.Q. . . . . *Louisiana Historical Quarterly*
M.C. Ltrs. . . . . Master Commandants' Letters, Naval Records in National Archives, Washington, D.C.
N.A. . . . . National Archives, Washington, D.C.
N.R. . . . . Naval Records in National Archives, Washington, D.C.
O.A.R. . . . . Old Army Records of U.S. Army in National Archives
P.R.O. . . . . Public Record Office in British Archives
U.S.N.I.P. . . . . *United States Naval Institute Proceedings*
WIA . . . . *Wounded in Action*

INTRODUCTION

1. Marquis James, *The Life of Andrew Jackson,* 3–18.
2. *Ibid.,* 17–25.
3. *Ibid.,* 25–26.
4. *Ibid.,* 28–29.
5. *Ibid.,* 31–41.
6. Zachary F. Smith, *The Battle of New Orleans,* 161.
7. M. James, *Jackson,* 91–130.
8. *Ibid.,* 137–48.
9. *Ibid.,* 149–50.
10. Glenn Tucker, *Poltroons and Patriots,* 2:440.
11. Dunbar Rowland, ed., *Official Letter Books of W. C. C. Claiborne, 1801–1816,* 4:212–13.
12. M. James, *Jackson,* 151–64; also, James Parton, *Life of Andrew Jackson,* 2:245.
13. John Reid and John H. Eaton, *Life of Andrew Jackson,* 49–51. Reid was Jackson's aide throughout the Creek War and the campaign on the Gulf Coast. He wrote about the

Creek War himself, but collaborated with Eaton, another associate of Jackson, who finished the biography after Reid's untimely death. It is a most valuable record of the Creek War, but is less valuable for later events.

14. M. James, *Jackson,* 151–58.

15. Tucker, *Poltroons and Patriots,* 2:452–54.

16. M. James, *Jackson,* 160–61.

17. *Ibid.,* 161–65.

18. Reid and Eaton, *Jackson,* 126–36; Tucker, *Poltroons and Patriots,* 2:462.

19. Henry Adams, *History of the United States of America,* 8:252–53.

20. Reid and Eaton, *Jackson,* 158–65; M. James, *Jackson,* 170–71; Tucker, *Poltroons and Patriots,* 2:463–67.

21. M. James, *Jackson,* 176–78.

22. Robert Hunt, F.R.S., "Sir Alexander F. I. Cochrane," *D.N.B.,* 10:159–60; William James, *Naval History of Great Britain,* 7:chap. 5.

23. Frank E. Ross, "William Darby," *D.A.B.,* 5:73.

24. Allan Westcott, "Daniel Todd Patterson," *D.A.B.,* 14:301–302; Dudley W. Knox, *History of the United States Navy,* 130–31; Walden L. Ainsworth, "An Amphibious Operation That Failed," *United States Naval Institute Proceedings* (hereinafter abbreviated to *U.S.N.I.P.*), 71 (February, 1945):193–202; Edwin McClellan, "The Navy at New Orleans," *U.S.N.I.P.,* 50 (December, 1924):2041–60.

25. Isaac J. Cox, "William Charles Coles Claiborne," *D.A.B.,* 4:115–16; François-Xavier Martin, *The History of Louisiana from the Earliest Period,* 2:241; Charles E. Gayarré, *History of Louisiana,* 4:156; David D. Porter, *Memoir of Commodore David Porter of the United States Navy,* 82.

26. Claiborne to Jackson, "personal," Dec. 22, 1814, John S. Bassett, ed., *Correspondence of Andrew Jackson,* 2:122, n. 1.

27. Edwin H. Carpenter, Jr., "Latour's Report on Spanish American Relations in Southwest," *Louisiana Historical Quarterly,* 30 (July, 1947):715.

28. Henry M. Chichester, "John Keane," *D.N.B.,* 10:1154–56.

29. Chichester, "Sir Edward Michael Pakenham," *D.N.B.,* 43:83–85; John W. Cole, *Memoirs of British Generals Distinguished during the Peninsular War,* 2:327–42.

30. Chichester, "Alexander Dickson," *D.N.B.,* 5:944–46.

31. Henry M. Stephens, "Sir John Fox Burgoyne," *D.N.B.,* 3:342–44; George Wrottesley, *Life and Correspondence of Field Marshal Sir John Burgoyne.*

32. Col. E. M. Lloyd, R.E., "Sir John Lambert," *D.N.B.,* 22 (supplement):950–51.

1. STATUS OF THE WAR WITH GREAT BRITAIN IN THE SOUTHWEST IN 1814

1. Secretary Armstrong to Jackson, May 22, 24, and 28, 1814, in John S. Bassett, ed., *Correspondence of Andrew Jackson,* 1:4–5.

2. Henry Adams, *History of the United States of America,* vol. 8, chap. 8, *passim.*

3. Alfred L. Burt, *The United States, Great Britain and British North America from the Revolution to the Establishment of Peace after the War of 1812,* 351.

4. *Ibid.,* 350–51.

5. *Niles' Weekly Register* (Baltimore, 1811–1849), Dec. 10, 1814, 7:218. This reprints the pamphlet from the *Quebec Gazette* of Oct. 16, 1814; Fred L. Engelman, *The Peace of Christmas Eve,* 123–24, cites the *Courier,* a paper close to the ministry, and the

Pamphleteer, another, which insisted on the cession of Florida and Louisiana by the United States.

6. Edward P. Brenton, Captain, R.N., *Naval History of Great Britain, 1783–1836,* 2:525; Sir A. Cochrane to Admiralty, July 23, 1814, Great Britain, Public Record Office (hereinafter abbreviated to P.R.O.), *Admiralty 1,* 506, and same to same, 681–82. The British wanted no repetition of the very serious losses from diseases that they had suffered during summer campaigns in the West Indies, especially in Havana in 1762. The British Commander of the Joint Forces, Sir Alexander Cochrane (who also urged a guarantee of Creek Indian lands in the treaty of peace similar to that provided for the Northwest Indians) had had previous amphibious warfare experience in the Caribbean.

7. Armstrong to Jackson, June 25, 1814, in Bassett, *Correspondence,* 2:11–12; Jackson to Armstrong, July 24, 1814, *ibid.,* 2:19–20; same to same, June 27, 1814, *ibid.,* 2:12–13; same to same, July 31, 1814, *ibid.,* 2:23.

8. Brenton, *Naval History,* 2:530. Brenton, an associate of Cochrane, relied on information obtained by him from Sir Alexander and his staff captains. He can be considered as primary source, though biased.

9. War Department, General Order, March 19, 1813, Old Army Records, National Archives (hereinafter abbreviated to O.A.R., N.A.), Book No. 98, 73; Secretary of War to Flournoy, July 4, 1813, Book No. 7, ordered 3rd away; same to same, Sept. 18, 1813, Book No. 7, sent 3rd to Fort Stoddert and named field officers for the new 44th Inf.

10. Alfred T. Mahan, *Sea Power in Its Relation to the War of 1812,* 2:291; Master Commandant Patterson to Secretary of Navy, Dec. 7, 1813, Ltr. No. 85, Master Commandants' Letters, Naval Records, National Archives (hereinafter abbreviated to M.C. Ltrs., N.R., N.A.).

11. H. Adams, *History,* 8:317.

12. Claiborne to Jackson, Aug. 24, 29, and Sept. 20, 1814, in Dunbar Rowland, *Official Letter Books of W. C. C. Claiborne, 1801–1816,* 6:16–17, 39, 271–72; Charles E. Gayarré, *History of Louisiana,* 4:296–98, 306–307; Claiborne to Jackson, Aug. 24, 1814, in Bassett, *Correspondence,* 2:29–30; Flournoy to Secretary of War, Jan. 24, 1814, in O.A.R., N.A., Book No. 7.

13. Jackson to Winchester, Nov. 22, 1814, Bassett, *Correspondence,* 2:106, and 3:205; Jackson to Claiborne, Aug. 22, 1814, *ibid.,* 2:27.

14. John W. Fortescue, *A History of the British Army,* 10:176; Pigot to Cochrane, June 8, 1814, P.R.O., *Admiralty 1,* 506; Cochrane to Bathurst, Sept. 2, 1814, P.R.O., *War Office 1,* 141.

15. William James, *Naval History of Great Britain,* 7:355; Fortescue, *British Army,* 10:139–49, tells of operations around Washington and Baltimore; Bathurst to Army Commander with Cochrane, Sept. 22, 1814, P.R.O., *War Office 6,* vol. 2.

16. Secretary of War to Jackson, Sept. 5, 1814, O.A.R., N.A., Book No. 7; same to same, Sept. 27, 1814, *ibid.;* same to same, Oct. 28, 1814, *ibid.*

17. Cochrane to Admiralty, July 23, 1814, P.R.O., *Admiralty 1,* 506.

18. John Reid and John H. Eaton, *Life of Andrew Jackson,* 148.

19. Marquis James, *The Life of Andrew Jackson,* 170.

20. Jackson to Armstrong, June 27, 1814, Bassett, *Correspondence,* 2:12.

21. Jackson to Coffee, July 17, 1814, *ibid.,* 2:16.

22. Jackson to Blount, Aug. 5, 1814, *ibid.,* 2:23–25.

23. Jackson to Butler, Aug. 27, 1814, *ibid.,* 2:31; Reid and Eaton, *Jackson,* 209.

24. Glenn Tucker, *Poltroons and Patriots,* 2:641.

25. For an interesting collection of Canadian, West Indian, and British opinions indicating their certainty that the American trans-Allegheny West would welcome British rule, see *Niles' Weekly Register,* Feb. 18, 1815, 7:407–408.

26. Reid and Eaton, *Jackson,* 211; Cochrane to Bathurst, July 14, 1814, P.R.O., *War Office* 1, 141.

27. M. James, *Jackson,* 183.

28. *Ibid.,* 184.

2. JEAN LAFFITE, THE BARATARIANS, AND THE LOUISIANA CREOLES

1. Jean Laffite, *The Journal of Jean Laffite,* 70; Jane L. de Grummond, *The Baratarians and the Battle of New Orleans,* 173; Stanley C. Arthur, *Jean Lafitte, Gentleman Rover;* Lyle Saxton, *Lafitte the Pirate.* The translator of Laffite's "journal," who claims to be a direct descendant of the Baratarian leader, says that it was written in the form of several letters to his children, between 1845 and 1850. Jean Laffite requested that his heirs not permit it to be published until 107 years after his death, and the request was honored. In due course, this book was released and published in an unedited English translation (from the French). It includes many glaring inaccuracies—lapses of memory on the part of an old man, no doubt—but it is also an amazing complement to the Case Papers (in the Archives of the U.S. District Court of the Louisiana District in New Orleans) for several famous cases between 1804 and 1825. At any rate, much of the obscurity that surrounded Laffite's early life and his final days has now been dispelled, and Jackson's willingness to accept his help is more readily explainable.

2. Capt. John Shaw to Secretary of Navy Paul Hamilton, Jan. 18, 1813, in Captains' Letters, N.R., N.A.; same to same, Apr. 11, 1812, *ibid.;* Patterson to Secretary of Navy, Nov. 23, 1813, in M.C. Ltrs., N.R., N.A. In the Jan. 18 letter, Shaw acknowledged receipt of the secretary of the navy's letter of Dec. 14, 1812, which censured him for having failed to suppress the activities of the Baratarian pirates and smugglers, and which was accompanied by a letter of complaint from someone in the office of the secretary of the treasury. Shaw referred to many earlier letters from the New Orleans station—letters from both Shaw and his predecessor—to the secretary of the navy on the subject of piracy, and reiterated the navy's inability to deal with the situation, owing to the uselessness of his assigned ships and the numerical weakness of his forces. In one such letter, dated Apr. 11, 1812, Shaw had reported the complete inadequacy of gunboats to protect commerce against "illicit practices on the coast of pirates and smugglers." Unless the naval gunboats could cripple the enemy craft with their first fire, the latter could always escape, since the smugglers and pirates were better sailors. Patterson, who relieved Shaw in command of the station (effective Dec. 10, 1813) also wrote (in the Nov. 23 letter cited) that he was very desirous of putting an end to piracy in the Gulf if he could get adequate ships and men for the task, but noted that he would be unable to do this with the naval forces then available to him.

3. Caspar F. Goodrich, "Our Navy and the West Indian Pirates," *U.S.N.I.P.,* 42 (January, 1916):1459–75.

4. George W. Cable, "Plotters and Pirates of Louisiana," *Century Magazine,* 25 (April, 1883):860. Hereinafter referred to as "Pirates."

5. Cable, "Who are the Creoles?" *Century Magazine,* 25 (January, 1883):395.

6. Cable, "The Creoles in the American Revolution," *Century Magazine,* 25 (Feb-

ruary, 1883):538; John W. Caughey, *Bernardo de Galvez in Louisiana, 1776–1783.*

7. Thomas A. Bailey, *A Diplomatic History of the American People,* 4th ed., 109; Elijah W. Lyon, *Louisiana in French Diplomacy, 1759–1804,* 242.

8. Philip C. Brooks, "Spain's Farewell to Louisiana, 1803–1821," *Mississippi Valley Historical Review,* 27 (July, 1940):29–42, *passim.*

9. François Barbé-Marbois, *History of Louisiana particularly of the Cession of that Colony to the United States* (trans. by William B. Lawrence), 182.

10. Henry Adams, *History of the United States of America,* 1:402–403.

11. Isaac J. Cox, *The West Florida Controversy, 1798–1813,* 487.

12. *Ibid.,* 488.

13. Hubert B. Fuller, *The Purchase of Florida,* 182–90.

14. William F. Galpin, "American Grain Trade to the Spanish Peninsula," *A.H.R.,* 28 (October, 1922):24–44; Julius W. Pratt, *Expansionists of 1812,* 70–73.

15. Claiborne to Jackson, Aug. 24, 1814, John S. Bassett, *Correspondence of Andrew Jackson,* 2:29–30.

16. Cable, "Pirates," 856.

17. Saxon, *The Pirate,* 30.

18. According to William Darby (*Geographical Description of the State of Louisiana, the Southern Part of the State of Mississippi, and the Territory of Alabama,* 184), the population of the city alone was reported in the 1810 census to be 17,242; it was probably over 23,000 by 1815.

19. Cable, "Pirates," 859.

20. Frank Dobie, "The Mystery of Lafitte's Treasure," *Yale Review,* 18 (September 1938):124.

21. de Grummond, *Baratarians,* 4–6; Arthur, *Gentleman Rover,* 19, 23, 255, 283.

22. Charles E. Gayarré, *History of Louisiana,* 4:303–306.

23. Walter B. Lister, "Portrait of a Pirate," *American Mercury,* 7 (February, 1926): 214.

24. Gayarré, *Louisiana,* 4:308; Shaw to Secretary of Navy, Jan. 18, 1813, Captains' Ltrs. (1813), N.R., N.A.; Patterson to Secretary of Navy, Jan. 31, 1814, M.C. Ltrs., N.R., N.A.

25. Alcée Fortier, *A History of Louisiana,* 3:87. This very partisan historian, of French descent, says: "The Laffites may without remorse be called pirates," 3:89.

26. Saxon, *The Pirate,* 120; Arthur, *Gentleman Rover,* 91; Glenn Tucker, *Poltroons and Patriots,* 2:643, n. 2.

27. Edgar S. Maclay, *A History of American Privateers,* 332.

28. Goodrich, "West Indian Pirates," 1461.

29. Cable, "Pirates," 960; Saxon, *The Pirate,* 43, 91.

30. Goodrich, "West Indian Pirates," 1461–75; Stanley Faye, "Privateersmen of the Gulf and Their Prizes," *L.H.Q.,* 22 (October, 1929):1012–94; Faye, "Privateers of Guadeloupe and Their Establishment in Barataria," *L.H.Q.,* 23 (April, 1940):428–44; Carlos G. Calkins, "The Repression of Piracy in the West Indies, 1814–1825," *U.S.N.I.P.,* 37 (December, 1911):1187–98; Violet Barbour, "Privateers and Pirates of the West Indies," *A.H.R.,* 17 (April, 1911):543–65.

31. Cable, "Pirates," 860.

32. Arthur, *Gentleman Rover,* 88.

33. David D. Porter, *Memoir of Commodore David Porter of the United States Navy,* 79.

34. John R. Kendall, "Shadow over the City," *L.H.Q.*, 22 (January, 1939):146; Fortier, *Louisiana*, 3:88.

35. Gayarré *Louisiana*, 4:132, 310.

36. de Grummond, *Baratarians*, 18–20; Saxon, *The Pirate*, 66.

37. Arthur, *Gentleman Rover*, 31–32; de Grummond, *Baratarians*, 21, n. 13.

38. Gayarré, *Louisiana*, 4:312.

39. Arthur, *Gentleman Rover*, 38.

40. Patterson to Secretary of Navy, July 8, 1814, acknowledges receipt of orders to destroy Barataria, M.C. Ltrs., N.R., N.A.; same to same, Aug. 20, 1814, reports arrival of *Carolina, ibid.*

41. Porter, *Memoir*, 76.

42. Edward A. Parsons, "Jean Lafitte in the War of 1812, a Narrative based on the Original Documents," *Proceedings of the American Antiquarian Society*, 50 (October, 1940):216.

43. Marquis James, *The Life of Andrew Jackson*, 191, citing the letter dated Sept. 4, 1814, now in *Bibliotheca Parsoniana*.

44. Parsons, "Jean Lafitte," 205–24.

45. Lister, "Portrait," 216.

46. Patterson to Secretary of Navy, Oct. 10, 1814, M.C. Ltrs., N.R., N.A.

47. M. James, *Jackson*, 193; Gayarré, "Historical Sketch of Pierre and Jean Lafitte," *Magazine of American History*, 10 (October and November, 1883):284–98; de Grummond, *Baratarians*, 24–25.

48. Gayarré, *Louisiana*, 4:359.

49. Theodore Roosevelt, *The Naval War of 1812*, 2:230.

50. Stephen Crane, *Great Battles of the World*, 217.

51. François-Xavier Martin, *The History of Louisiana from the Earliest Period*, 2:339. Martin became a member of the Louisiana Supreme Court in January, 1814. He was chief justice of that court when he wrote his history. He was attorney general when the British made their attack.

3. GULF OPERATIONS TO DECEMBER 1, 1814

1. Marquis James, *The Life of Andrew Jackson*, 182.

2. John Reid and John H. Eaton, *Life of Andrew Jackson*, 210; Manrique to Jackson, Aug. 30, 1814, John S. Bassett, *Correspondence of Andrew Jackson*, 2:37–40.

3. Jackson to Manrique, Sept. 9, 1814, Bassett, *Correspondence*, 2:44–46.

4. Arsène L. Latour, *Historical Memoir of the War in West Florida and Louisiana, 1814–15* (trans. from French by H. R. Nugent), 33.

5. William James, *A Full and Correct Account of the Military Occurrences in the Late War between Great Britain and the United States of America*, 2:341–44. Hereinafter this will be referred to as *Occurrences*.

6. Latour, *Memoir*, 36–38, quoting Lawrence Battle Report to Jackson, Sept. 16, 1814; W. James, *Occurrences*, 2:342. James was also a naval historian and can be believed concerning British data, if not American. Percy to Cochrane, Sept. 16, 1814, P.R.O., *Admiralty* 1, 505, is the British Battle Report.

7. Latour, *Memoir*, 36–38; Jackson to Secretary of War, Sept. 17, 1814, Bassett, *Correspondence*, 2:50–51.

8. Glenn Tucker, *Poltroons and Patriots,* 2:648; W. James, *Occurrences,* 355.

9. Alfred T. Mahan, *Sea Power in Its Relation to the War of 1812,* 2:387–88.

10. M. James, *Jackson,* 188–89.

11. Jackson to Blount, Sept. 9, 1814, Jackson Papers, Library of Congress (herein-after abbreviated to L.C.); Edward A. Parsons, "Jean Lafitte in the War of 1812, a Narrative based on the Original Documents," *Proceedings of the American Antiquarian Society,* 50 (October, 1940):210.

12. Gerald W. Johnson, *Andrew Jackson, Epic in Homespun,* 168.

13. Irving Brant, *James Madison, The President 1809–1813,* 336, 418, 439.

14. Hamilton to Shaw, Oct. 12, 1814, Secretary of Navy Letters, N.R., N.A., 10:174.

15. Shaw to Hamilton, Aug. 23, 1812 and Nov. 9, 1812, Captains' Ltrs., N.R., N.A.

16. Gaillard Hunt, *Life of James Madison,* 329.

17. Edwin N. McClellan, "The Navy at New Orleans," *U.S.N.I.P.,* 50 (December, 1924): 2041.

18. Patterson to Jones, Sept. 4, 1814, M.C. Ltrs., N.R., N.A.; Patterson to Jackson, Sept. 2, 1814, Jackson Papers, L.C.; Jackson to Secretary of War, Sept. 8, 1814, vol. 8, Register of Letters Rec'd., War Office, O.A.R., N.A.

19. Jackson to Secretary of War, Sept. 20, 1814, vol. 8, Register of Letters Rec'd., War Office, O.A.R., N.A.

20. Jackson to Patterson, Oct. 14, 1814, Bassett *Correspondence,* 2:80, n. 2; Bassett, *The Life of Andrew Jackson,* 158.

21. Jackson to Patterson, Oct. 23, 1814, Bassett, *Correspondence,* 2:80–81.

22. Henry P. Dart, ed., "Andrew Jackson and Judge D. A. Hall," *L.H.Q.,* 5 (October, 1922):555–58.

23. Dunbar Rowland, *Official Letter Books of W.C.C. Claiborne,* 6:213–15.

24. There are 15 letters between the dates of Aug. 10 and Nov. 17 from McRae to Jackson and 7 from Jackson to McRae, in the Jackson Papers, L.C. Jackson's Military Papers have many more, which are from his Adjutant General's Office to McRae, to Col. William Piatt, D.Q.M., and to Capt. John T. Pemberton, D.P.M., during this period.

25. Reid and Eaton, *Jackson,* 223.

26. Charles Cassidy to Jackson, Sept. 25, 1814, Jackson Papers, L.C.; Bassett, *Jackson,* 142–43.

27. M. James, *Jackson,* 196.

28. *Ibid.,* 198.

29. Reid and Eaton, *Jackson,* 227.

30. *Ibid.,* 231–34; Jackson to Secretary of War, Nov. 14, 1814, Bassett, *Correspondence,* 2:96–99.

31. Ruth A. Fisher, "The Surrender of Pensacola as Told by the British," *A.H.R.,* 54 (January, 1949):329; Cochrane to Admiralty, Dec. 7, 1814, P.R.O., *Admiralty* 1:508, enclosed Percy to Cochrane, Nov. 9, 1814, and Gordon to Cochrane, same date. The latter had arrived to relieve Percy of command in the midst of the operation. Cochrane submitted their reports of the occurrences at Pensacola and said he would order a court of inquiry. If he did, the record of its findings is not available in the United States.

32. Jackson to Monroe, Nov. 14, 21, and 22, Bassett, *Correspondence,* 2:96–101.

33. Fisher, "Surrender of Pensacola," 326–29; Percy to Cochrane, Nov. 9, 1814 (see n. 31 above).

34. M. James, *Jackson,* 183.

35. Isaac J. Cox, *The West Florida Controversy, 1798–1813,* 612.

36. Latour, *Memoir*, 49.

37. Cochrane to Admiralty, Feb. 25, 1815, P.R.O. *Admiralty* 1:518, refers to his return of Spanish soldiers after peace.

38. Reid and Eaton, *Jackson*, 238.

39. *Ibid.*, 239, quotes Jackson's own words.

40. Henry S. Halbert and Timorthy H. Ball, *The Creek War of 1813–14*, 280.

41. Albert J. Pickett, *History of Alabama*, 609. Pickett was mistaken in at least one particular: Major Blue's reports to Jackson are a matter of record in the Jackson Papers.

42. Hawkins to Jackson, Oct. 30, Nov. 26, and Dec. 17, 1814; Jackson to Hawkins, Oct. 3, Nov. 5, 1814; and Blue to Jackson, Oct. 25, Dec. 7, 18, 27, 1814, and Jan. 28 and 29, 1815, all in Jackson Papers, L.C.; General Order, Nov. 16, 1814, Bassett, *Correspondence*, 2:100–101.

43. W. James, *Occurrences*, 2:370.

44. George R. Gleig, *The Campaigns of the British Army at Washington and New Orleans*, 2nd ed., 264–70. This story is in all five editions of Gleig's work but it is hard to believe.

45. M. James, *Jackson*, 181, n. 38.

46. Jackson to Winchester, Nov. 22, 1814, Bassett, *Correspondence*, 2:106. Jackson was neither a professional military engineer nor a coast artilleryman. Fort Bowyer was indefensible against a landing attack by capable troops using siege tactics, as the British would demonstrate the following February.

47. *Ibid.*, 107.

48. M. James, *Jackson*, 199.

49. *Ibid.*, 200, citing Cassidy's letter seen by him.

4. AMERICAN PLANS AND PREPARATIONS

1. William Darby, *Geographical Description of the State of Louisiana, the Southern Part of the State of Mississippi, and the Territory of Alabama*, 40. His reference to the extent of his survey is on page 279.

2. *Ibid.*, 146.

3. Howell Tatum, "Major Howell Tatum's Journal," ed. by John S. Bassett, in *Smith College Studies in History*, 7 (October, 1921, January and April, 1922):96–97. Besides Tatum's evidence as to Jackson's arrival on Dec. 1, there is that of John Reid, Jackson's aide, in John Reid and John H. Eaton, *Life of Andrew Jackson*, 240; Charles E. Gayarré, *History of Louisiana*, 4:379, who cites Claiborne's dispatch to Monroe, Dec. 9, 1814; Marquis James, *The Life of Andrew Jackson*, 210, who cites Jackson to Coffee, Dec. 10, 1814, in Bassett, *Correspondence of Andrew Jackson*, 2:112. On the other hand, the hypercritical Henry Adams asserts that Jackson did not arrive until Dec. 2, as do: Arsène L. Latour, *Historical Memoir of the War in West Florida and Louisiana 1814–15*, 5, and François-Xavier Martin, *The History of Louisiana from the Earliest Period*, 2:335. Fortier, Walker, Tucker, Mahan, and others echo the latter group. Time was of the essence in the defense of New Orleans by that date, so exactness is historically important. The testimony of two of Jackson's official family (one of them keeping a daily journal of their travel) and Claiborne's official dispatch establishes the date as Dec. 1, 1814.

4. Alexander Walker, *Jackson and New Orleans*, 14.

5. William H. Coleman, ed., *Historical Sketchbook and Guide to New Orleans*, 15; Donald B. Chidsey, *The Battle of New Orleans*, 112.

6. Martin, *Louisiana*, 2:341. Judge Martin, who was born in France, did not become a Louisianian until late in life. He emigrated to the United States as a young man, studied Anglo-Saxon law in North Carolina, and in time became an eminent jurist there. Jefferson appointed him to the federal court of Louisiana while it was still a territory. When it became a state, he resigned from the federal bench and went to the state supreme court in January, 1815. However, he was serving as attorney general at the time of the British invasion. His sympathies were definitely pro-Creole, but he was an eyewitness to the events he discussed, and he is very difficult to refute.

7. Gayarré, *Louisiana*, 4:156. Charles Gayarré was born in 1805 in New Orleans, of French and Spanish descent, so that he was not a Creole in the truest sense, though he was certainly partial to their point of view. Since he wrote the fourth volume of his history in 1866, he had recourse to many records, such as Claiborne's letters and other documents, which Martin did not have. Gayarré undoubtedly did have much eyewitness information about participants in the battle to draw upon, because he had spent all his life in New Orleans. He became a distinguished historian and was president of the Louisiana Historical Society from 1850 to 1888.

8. M. James, *Jackson*, 202. Livingston had migrated to New Orleans from New York after being involved in a financial scandal there. Jackson had met and liked him when they were together in Congress, 1796–98, before the scandal. He had corresponded with him over defense problems at New Orleans during the summer of 1814, and Livingston became one of Jackson's aides. He always thoroughly disliked New Orleans and its people, and left there after the war as soon as his fortunes mended.

9. Gayarré, *Louisiana*, 4:102; Glenn Tucker, *Poltroons and Patriots*, 2:650.

10. Thomas P. Abernethy, *The South in the New Nation 1789–1819*, 266, 269, 279; William S. Carpenter, "Edward Livingston," *D.A.B.* 11:309–12.

11. Gayarré, *Louisiana*, 4:105.

12. Grace King, trans. and ed. "Martigny's Reflections on New Orleans Campaign," *L.H.Q.*, 6 (January, 1923):61–85. Martigny's *Reflections* had been published in French about 1830, but went unnoticed then. Hereinafter this is referred to as "Marigny."

13. Sir Harry Smith, *The Autobiography of Lieutenant General Sir Harry Smith*, ed. by G. M. Smith, 1:240. Smith was Pakenham's assistant adjutant general until Jan. 6, 1815.

14. Stanley C. Arthur, *Jean Lafitte, Gentleman Rover*, 88.

15. M. James, *Jackson*, 205, citing Jackson to Senator James Brown, Feb. 4, 1815.

16. Latour, *Memoir*, 79–81.

17. George R. Gleig, *The Campaigns of the British Army at Washington and New Orleans*, 2nd ed., 253. There are five editions of this account by a man who later became Chief of Chaplains of the British Army. They differ somewhat, and some statements are disproved by other chroniclers and official records. The second edition is quoted throughout this discussion unless otherwise noted.

18. Darby, *Description*, 187.

19. Jackson's Adjutant General to Officer Commanding 7th U.S. Inf., Dec. 12, 1814, O.A.R., N.A. Similar orders to other individuals are discussed by various historians. This is the only written order located by this writer.

20. Tatum, "Journal," 101.

21. Jackson to Monroe, Dec. 10, 1814, Bassett, *Correspondence*, 2:111.

22. Jackson to Coffee, Dec. 10, 1814, *ibid.*, 2:112.
23. Martin, *Louisiana*, 2:340.
24. George C. Eggleston, *Red Eagle*, 147–48.
25. Gayarré, *Louisiana*, 4:344; and Martin, *Louisiana*, 2:341.
26. "Marigny," 65.
27. Gayarré, *Louisiana*, 4:392–94.
28. *Ibid.*, 379–80.
29. Latour, *Memoir*, 53.
30. Gayarré, *Louisiana*, 4:384.
31. *Ibid.*, 388.
32. Jones to Patterson, Mar. 7, 1814, Secretary of Navy Letters (1814), N.R., N.A., received and acknowledged by Patterson, Apr. 22, 1814, M.C. Ltrs., N.R., N.A.
33. Howard I. Chapelle, *History of the American Sailing Navy*, 179–209, 245, 294, 534, 555.

5. BRITISH PLANS AND OPERATIONS TO DECEMBER 20, 1814

1. Alfred T. Mahan, *Sea Power in Its Relation to the War of 1812*, 2:389.
2. "Subaltern in America," *Blackwood's Edinburgh Magazine*, 21 (June, 1827):420. The author appears to have served in the Light Company of the 4th Regiment. Hereinafter he will be referred to as "Subaltern."
3. Cochrane to Admiralty from off Pensacola, Dec. 7, 1814, P.R.O., *Admiralty* 1, 508.
4. Mahan, *War of 1812*, 2:388.
5. Instructions to Ross, undated, P.R.O., *War Office* 6, vol. 2; Bathurst to Ross, Sept. 6, 1814, *ibid.*; same to Keane, Sept. 12, 1814, *ibid.*, same to Lambert, Oct. 5 and Oct 18, 1814, *ibid.*; Bathurst to Pakenham, Oct. 24, 1814, *ibid.*
6. Arthur Wellesley, Duke of Wellington, "Letter of Duke of Wellington, May 22, 1815, on the Battle of New Orleans, "*L.H.Q.*, 9 (January, 1926):5–10; Sir Harry Smith, *The Autobiography of Lieutenant General Sir Harry Smith*, ed. by G. M. Smith, 1:30.
7. John W. Fortescue, *A History of the British Army*, 10:149–52. Author is refuted by all naval historians, but Smith, *Autobiography*, 1:30, alleged that the Duke of Wellington believed it, too.
8. Edward P. Brenton, Captain, R.N., *Naval History of Great Britain*, 2:527–30.
9. Arsène L. Latour, *Historical Memoir of the War in West Florida and Louisiana 1814–15*, 105; "Subaltern," Blackwood's, 22 (July, 1827):77.
10. George R. Gleig, *The Campaigns of the British Army at Washington and New Orleans*, 257, is the source of the quotation, but Gleig did not see the Lake Borgne battle. Patterson to Secretary of Navy, Mar. 17, 1815, encloses Jones to Patterson (Battle Report), Mar. 12, 1815, M.C. Ltrs., N.R., N.A. Patterson to Secretary of Navy, Dec. 16, 1814, encloses report of eyewitness Sailing Master William Johnson to Patterson, *ibid.* British Battle Report is Lockyer to Cochrane, Dec. 16, 1814, enclosed in Cochrane to Admiralty, Dec. 16, 1814, P.R.O., *Admiralty* 1, 508.
11. George L. Chesterton, *Peace, War and Adventure*, 1:290.
12. John Reid and John H. Eaton, *Life of Andrew Jackson*, 281.
13. William James, *A Full and Correct Account of the Military Occurrences in the Late War between Great Britain and the United States of America*, 2:353.

14. Jones to Patterson, Battle Report, Mar. 12, 1815, N.R., N.A.

15. William James, *Occurrences,* 2:360.

16. Howard I. Chapelle, *History of the American Sailing Navy,* 264.

17. Gleig, *Campaigns,* 260–61; "Subaltern," *Blackwood's,* 21:720.

18. James Parton, *Life of Andrew Jackson,* 2:56.

19. Marquis James, *The Life of Andrew Jackson,* 210–11.

20. Mrs. Dunbar (Eron) Rowland, *Andrew Jackson's Campaign against the British,* 70–78, *passim.*

21. François Xavier Martin, *The History of Louisiana from the Earliest Period,* 2:346.

22. Patterson to Secretary of Navy, Dec. 16, 1814, M.C. Ltrs., N.R., N.A.

23. Charles E. Gayarré, *History of Louisiana,* 4:402–403.

24. Parton, *Jackson,* 2:60, citing Jackson's General Order of Dec. 16, 1814.

25. Latour, *Memoir,* 72.

26. Reid and Eaton, *Jackson,* 302.

27. Patterson to Secretary of Navy, Oct. 10, 1814, M.C. Ltrs., N.R., N.A., re Barataria expedition.

28. Grace King, trans. and ed., "Marigny's Reflections on New Orleans Campaign," *L.H.Q.,* 22 (January, 1939):65.

29. Livingston was Jackson's aide and military secretary, to whom Jackson had dictated the letters to Washington describing his military ammunition and ordnance inventories. Lyle Saxon, *(Lafitte the Pirate,* 173–75), first advanced the explanation that Lafitte had flints and ammunition secretly cached that he bartered to Jackson for his recommendation for a pardon. Jane de Grummond, *(The Baratarians and the Battle of New Orleans)* confirms this. *The Journal of Jean Laffite* is an extravagant and doubtless erroneous account of the extensive aid provided by the Baratarians, but at last it is explained why Jackson accepted aid from the "hellish banditti."

30. Edwin H. Carpenter, Jr., "Latour's Report on Spanish American Relations in Southwest," *L.H.Q.,* 30 (July, 1947):716.

31. Latour, *Memoir,* 72.

32. Saxon, *The Pirate,* 174.

33. Gayarré, *Louisiana,* 4:411; citing Martin, Latour *(Memoir,* 71) tells of companies of "marines."

34. Livingston to Jackson, Dec. 29, 1814, Jackson Papers, L.C.

35. Alexander Walker, *Jackson and New Orleans,* 143.

36. M. James, *Jackson,* 214.

37. John S. Jenkins, *Life and Public Service of General Andrew Jackson,* 100.

38. M. James, *Jackson,* 215.

39. Keane to Pakenham, Dec. 28, 1814, appendix to Latour, *Memoir,* cviii.

6. THE BRITISH LANDING

1. Cochrane to Admiralty, Jan. 18, 1815, P.R.O., *Admiralty* 1, 508. In his letter of Dec. 7, 1814, to the Admiralty, *ibid.,* he mentions planning to land on the shores of Lake Pontchartrain from Mobile. William Surtees, *Twenty-five Years in the Rifle Brigade,* 339, tells of the visit of five or six French Americans to Pine Island from New Orleans, but he also mentions a visit of Spanish fishermen who he believed brought the news of

Bayou Bienvenue. George R. Gleig, *The Campaigns of the British Army at Washington and New Orleans*, 262 and 272, tells of the American deserters and what he called the "Bayou Catalan" route.

2. Keane to Pakenham, Dec. 28, 1814, P.R.O., *War Office* 1, vol. 141; Wellington, *Supplementary Despatches and Memoranda of Field Marshal Arthur Duke of Wellington*, 10, 395. This is a copy of the letter written to Pakenham, mentioned elsewhere herein.

3. Colonel Sir Alexander Dickson, "Artillery Services in North America in 1814 and 1815, "*J.S.A.H.R.*, 8 (April, July, and October, 1929):173 .

4. Arsène L. Latour, *Historical Memoir of the War in West Florida and Louisiana 1814–15*, 102–105; Jackson to Secretary of War , Dec. 26, 1814, Register of Letters Rec'd, War Office, O.A.R., N.A.; Jackson to Holmes, Dec. 5, 1814, and Jackson to Blount, Feb. 6, 1815, in Jackson Papers, L.C.

5. Charles E. Gayarré, *History of Louisiana*, 4:418. Italics supplied by writer.

6. John Reid and John H. Eaton, *Life of Andrew Jackson*, 306.

7. William Cobbett (M.P. for Oldham), *Life of Andrew Jackson*, 92.

8. William James, *A Full and Correct Account of the Military Occurrences in the Late War between Great Britain and the United States of America*, 2:360.

9. Cochrane to Admiralty, Jan. 18, 1815, P.R.O., *War Office* 1, 141.

10. Gleig, *Campaigns*, 272.

11. Sir William F. P. Napier, *History of the War in the Peninsula and in the South of France*, 4:252.

12. Brooke to Bathurst, Sept. 17, 1814, P.R.O., *War Office* 1, 141; Hugh F. Rankin, ed., *The Battle of New Orleans, A British View*, 24; Dickson, "Artillery Services," 80–82; Bathurst to Ross, Sept. 29, 1814, P.R.O., *War Owce* 6, vol. 2. Illustrative of British attempts to minimize their strength are different editions of Gleig. In the 1821 edition, he gives the aggregate of Keane's force at Jamaica as 6,000, with 4,400 of them dependable troops (page 241). In the 1847 edition, he reduced his estimate by 1,000 men in both cases (page 131).

13. MacDougall is quoted in John W. Cole, *Memoirs of British Generals Distinguished during the Peninsular War*, 2:364.

14. Sir John H. Cooke, *A Narrative of Events in the South of France and in the Attack on New Orleans in 1814 and 1815*, 200. The author was a captain in the 43rd Light Infantry, which arrived at New Orleans on Jan. 6, 1815. This was one of the Iron Duke's favorite regiments on the Peninsula. What Cooke has to tell of events at New Orleans before the day of his arrival is hearsay evidence, as set forth twenty years later by a very opinionated young nobleman. Perhaps one could accept some of it as *res gestae*, however.

15. Lewis W. G. Butler, *Annals of the King's Royal Rifle Corps*, 2:136; Surtees, *Rifle Brigade*, 39–40, 334.

16. Richard Johns and Philip H. Nicolas, *Naval and Military Heroes of Great Britain, or the Calendar of Victory*, 20–32.

17. John Buchan, *History of the Royal Scots Fusiliers, 1678–1918;* John W. Fortescue, *A History of the British Army*, 10:179, quotes George C. M. Smith, ed., *The Autobiography of Lieutenant General Sir Harry Smith,* ed. by G. M. Smith, 1.232, to belittle the 21st and 44th.

18. Johns and Nicolas, *Calendar of Victory*, 32–48.

19. Surtees, *Rifle Brigade*, 341; Latour, *Memoir*, 100.

20. Alexander Walker, *Jackson and New Orleans*, 157; Surtees, *Rifle Brigade*, 343.
21. Latour, *Memoir*, 83–85.
22. Jackson to Monroe, Dec. 26, 1814, Register of Letters Rec'd., War Office, vol. 8, O.A.R., N.A. The traditional story of who first reported the presence of the British to Jackson has been told many times. Alexander Walker, in his *Jackson and New Orleans*, named one Augustin Rousseau, presumably one of the refugees mentioned by Latour. He could not have preceded Tatum by many minutes. Tatum does not mention his having personally reported it, merely that the general received the information that the enemy had effected a landing from Latour. Reid, Jackson's aide, gives the credit solely to Tatum. Both Martin and Gayarré are silent as to the identity of the informant. Walker draws a romantic picture of Major Villeré arriving on the heels of Rousseau, accompanied by two Creole friends, to report his escape from the British, two crossings of the Mississippi River, and a mad ride between them. Still, according to Walker, they were ahead of Tatum, Jackson's senior engineer, who had no rivers to cross—and who was also in rather a hurry. Walker even adds the touching story of Major Villeré's having been forced to kill his favorite dog to prevent its betraying his hiding place to British pursuers. This story is told by Gayarré, but only as a report. Martin does not mention it. Alcée Fortier calls the story a myth. Marquis James accepts Walker's story because, as James puts it, Walker "was in New Orleans at the time and knew all persons concerned" —a rationale that is not persuasive since, in point of fact: Walker was born in 1818, he visited New Orleans for the first time in 1840, and he published his account of the battle in 1856! Though one cannot be sure of what actually happened, Walker's story of Major Villeré's frantic journey can safely be dismissed as nothing more than a fairy tale.
23. Mrs. Dunbar (Eron) Rowland, *Andrew Jackson's Campaign Against the British*, 278, 279 (n. 1), 296–97, 298. This work depends heavily upon state archives of Mississippi and Louisiana.
24. Latour, *Memoir*, 87; Howell Tatum, "Major Howell Tatum's Journal," ed. by John S. Bassett, in *Smith College Studies in History*, 7 (October, 1921, January and April, 1922):107; Reid and Eaton, *Jackson*, 384; Gayarré, *Louisiana*, 4:421; Alcée Fortier, *A History of Louisiana*, 3:110; Marquis James, *The Life of Andrew Jackson*, 820 (n. 55); Robert P. McCutcheon, "Alexander Walker," *D.N.B.*, 19:37–38.
25. Gayarré, *Louisiana*, 4:422.
26. Mrs. Rowland, *Jackson's Campaign*, 299.
27. Gleig, *Campaigns*, 283, is quoted. Surtees, *Rifle Brigade*, 344, said one of his better officers thought the British were in a dangerous situation that afternoon.
28. Gayarré, *Louisiana*, 4:422.
29. Dickson, "Artillery Services," 158, records that the local times of sunrise and sunset on Jan. 8, 1815 were 6:57 A.M. and 5:15 P.M. Sunset on Dec. 23, 1814 would therefore have been about 5:00 P.M.

7. THE NIGHT ATTACK AND ITS RESULTS, DECEMBER 23–31, 1814

1. George R. Gleig, *The Campaigns of the British Army at Washington and New Orleans*, 284.
2. John W. Fortescue, *A History of the British Army*, 10:157; William Surtees, *Twenty-five Years in the Rifle Brigade*, 351. Surtees says the 95th lost 120 men, the 85th a great many more than that.

3. Keane to Pakenham, Dec. 26, 1814, P.R.O., *War Office* 1, vol. 141. After the battle, Keane sent his journal to the Duke of Wellington, repeating his inaccuracies about the night action. See Wellington, *Supplementary Despatches and Memoranda of Field Marshal Arthur Duke of Wellington*, 10:388.

4. Gleig, *Campaigns*, 292, said the losses were enormous, but minimizes them in his 5th edition.

5. Arsène L. Latour, *Historical Memoir of the War in West Florida and Louisiana 1814–15*, 110; Charles E. Gayarré, *History of Louisiana*, 4:428.

6. Vincente Nolte, *Fifty Years in Both Hemispheres* (trans. from German), 210; Jackson MS, "Story of the Battle of New Orleans," in L.C. tells of marines; Howell Tatum, "Major Howell Tatum's Journal," ed. by John S. Bassett, in *Smith College Studies in History*, 7 (October, 1921, January and April, 1922):109. Tatum does not mention the marines having faltered.

7. Latour, *Memoir*, 99; "Subaltern in America," *Blackwood's Edinburgh Magazine*, 21 (July, 1827):82. It has been alleged that "Subaltern" of the serial story in *Blackwood's* was Gleig writing under a *nom de plume*. This would appear to be most unlikely indeed, since there is very little similarity in their accounts of the battle, and no similarity of style.

8. Keane to Pakenham, Dec. 26, 1814, P.R.O., *War Office* 1, vol. 141; Jackson to Monroe, Dec. 7, 1814, John S. Bassett, *Correspondence of Andrew Jackson*, 2:126–28.

9. Cochrane to Admiralty, Jan. 18, 1814, P.R.O., *Admiralty* 1, vol. 508, encloses Captain Thomas Trowbridge's report of naval forces ashore. In this report Trowbridge mentions as his own enclosure a report of navy and marine casualities, but no such enclosure is to be found in the Library of Congress. Admiralty to Cochrane, Letter No. 20, 1815, P.R.O., *Admiralty* 2, vol. 833, acknowledges the Cochrane and Trowbridge letters but states that the list of casualties was not received by the Admiralty. No other record of the missing data has been found by this writer.

10. Adjutant General's return for that date in Jackson Military Papers, L.C.; Keane to Pakenham, Dec. 26, 1814, P.R.O., *War Office* 1, vol. 141.

11. Gleig, *Campaigns*, 248.

12. Fortescue, *British Army*, 10:259.

13. Gleig, *Campaigns*, 299–300.

14. Keane's two reports, one to Pakenham and the other to the Duke of Wellington, agree on this point—and with Gleig—concerning the rapid debarkation of the entire British landing force.

15. Gleig, *Campaigns*, 277.

16. *Ibid.*, 300.

17. François-Xavier Martin, *The History of Louisiana from the Earliest Period*, 2: 359; Latour, *Memoir*, 113.

18. Jackson MS, "Battle," in L.C., 12.

19. Colonel Sir Alexander Dickson, "Artillery Services in North America in 1814 and 1815," *J.S.A.H.R.*, 8 (April, July, and October, 1929):97, says that British Indian allies seeking horses for the British artillery in that area were afterwards fired on by the jittery British outposts, probably as a result of this American activity. Latour, *Memoir*, 117, says that the break was made by Major Bartholomew Lafon.

20. Nolte, *Fifty Years*, 213. This is an arresting story, easy to believe, but nowhere confirmed.

21. Jackson MS, "Battle," in L.C., 12–18; Bassett, *Jackson*, 189–90.

22. Girod to Jackson, Dec. 25, 1814, Bassett, *Correspondence*, 2:125.

23. Martin, *Louisiana*, 2:365.

24. Gleig, *Campaigns,* 302; Surtees, *Rifle Brigade*, 354.

25. Gleig, *Campaigns*, 306, is quoted.

26. "R.S.," "Battle of New Orleans, 8th January, 1815," *Blackwood's Edinburgh Magazine*, 24 (September, 1828): 354–57. The author, a British officer who tells of being wounded and captured on Jan. 8, 1815, probably was Major Robert Simpson, 43rd Foot.

27. Stanley C. Arthur, *The Story of the Battle of New Orleans*, 160. Arthur quotes a pamphlet by John R. Ogilvy, "Kentucky at New Orleans." Ogilvy, an enlisted man "eyewitness" to the Battle of New Orleans, was a Presbyterian clergyman when he wrote the pamphlet. This writer has not seen the pamphlet, but it is also quoted by Zachary Smith.

28. Gayarré, *Louisiana*, 4:442; Bassett, *Jackson*, 183.

29. Fortescue, *British Army*, 10:161–62; George Wrottesley, ed., *Life and Correspondence of Field Marshal Sir John Burgoyne*, 1:304. Fortescue alleges that Pakenham did not trust Cochrane, but no other British source has been found (by this writer) to confirm the allegation.

30. William James, *A Full and Correct Account of the Military Occurrences in the Late War Between Great Britain and the United States of America*, 2:360, re Petites Coquilles; Alexander Walker, *Jackson and New Orleans*, is quoted.

31. Edward P. Brenton, Captain, R.N., *Naval History of Great Britain*, 2:534.

32. Robert Hunt, F.R.S., "Sir Alexander F. I. Cochrane," *D.N.B.*, 10:160.

33. Benson E. Hill, *Recollections of an Artillery Officer*, 2:294–95.

34. Dickson, "Artillery Services," 98–99.

35. Patterson to Secretary of Navy, Dec. 28, 1814, M.C. Ltrs., N.R., N.A.

36. Sir Harry Smith, *The Autobiography of Lieutenant General Sir Harry Smith*, ed. by G. M. Smith, 1:237. James Parton, *Life of Andrew Jackson*, 2:131–32, began the American practice of criticizing the British for not also burning the *Louisiana*.

37. Patterson to Secretary of Navy, Dec. 28, 1814.

38. Tatum, "Journal," 113.

39. Fortescue, *British Army*, 10:163.

40. Gleig, *Campaigns*, 305, 307; Surtees, *Rifle Brigade*, 356.

41. Gleig, *Campaigns*, 309; Surtees, *Rifle Brigade*, 359.

42. "Subaltern," *Blackwood's*, 22 (December, 1827):319; Surtees, *Rifle Brigade*, 361.

43. "Subaltern," *Blackwood's*, 22 (December, 1827):316–17, took part in the action in the woods and was very sure that the American left could have been turned that day. Jackson's MS "Battle," in L.C., 18, indicates that he was of the same opinion.

44. Livingston to Jackson, Dec. 25, 1814, Bassett, *Correspondence*, 2:125. Bassett, *The Life of Andrew Jackson*, 205, cites as one of Jackson's mistakes his decision not to extend his line into the swamp before the 28th. Bassett is one of Jackson's most critical biographers. Coffee's men occupying the line into the swamp lived very miserably there, and after the battle many of them died of sickness caused by their long exposure.

45. Fortescue, *British Army*, 10:163.

46. W. James, *Occurrences*, 2:542.

47. "Subaltern," *Blackwood's*, 22 (December, 1827):323.

48. Theodore Roosevelt, *The Naval War of 1812*, 2:236.

49. Patterson to Secretary of Navy, Dec. 29, 1814, M.C. Ltrs., N.R., N.A.; Jane L. de Grummond, *The Baratarians and the Battle of New Orleans*, 108–109. Dr. de Grummond seems convinced that the crew of the *Louisiana* were Baratarians, but the fact is

that this crew had been enlisted from idle seamen in New Orleans before Jackson raised the ban on Laffite and his men. Few Baratarians would ever have enlisted under the hated Patterson's command, even if he would have accepted them, which is unlikely.

50. Tatum, "Journal," 118.

51. Sir John H. Cooke, *A Narrative of Events in the South of France and in the Attack on New Orleans in 1814 and 1815*, 205. Bassett, *Jackson*, 186, on the contrary, thinks the American defense could have been swept away on the 28th. Historians and war correspondents frequently seem to know so much more of the military arts and sciences than professional soldiers do!

52. Fortescue, *British Army*, 10:164.

53. "Subaltern," *Blackwood's*, 22 (December, 1827):320.

54. Mrs. Dunbar (Eron) Rowland, *Andrew Jackson's Campaign Against the British*, 324–35. No British corroboration of this exchange has been found. It may well be another myth, and yet it *sounds* like Jackson. Harry Smith, who would normally have taken a flag of truce forward for Pakenham, does not mention it in his memoirs, but he could well have forgotten the incident over the years. Smith did remember Jackson's having forbidden the use of French on one occasion (noted above), but that was after January 8.

55. Gayarré, *Louisiana*, 4:539–57; Henry P. Dart, "Jackson and the Louisiana Legislature, 1814–1815," *L.H.Q.*, 9 (April, 1926):221–80.

56. Latour, *Memoir*, 134; Nolte, *Fifty Years*, 216, 232. Ogilvy (quoted by Arthur, *New Orleans*, 133) said they proved useless and were abandoned except for flooring and for bedding for troops behind the lines (especially Coffee's men in the swamp). Fortescue, *British Army*, 10:164, accepts the story as true. Also see Parton, *Jackson*, 3:633, and Bassett, *Jackson*, 188.

57. Marquis James, *The Life of Andrew Jackson*, 823, n.5; Nolte, *Fifty Years*, 216.

58. Patterson to Secretary of Navy, Dec. 29, 1814, tells of the transfer of naval personnel to the army. Roosevelt, *Naval War of 1812*, 2:232, called them "New Englanders."

59. Edwin N. McClellan, "The Navy at New Orleans," *U.S.N.I.P.*, 50 (December, 1924):2054.

60. Patterson to Secretary of Navy, Dec. 29, 1814.

61. Dickson, "Artillery Services," 170–71. To demonstrate how determined the British War Office was to succeed at New Orleans, one has only to note that the ordnance that arrived late comprised the following:

- 6   18-pounders on traveling carriages (2,100 rounds of all natures per gun)
- 4   12-pounders on traveling carriages (1,100 rounds per gun)
- 4   12-pounders on garrison carriages (1,100 rounds per gun)
- 2   8-inch Howitzer traveling carriages (800 rounds per gun)
- 4   24-pounders on garrison carriages (1,200 rounds per gun)
- 4   24-pounders on carronades (1,200 rounds per gun)
- 2   10-inch mortars (800 rounds per gun)

8. THE ARTILLERY DUEL AND ITS RESULTS

1. John W. Fortescue, *A History of the British Army*, 10:163.

2. Bathurst to Pakenham, Oct. 24, 1814, P.R.O., *War Office* 6, vol. 3 (3rd letter that date).

3. When Prime Minister Lord Liverpool wrote Wellington on Feb. 28, 1815 (*Supplementary Despatches and Memoranda of Field Marshal Arthur Duke of Wellington,* 9:582) that everything had been done to make certain that Sir Edward would end the American war with a brilliant victory, he meant it. Reinforcements under Major General Sir Manley Power had been ordered to New Orleans from Canada. Sir Harry Smith (*The Autobiography of Lieutenant General Sir Harry Smith,* ed. by G. M. Smith, 1:244) reports that they arrived late—but before the British Landing Force left the Gulf—and so did the 40th Foot and an artillery siege train sent from England. In addition, Major General George Johnson was ordered from Cork (Bathurst to Johnson, Jan. 9, 1815, P.R.O., *War Office* 6, vol. 3) with five additional regiments of foot troops (plus detachments of artillery, dragoons, and special troops). As it happened, they never sailed.

4. George L. Chesterton, *Peace, War and Adventure,* 1:192–93, describing Dickson's reputation with the British artillery.

5. The Duke once said that Pakenham was "one of the best we had" (Wellington to Horse Guards, cited by Charles B. Brooks, *The Siege of New Orleans,* 209). This statement has been quoted by many historians, British and American, and Brooks located the original. The Duke was naturally anxious that his young kinsman by marriage do well in his first independent command. Though Wellington was stationed in Paris, his correspondence, as shown in the voluminous collections of his son, was very heavy on a score of matters. The War Office, from Lord Bathurst, Secretary of State for War, on down to the minor officials, sought the Iron Duke's opinion constantly. There are no complete records of his conversations with the many people who sought out his advice in person. So far as is known, there is nothing in writing to indicate that the Duke had a hand in choosing Pakenham to command the New Orleans expedition, and there is no record of any correspondence between, or meeting of, Wellington and Pakenham before the latter's departure from England. But the human logic of the situation makes it seem far more likely than not that counsel would have been given the young man, probably through an intermediary such as one of the Duke's aides. And it is not hard to guess why the Duke would desire that no record be kept of the matter, for he would almost certainly wish to avoid weakening the position of his wife's younger brother by opening up the possibility of some later charge of nepotism. In any case, although the Duke considered Pakenham "one of the best we had," he did acknowledge that Sir Edward was "not the brightest genius," and if Wellington did entertain hopes for his wife's brother's success, it would be surprising if he did not have a hand in providing him with two of the best staff commanders of the Peninsular Army, Burgoyne and Dickson.

6. Colonel Sir Alexander Dickson, "Artillery Services in North America in 1814 and 1815," *J.S.A.H.R.,* 8 (April, July, and October, 1929):106–12; John B. Trussell, Jr., "Thunder by the River," *Field Artillery Journal,* 39 (July–August, 1949):173–75, an American artilleryman's account of the battle.

7. Arsène L. Latour, *Historical Memoir of the War in West Florida and Louisiana 1814–15,* 147.

8. Theodore Roosevelt, *The Naval War of 1812,* 2:232, n. 1; Dickson, "Artillery Services," 93.

9. Hugh F. Rankin, ed., *The Battle of New Orleans, A British View,* 36–37, quotes Pakenham's order verbatim. This is the journal of Pakenham's assistant quartermaster general, Major Charles R. Forrest.

10. Fortescue, *British Army,* 10:164, gave the time as 8 A.M.; Rankin, *British View,*

37, 9 A.M.; Marquis James, *Life of Andrew Jackson*, 238, 8 A.M.; Charles E. Gayarré, *History of Louisiana*, 4:455, 10 A.M.; John Reid and John H. Eaton, *Life of Andrew Jackson*, 253, 9 A.M.; and finally Dickson, "Artillery Services," the only artillery expert among the historians cited, said that it was "after 9 o'clock." This writer believes Gayarré to be correct.

11. Gayarré, *Louisiana*, 4:455, is quoted.

12. George R. Gleig, *The Campaigns of the British Army at Washington and New Orleans*, 317; Dickson, "Artillery Services," 147–48.

13. Stephen Crane, *Great Battles of the World*, 231.

14. Lambert to Bathurst, Jan. 10, 1815, P.R.O., War Office 7, vol. 141; Dickson, "Artillery Services," 148.

15. Sir Edward Codrington, *Memoirs of Admiral Sir Edward Codrington*, ed. by Lady Jane B. Bouchier, 1:334.

16. Fortescue, *British Army*, 10:164; Smith, *Autobiography*, 232–33; Dickson, "Artillery Services," 149–50.

17. Gleig, *Campaigns*, 318–19, is quoted.

18. William Surtees, *Twenty-five Years in the Rifle Brigade*, 366.

19. Patterson to Secretary of Navy, Jan. 2, 1815, M.C. Ltrs., N.R., N.A.

20. Gleig, *Campaigns*, 318; "Subaltern in America," *Blackwood's Edinburgh Magazine*, 22 (December, 1827):324.

21. Sir John H. Cooke, *A Narrative of Events in the South of France and in the Attack on New Orleans in 1814 and 1815*, 284; John S. Cooper, *Rough Notes of Seven Campaigns in Portugal, Spain, France, and America During the Years 1809–15*, 136. The latter was the journal of a sergeant of the 7th Royal Fusiliers, first published in 1869.

22. Fortescue, *British View*, 10:176, citing Bathurst to Ross, Sept. 29, 1814.

23. *Ibid.*, 10:164.

24. *Ibid.*, 10:166; Smith, *Autobiography*, 1:230.

25. Surtees, *Rifle Brigade*, 369; George L. Chesterton, *Peace, War and Adventure*, 1:205; "Subaltern," 323.

26. Cooke, *Narrative*, 250.

27. Fortescue, *British Army*, 10:166; Dickson, "Artillery Services," 153–54.

28. Dickson, "Artillery Services," 155.

29. Smith, *Autobiography*, 1:324; Codrington (*Memoirs*, 1:235), said "Sir Edward did not place much dependence upon it"; and Major Duncan MacDougall, Pakenham's aide, testifying that the general "did not consider the attack on the right bank of any importance to the attack on the left," in William Espy, ed., "General Court Martial for the trial of Brevet Lieutenant Colonel Hon. Thomas Mullins, July 11 to August 1, 1815," *L.H.Q.*, 9 (January, 1926):34.

30. Cooper, *Rough Notes*, 134; Dickson, "Artillery Services," 156.

31. Latour, *Memoir*, 137; Gayarré, *Louisiana*, 4:457.

32. Dickson, "Artillery Services," 156.

33. Latour, *Memoir*, 146–47, 151.

34. Zachary F. Smith, *The Battle of New Orleans*, 116.

35. M. James, *Jackson*, 207.

36. Wooley to Jackson, Jan. 1, 1815, Jackson Papers, L.C.

37. Z. Smith, *New Orleans*, 73, 77–78.

38. *Ibid.*, 98–99.

39. *Ibid.*, 74.

40. Jackson Military Papers, 5:101–18, L.C., for morning reports, Jan. 8, 1815.
41. *Ibid.*, 124–25.
42. *Ibid.*, 166–68.
43. Edwin N. McClellan, "The Navy at New Orleans," *U.S.N.I.P.*, 50 (December, 1924):2057.
44. Z. Smith, *New Orleans*, 95–97; Latour, *Memoir*, 160–68.
45. Roosevelt, *Naval War of 1812*, 2:241.
46. Gayarré, *Louisiana*, 4:480.
47. Latour, *Memoir*, 170.
48. McClellan, "The Navy at New Orleans," 2058.
49. M. James, *Jackson*, 241.
50. Cooke, *Narrative*, 169.
51. Latour, *Memoir*, 203.
52. "R.S." [Robert Simpson], "Battle of New Orleans, 8th January, 1815," *Blackwood's Edinburgh Magazine*, 24 (September, 1828) : 357.
53. Wellington, *Supplementary Despatches*, 10:394–400, is a copy of Pakenham's explicit order to his generals. Rankin, *British View*, 40–42, is a copy of a memorandum order signed by Sir Edward to the troop commanders. Fortescue, *British Army*, 10:168, n. 1, said: "Cooke, Surtees and Gleig are all different and all wrong."
54. Dickson, "Artillery Services," 159–60; Cooke, *Narrative*, 250.
55. Fortescue, *British Army*, 10:167–68.
56. M. James, *Jackson*, 243.

9. THE GRAND ASSAULT AND ITS AFTERMATH

1. Marquis James, *The Life of Andrew Jackson*, 241; Patterson to Secretary of Navy, Jan. 13, 1815, M.C. Ltrs, N.R., N.A., re capture of British supply ship; Arsène L. Latour, *Historical Memoir of the War in West Florida and Louisiana 1814–1815*, 139; Colonel Sir Alexander Dickson, "Artillery Services in North America in 1814 and 1815," *J.S.A.H.R.*, 8 (April, July, and October, 1929):154, re Kemper's reconnaissance. From a prisoner taken from Kemper's group the British first learned of the arrival of the Kentuckians.
2. Dickson, "Artillery Services," 159.
3. Augustus C. Buell, *A History of Andrew Jackson*, 212.
4. John W. Fortescue, *A History of the British Army*, 10:165–66; Wellington, *Supplementary Despatches and Memoranda of Field Marshal Arthur Duke of Wellington*, 10:105; Lambert to Bathurst, Jan. 10, 1815, P.R.O., *War Office* 7, vol. 141.
5. Dickson, "Artillery Services," 160; Fortescue, *British Army*, 10:166.
6. Dickson, "Artillery Services," 161.
7. Sir John H. Cooke, *A Narrative of Events in the South of France and in the Attack on New Orleans in 1814 and 1815*, 247, describes and discusses the tradition of engineers' part in storm attempts.
8. Fortescue, *British Army*, 10:169.
9. William Surtees, *Twenty-five Years in the Rifle Brigade*, 374.
10. William Espy, ed., "General Court Martial for the trial of Brevet Lieutenant Colonel Hon. Thomas Mullins, July 11 to August 1, 1815," *L.H.Q.*, 9 (January, 1926) : 33–110; Sir Harry Smith, *The Autobiography of Lieutenant General Sir Harry Smith*,

ed. by G. M. Smith, 1:245; John S. Bassett, *The Life of Andrew Jackson*, 194, says that the entire British Army knew Mullins was worthless. His statement is not corroborated by anyone.

11. Fortescue, *British Army*, 10:170; Smith, *Autobiography*, 1:235–36; Espy, "Court Martial," 42–44, and John W. Cole, *Memoirs of British Generals Distinguished during the Peninsular War*, 2:350–64, produced more corroborative evidence from Mac-Dougall. However, it is to be remembered that, according to Robert H. Vetch, "Sir Duncan MacDougall (1787–1862)," *D.N.B.*, 22:992, MacDougall was seventy when he wrote his recollections of the battle for Cole.

12. Fortescue, *British Army*, 10:171.

13. "R.S." [Robert Simpson], "Battle of New Orleans, 8th January 1815," *Blackwood's Edinburgh Magazine*, 24 (September, 1828):354–55; Cooke, *Narrative*, 251; Surtees, *Rifle Brigade*, 374–75; John S. Cooper, *Rough Notes of Seven Campaigns in Portugal, Spain, France, and America During the Years 1809–15*, 139–40.

14. Dickson, "Artillery Services," 163.

15. *Ibid.*, 157.

16. Stanley C. Arthur, *The Story of the Battle of New Orleans*, 185, citing the account given by Colonel Robert Butler, Jackson's adjutant general, who was with Jackson on the left of the American line. Butler gave his account to Buell in 1874. "R.S.," "New Orleans," 355, writing in 1828, said that the British artillery opened fire on the rocket signal. Surtees, *Rifle Brigade*, 373, said that the American artillery opened fire when the rocket flared and the British replied immediately. This almost concurs with Butler, and is believed by this writer to be correct. Butler was quite old when he talked to Buell, but Arthur also relied on Ogilvy, who corroborated this point.

17. Espy, "Court Martial," 49.

18. "Subaltern in America," *Blackwood's Edinburgh Magazine*, 22:325.

19. Arthur, *New Orleans*, 187, quoting Ogilvy.

20. Surtees, *Rifle Brigade*, 374, did not participate in this attack, but he was in position to observe it. He described best the break of the British attacking columns.

21. Thomas E. Watson, *Life and Times of Andrew Jackson*, 217, quoted the British medical report of British losses, which only he has seen, as follows: KIA, 381, DOW, 477; total deaths, 858; WIA-permanently disabled, 1,251, temporarily disabled, 1,217—total, 3,326. Of these numbers, 3,000 were struck by rifle bullets. Much has been written to minimize the number of casualties due to small-arms fire, and to credit the greater proportion to artillery fire. Watson's figures are therefore very surprising, unless one recalls that Crawley's Battery #4 was a naval 32-pounder loaded with musket balls, and that it was observed by Surtees and "Subaltern" to have done much damage.

22. Surtees, *Rifle Brigade*, 275; Fortescue, *British Army*, 10:171.

23. H. Smith, Autobiography, 1: 236.

24. Cooke, *Narrative*, 254.

25. Latour, *Memoir*, 158; Howell Tatum, "Major Howell Tatum's Journal," ed. by John S. Bassett in *Smith College Studies in History*, 7 (October, 1921, January, and April, 1922):125; Smith, *Autobiography*, 1:247; Theodore Roosevelt, *The Naval War of 1812*, 2:245–46; Surtees, *Rifle Brigade*, 376; "Subaltern," 328.

26. Fortescue, *British Army*, 10:171.

27. Surtees, *Rifle Brigade*, 375.

28. Fortescue, *British Army*, 10:172–73.

29. M. James, *Jackson*, 242.

30. Lambert to Bathurst, Jan. 10, 1815, P.R.O., gave British official army casualties;

Jackson to Monroe, January 9 and 13, 1815, vol. 8, Register of Letters Received, War Office, O.A.R., N.A., told of his decision against a counterattack.

31. Fortescue, *British Army*, 10:165.

32. Charles E. Gayarré, *History of Louisiana*, 4:484; Thornton to Pakenham, Jan. 8, 1815, P.R.O., *War Office* 6, vol. 141; Dickson, "Artillery Services," 160.

33. Jackson to Patterson, Jan. 6, 1815, Jackson Papers, L.C.

34. Jackson to Robert Hayes, Jan. 26, 1815, Bassett, *Correspondence of Andrew Jackson*, 2:156.

35. Gayarré, *Louisiana*, 4:480; Fortescue, *British Army*, 10:172; George R. Gleig, *The Campaigns of the British Army at Washington and New Orleans*, 327. Gleig was present in action on the west bank.

36. Gayarré, *Louisiana*, 4:484; Zachary F. Smith, *The Battle of New Orleans*, 100–101; David B. Morgan, "General Morgan's Defense of Conduct of Louisiana Militia," *L.H.Q.*, 9 (January, 1926):16–29.

37. Fortescue, *British Army*, 10:172; Gayarré, *Louisiana*, 4:429.

38. Gayarré, *Louisiana*, 4:486; Z. Smith, *New Orleans*, 102–103; Patterson to Secretary of Navy, Jan. 13, 1815, M.C. Ltrs.; Jackson to Monroe, Jan. 9 and 13, 1815; Bassett, *Correspondence*, 2:12.

39. Lambert to Bathurst. Jan. 10, 1815, P.R.O., Dickson, "Artillery Services," 173–74.

40. Z. Smith, *New Orleans*, 118; Cooke, *Narrative*, 260.

41. Jackson to Monroe, Jan. 9, 13, and 19, 1815, in Bassett, *Correspondence*, 2:136–38, 142–44, 148–49. Patterson to Secretary of Navy, Jan. 2, 1815, M.C. Ltrs., N.R., N.A.

42. M. James, *Jackson*, 243; Cooke, *Narrative*, 254, for quote.

43. Fortescue, *British Army*, 10:174; George Wrottesley, ed., *Life and Correspondence of Field Marshal Sir John Burgoyne*, 306, for quote.

44. Fortescue, *British Army*, 10:172; H. Smith, *Autobiography*, 1:238–39, for quote; Gleig, *Campaigns*, 330.

45. Jackson to Monroe, Jan. 9, 1815; H. Smith, *Autobiography*, 1:240.

46. Tatum, "Journal," 133–35; Patterson to Secretary of Navy, Jan. 13, 1815; Gleig, *Campaigns*, 185; Cooper, *Rough Notes*, 143; Cooke, *Narrative*, 267–69; Surtees, *Rifle Brigade*, 383–84.

47. Overton to Jackson, Jan. 19, 1815, quoted in Latour, *Memoir*, 192–95.

48. Hinds to Jackson, Jan. 25, 1815, an enclosure to Jackson MS, "Story of the Battle of New Orleans," in L.C. This development further estranged Jackson and the Kentuckians. Zachary Smith does not mention it. Neither does any other account of the battle found by this writer.

49. Fortescue, *British Army*, 10:174–76.

50. Jackson to Secretary of War, Feb. 24, 1815, in vol. 8, Register of Letters Rec'd., War Office, O.A.R., N.A.; Fortescue, *British Army*, 10:176.

51. Henry P. Dart, ed., "Andrew Jackson and Judge D. A. Hall," *L.H.Q.*, 5 (October, 1922) : 509–70; M. James, *Jackson*, 254–64.

52. Fortescue, *British Army*, 10:181.

10. SUMMARY AND CONCLUSIONS

1. Robert S. Henry, "Tennesseans and Territory," *Tennessee Historical Quarterly*, 12 (September, 1953):195.

2. Fred L. Engelman, *The Peace of Christmas Eve*, 288. This unfooted monograph,

published in 1962, constitutes the first major study of the Ghent negotiations, by an American, since 1915. However, its extensive bibliography includes absolutely no reference to the Public Record Office material in the War Office and Admiralty records—an omission that seems to weaken seriously the persuasiveness of the work's rather dogmatic conclusions.

3. Liverpool to Wellington, Feb. 28, 1815, Wellington, *Supplementary Despatches and Memoranda of Field Marshal Arthur Duke of Wellington,* 9:582.

4. Thomas P. Abernethy, *The South in the New Nation, 1789–1819,* 402.

5. Engelman, *The Peace of Christmas Eve,* 284.

6. Alfred L. Burt, *The United States, Great Britain and British North America from the Revolution to the Establishment of Peace after the War of 1812,* 344 and n. 1, said that the governor of Massachusetts had already made such overtures to the authorities in Halifax.

7. Bathurst to Pakenham, secret, Oct. 24, 1814, 3rd letter same to same of that date, P.R.O., *War Office* 6, vol. 2.

8. Baker to Castlereagh, Feb. 18, 1815, P.R.O., *Foreign Office* 5, vol. cvii.

9. Engelman, *Peace of Christmas Eve,* 289; John W. Fortescue, *A History of the British Army,* 10:195; Charles B. Brooks, *The Siege of New Orleans,* 267.

10. Samuel F. Bemis, *A Short History of American Foreign Policy and Diplomacy,* 91.

11. *Ibid.,* 67, 96.

12. Walton L. Ainsworth, "An Amphibious Operation that Failed," *U.S.N.I.P.,* 71 (February, 1945):195.

13. Edward A. Channing, *The Jeffersonian System,* 79.

14. Edward P. Brenton, Captain, R.N., *Naval History of Great Britain,* 2:529–30 and n. 1, 536.

15. Cecil S. Forester, *The Age of Fighting Sail,* 265.

16. Colonel Sir Alexander Dickson, "Artillery Services in North America in 1814 and 1815," *J.S.A.H.R.,* 8 (October, 1929):170; Cochrane to Admiralty, Jan. 21 and 24, 1815, P.R.O., *Admiralty* 1, vol. 508; Bathurst to Ross, Sept. 10 and 29, 1814, P.R.O., *War Office* 6, vol. 2.

17. Henry Adams, *History of the United States of America,* 8:315–16; *Niles Weekly Register,* Feb. 18, 1815, 7:389.

18. Cochrane to Admiralty, Dec. 7, 1814, P.R.O., *Admiralty* 1, vol. 508.

19. *Ibid.;* Brenton, *Naval History,* 2:530.

20. Abernethy, *South in New Nation,* 384, told this story. Walker could have been expected to advance such a story, but did not. One could expect it from Dr. de Grummond, but she has not mentioned it either. George R. Gleig, *The Campaigns of the British Army at Washington and New Orleans,* 277, feared treachery. Edward Codrington, *Memoirs of Admiral Sir Edward Codrington,* ed. by Lady Jane B. Bouchier, 1:331–32, expected to attack at the Rigolets until his letter of Dec. 16, 1814.

21. Arthur Wellesley, Duke of Wellington, "Letters of Duke of Wellington (May 22, 1815) on the Battle of New Orleans," *L.H.Q.,* 9 (January, 1926):5–10; *Niles Weekly Register* (Baltimore), Feb. 18, 1815, 7:390, quoted a British estimate that booty at New Orleans would exceed $20,000,000.

22. Abernethy, *South in New Nation,* 384.

23. William James, *A Full and Correct Account of the Military Occurrences in the Late War between Great Britain and the United States of America,* 2:360.

24. John W. Fortescue, *A History of the British Army,* 10:156.

25. H. Adams, *History*, 8:229.

26. John Armstrong, *Notices of the War of 1812*, 2:178–79; James Wilkinson, *Memoirs of My Own Times*, 1:537; Charles F. Adams, *Studies, Military and Diplomatic*, 174–202. These are examples only. There is much similar criticism from self-styled experts of no battle experience.

27. Jackson to Patterson, Dec. 6, 1814, Jackson Papers, L.C., and Patterson to Jackson (two letters), Dec. 7, 1814, John S. Bassett, *Correspondence of Andrew Jackson*, 2:132.

28. Fortescue, *British Army*, 10:165.

29. Emory Upton, *The Military Policy of the United States*, 96–98.

30. Claiborne to Secretary of War, Dec. 9, 1814, vol. 8, Register of Letters Rec'd., War Office, O.A.R., N.A.

31. Jackson to Secretary of War, Aug. 25, 1814, and Monroe to Jackson, Dec. 7, 1814, Jackson Papers, L.C.

32. Brenton, *Naval History*, 2:536. Codrington's *Memoirs*, 1:336, said he opposed the storm attempt, but made no comment on Lambert's decision to retreat. Cochrane to Admiralty, Feb. 15, 1815 (P.R.O., *Admiralty* 1, vol. 508), shouldered off all blame.

33. "Wellington's Letter," 8–9; Fortescue, *British Army*, 10:177; and especially Wellington to Liverpool, Nov. 9, 1814, in *Supplementary Despatches*, 10:534.

34. George L. Chesterton, *Peace, War and Adventure*, 1:325. In this account of the author's personal conversation with the Duke many years after the campaign, Wellington is quoted as saying, again, that he had specifically advised against landing on the shore of Lake Borgne.

BIBLIOGRAPHY

BOOKS

Abernethy, Thomas P. *The South in the New Nation, 1789–1819.* Baton Rouge: Louisiana State University Press, 1961.

Adams, Charles F. "The Battle of New Orleans." *Studies Military and Diplomatic.* New York: Macmillan Co., 1911.

———. "A Plea for Military History." *Lee at Appomattox and Other Papers.* Boston and New York: Macmillan Co., 1911.

Adams, Henry. *History of the United States of America.* 9 vols. New York: Charles Scribner's Sons, 1921.

Armstrong, John. *Notices of the War of 1812.* 2 vols. New York: Wiley & Putnam, 1840.

Arthur, Stanley C. *Jean Laffite, Gentleman Rover.* New Orleans: Harmanson, 1952.

———. *The Story of the Battle of New Orleans.* New Orleans: Louisiana Historical Society, 1915.

Bailey, Thomas A. *A Diplomatic History of the American People.* 4th ed. New York: Appleton-Century-Crofts, Inc., 1950.

Barbé-Marbois, François. *History of Louisiana Particularly of the Cession of that Colony to the United States.* Translated from the French by William B. Lawrence. Philadelphia: Cary & Lea, 1830.

Bassett, John S., ed. *Correspondence of Andrew Jackson.* 6 vols. Washington: Carnegie Institution, 1926–1927.

———. *The Life of Andrew Jackson.* New York: The Macmillan Co., 1928.

Beirne, Francis F. *The War of 1812.* New York: E. P. Dutton, 1949.

Bemis, Samuel F. *A Diplomatic History of the United States.* 3rd ed. New York: Henry Holt & Co., 1950.

———. *A Short History of American Foreign Policy and Diplomacy.* New York: Holt, Rinehart & Winston, 1959.

Brannon, John, ed. *Official Letters of the Military and Naval Officers of the United States during the War with Great Britain in the Years 1812, '13, '14 & '15.* Washington City: Way & Gidion, 1823.

Brant, Irving. *James Madison the President 1809–1813.* Indianapolis and New York: Bobbs-Merrill Co., Inc., 1956.

Brenton, Edward P., Captain, R.N. *Naval History of Great Britain, 1783–1836.* 2 vols. London: Henry Colburn, 1837.

Brooks, Charles B. *The Siege of New Orleans.* Seattle: University of Washington Press, 1961.

Buchan, John. *The History of the Royal Scots Fusiliers, 1678–1918.* London: Thomas Nelson & Sons, 1925.

Buell, Augustus C. *A History of Andrew Jackson.* 2 vols. New York: Charles Scribner's Sons, 1904.

Burt, Alfred L. *The United States, Great Britain, and British North America from the Revolution to the Establishment of Peace after the War of 1812*. New Haven: Yale University Press, 1940.

Butler, Lewis W. *Annal's of the King's Royal Rifle Corps*. 4 vols. London: John Murray, 1923.

Caughey, John W. *Bernardo de Galvez in Louisiana, 1776–1783*. Berkeley: University of California Press, 1934.

Channing, Edward A. *The Jeffersonian System*. Vol. 12 of *The American Nation Series*. New York: Harper & Bros., 1906.

Chapelle, Howard J. *History of the American Sailing Navy*. New York: W. W. Norton, 1949.

Chesterton, George L. *Peace, War and Adventure*. 2 vols. London: Longman, Brown, Green, & Longmans, 1953.

Chidsey, Donald B. *The Battle of New Orleans*. New York: Crown Publishers, Inc., 1961.

Cobbett, William. *Life of Andrew Jackson*. New York: Harper & Bros., 1834.

Codrington, Sir Edward. *Memoirs of Admiral Sir Edward Codrington*. 2 vols. Ed. by his daughter, Lady Jane B. Bouchier. London: Longmans, Green & Co., 1873.

Cole, John W. *Memoirs of British Generals Distinguished during the Peninsular War*. 2 vols. London: R. Bentley, 1856.

Coleman, William H., ed. *Historical Sketchbook and Guide to New Orleans*. New York: W. H. Coleman, 1885.

Cooke, Sir John H. *A Narrative of Events in the South of France and of the attack on New Orleans, in 1814 and 1815*. London: T. & W. Boone, 1835.

Cooper, John S. *Rough Notes of Seven Campaigns in Portugal, Spain, France and America During the Years 1809–15*. 2d. ed. Carlisle: G. & T. Coward, Ltd., 1914.

Corey, Albert B. *The Crisis of 1830–1842 in Canadian American Relations*. Toronto: Ryerson Press, 1941.

Cox, Isaac J. *The West Florida Controversy 1798–1813*. Baltimore: Johns Hopkins Press, 1918.

Crane, Stephen. *Great Battles of the World*. Philadelphia: J. B. Lippincott & Co., 1900.

Darby, William. *Geographical Description of the State of Louisiana, the Southern Part of the State of Mississippi and the Territory of Alabama*. New York: James Olmstead, 1817.

Eaton, John H. *Life of Andrew Jackson*. Philadelphia: Samuel F. Bradford, 1824.

Eggleston, George C. *Red Eagle and the wars with the Creek Indians of Alabama*. New York: Dodd, Mead & Co., 1878.

Engelman, Fred L. *The Peace of Christmas Eve*. New York: Harcourt, Brace & World, Inc., 1962.

Forester, Cecil S. *The Age of Fighting Sail, the Story of the Naval War of 1812*. Garden City: Doubleday, 1956.

Fortescue, Hon. John W. *A History of the British Army*. 13 vols. London: Macmillan & Co., Ltd., 1899–1930.

Fortier, Alcée. *A History of Louisiana*. 4 vols. New York: Goupil & Co., of Paris, 1904.

Fuller, Hubert B. *The Purchase of Florida*. Cleveland: Burrows Brothers Co., 1906.

Gayarré, Charles E. *History of Louisiana*. 4 vols. Vol. 4, 4th ed. New Orleans: F. F. Hansell & Bros., Ltd., 1903.

Gleig, George R. *The Campaigns of the British Army at Washington and New Orleans*. London: John Murray, 1821.

Griffin, Charles C. *The United States and the Disruption of the Spanish Empire.* New York: Columbia University Press, 1937.

Grummond, Jane L. de. *The Baratarians and the Battle of New Orleans.* Baton Rouge: Louisiana State University Press, 1961.

Halbert, Henry S., and Timothy H. Ball. *The Creek War of 1813–14.* Montgomery: White, Woodruff & Fowler, 1895.

Hill, Benson E. *Recollections of an Artillery Officer including scenes and adventures in Ireland, America, Flanders and France.* 2 vols. London: R. Bentley, 1836.

Hunt, Gaillard. *Life of James Madison.* New York: Doubleday & Page, 1902.

James, Marquis. *The Life of Andrew Jackson.* Indianapolis and New York: Bobbs-Merrill Co., 1938.

James, William. *A Full and Correct Account of the Military Occurrences in the Late War between Great Britain and United States of America.* 2 vols. London: Printed for author, 1818.

———. *Naval History of Great Britain.* London: R. Bentley, 1837.

Jenkins, John S. *Life and Public Service of General Andrew Jackson.* Buffalo: George H. Derby, 1850.

Johns, Richard, Major, R.M., and Philip H. Nicholas, Lieutenant Colonel, R.M. *Naval and Military Heroes of Great Britain or the Calendar of Victory.* London: Henry G. Bonn, 1860.

Johnson, Gerald W. *Andrew Jackson, Epic in Homespun.* New York: Milton Balch & Co., 1927.

Keenlyside, Hugh L. *Canada and the United States.* New York: Alfred A. Knopf, Inc., 1929.

Knox, Dudley W. *History of the United States Navy.* New York: G. P. Putnam & Sons, 1936.

Laffite, Jean. *The Journal of Jean Laffite; the privateer-patriot's own story.* New York: Vantage Press, 1958.

Latour, Arsène L. *Historical Memoir of the War in West Florida and Louisiana 1814–15.* Translated from the French by H. P. Nugent. Philadelphia: John Conrad & Co., 1816.

Lee, Sidney, ed., *et al. Dictionary of National Biography.* London: Smith, Elder & Co., 1885–1900.

Lyon, Elijah W. *Louisiana in French Diplomacy 1759–1804.* Norman: University of Oklahoma Press, 1934.

Maclay, Edgar S. *A History of American Privateers.* New York and London: D. Appleton & Co., 1924.

Mahan, Alfred T. *Sea Power in Its Relation to the War of 1812.* 2 vols. Boston: Little Brown & Co., 1905.

Malone, Dumas (ed.). *Dictionary of American Biography.* New York: Charles Scribner's Sons, 1934.

Martin, François-Xavier. *The History of Louisiana from the Earliest Period.* 2 vols. New Orleans: Lyman & Beardslee, 1827–1829. Reprinted by J. A. Gresham, 1882.

Napier, Sir William F. P. *History of the War in the Peninsula and in the South of France from A. D. 1814.* 5 vols. New York: Armstrong, n. d.

Nolte, Vincent. *Fifty Years in Both Hemispheres or Reminiscences of the Life of a Former Merchant.* Translated from the German. New York. Redfield, 1854.

Parton, James. *Life of Andrew Jackson.* 3 vols. New York: Mason & Bros., 1860.

Patrick, Rembert W. *Florida Fiasco*. Athens: University of Georgia Press, 1954.

Pickett, Albert J. *History of Alabama*. 2 vols. Birmingham: Webb Book Co., 1900.

Porter, David D. *Memoir of Commodore David Porter of the United States Navy*. Albany: J. Munsell, 1875.

Pratt, Julius W. *Expansionists of 1812*. New York: P. Smith, 1949.

Pringle, Norman P. *Letters by Major Norman Pringle, Late of the 21st Royal Scot Fusiliers, vindicating the Character of the British Army employed in North America in the years 1814–15, from aspersions cast upon it*. Edinburgh: William Blackwood, 1834.

Rankin, Hugh, ed. *The Battle of New Orleans: A British View*. New Orleans: The Hauser Press, 1961.

Reid, John, and John H. Eaton. *Life of Andrew Jackson*. Philadelphia: Samuel F. Bradford, 1820.

Roosevelt, Theodore. *The Naval War of 1812*. Vols. 1 & 2 of *Works of Theodore Roosevelt*, Elkhorn Edition. 28 vols. New York: Charles Scribner's Sons, 1902–1916.

Rowland, Dunbar, ed. *Official Letter Books of W. C. C. Claiborne 1801–1816*. Jackson: Mississippi State Department of Archives & History, 1917.

Rowland, Mrs. Dunbar (Eron). *Andrew Jackson's Campaign against the British*. New York: Macmillan Co., 1926.

Saxon, Lyle. *Lafitte the Pirate*. New York: The Century Co., 1930.

Smith, Sir Harry. *The Autobiography of Lieutentant General Sir Harry Smith, Baronet of Olival on the Sutlej*. Ed. by George C. M. Smith. 2 vols. London: John Murray, 1902.

Smith, Zachary F. *The Battle of New Orleans*. (Filson Club Publication No. 19). Louisville, Ky.: John P. Morton & Co., 1904.

Steele, Matthew F. *American Campaigns*. 2 vols. (War Dept. Document #324). Washington: United States Infantry Association, 1922.

Surtees, William. *Twenty-five years in the Rifle Brigade*. Edinburgh and London: William Blackwood and T. Cadell, respectively, 1833.

Tucker, Glenn. *Poltroons and Patriots*. 2 vols. Indianapolis: Bobbs-Merrill Co., Inc., 1954.

Updyke, Frank A. *The Diplomacy of the War of 1812*. Baltimore: Johns Hopkins University Press, 1915.

Upton, Emory. *The Military Policy of the United States*. Washington: Government Printing Office, 1904.

Walker, Alexander. *Jackson and New Orleans*. New York: J. C. Derby, 1856.

Ward, Christopher. *The War of the Revolution*. 2 vols. New York: Macmillan Co., 1952.

Watson, Thomas E. *Life and Times of Andrew Jackson*. Thompson, Ga.: Jeffersonian Publishing Co., 1912.

Wellesley, Arthur, Duke of Wellington. *Supplementary Despatches and Memoranda of Field Marshal Arthur Duke of Wellington*. Ed. by his son, the Duke of Wellington. Vols. 6, 9, and 10 (July, 1807 to December, 1810). London: John Murray, 1860.

Whitaker, Arthur P. *The Mississippi Question, 1795–1803*. New York: D. Appleton-Century Co., Inc., 1934.

———. *Spanish American Frontier, 1783–1795*. New York: Houghton Mifflin Co., 1927.

Wilkinson, James. *Memoirs of My Own Times*. 3 vols. Philadelphia: Abraham Small, 1816.

Wrottesley, George. *Life and Correspondence of Field Marshal Sir John Burgoyne.* London: R. Bentley & Son, 1873.

UNPUBLISHED MATERIAL

Anderson, Conwell A. "Spanish Caribbean and Gulf Defense, 1763–1783." Unpublished doctoral dissertation, Department of History, University of Alabama, 1954.

Brown, Wilburt S. "The Preliminary Operations of the Amphibious Campaign for New Orleans, 1814–1815." Unpublished Master's thesis, Department of History, University of Alabama, 1957.

ARTICLES AND PERIODICALS

Adams, Reed McC. B. "New Orleans and the War of 1812," *Louisiana Historical Quarterly,* 16 (April, July, October, 1933):221–34, 478–503, 681–703, and 17 (January, April, July, 1934):169–82, 349–63, 502–23.

Ainsworth, Walden L. "An Amphibious Operation that Failed," *United States Naval Institute Proceedings,* 71 (February, 1945):193–202.

Barbour, Violet. "Privateers and Pirates of the West Indies," *American Historical Review,* 17 (April 1911):543–65.

Bassett, John S., ed. "Major Howell Tatum's Journal," *Smith College Studies in History,* 7 (October, 1921, January and April, 1922):96–138.

Bridgewater, William. "Jean Lafitte," *Dictionary of American Biography,* 10:340–41.

Brooks, Philip C. "Spain's Farewell to Louisiana, 1803–1821," *Mississippi Valley Historical Review,* 27 (July, 1940):29–42.

Cable George W. "The Creoles in the American Revolution," *Century Magazine,* 25 (February, 1883):538–50.

———. "The End of Foreign Dominion in Louisiana," *Century Magazine,* 25 (March, 1883):643–54.

———. "Plotters and Pirates of Louisiana," *Century Magazine,* 25 (April, 1883):852–66.

———. "Who are the Creoles?" *Century Magazine,* 25 (January, 1883):384–98.

Calkins, Carlos G. "The Repression of Piracy in the West Indies, 1814–1825," *United States Naval Institute Proceedings,* 37 (December, 1911):1187–98.

Carpenter, Edwin H., Jr. "Latour's Report on Spanish American Relations in Southwest," *Louisiana Historical Quearterly,* 30 (July, 1947):715–17.

Carpenter, William S. "Edward Livingston," *Dictionary of American Biography,* 11:309–12.

Chichester, Henry M. "Alexander Dickson," *Dictionary of National Biography,* 5:944–46.

———. "John Keane," *Dictionary of National Biography,* 10:1154–56.

———. "Sir Edward Michael Pakenham," *Dictionary of National Biography,* 43:83–85.

"A Contemporary Account of Battle of New Orleans by a Soldier in the Ranks," *Louisiana Historical Quarterly,* 9 (January, 1926):11–15.

Cusacks, Gaspar. "Lafitte, the Louisiana Pirate and Patriot," *Louisiana Historical Quarterly*, 2 (October, 1919):418–38.

Dart, Henry P., ed. "Andrew Jackson and Judge D. A. Hall," *Louisiana Historical Quarterly*, 5 (October, 1922):509–70.

———. "Jackson and the Louisiana Legislature, 1814–15," *Louisiana Historical Quarterly*, 9 (April, 1926):221–80.

Dickson, Colonel Sir Alexander. "Artillery Services in North America in 1814 and 1815," *Journal of the Society for Army Historical Research*, 8 (April, July and October, 1929):79–112, 147–78, 213–26.

Dobie, J. Frank. "'The Mystery of Lafitte's Treasure," *Yale Review*, 18 (September, 1938):116–34.

Espy, William, ed. "General Court Martial held at the Royal Barracks, Dublin, for the trial of Brevet Lieutenant Colonel Hon. Thomas Mullins, Captain of the 44th Regiment of Foot, July 11 to August 1, 1815," *Louisiana Historical Quarterly*, 9 (January, 1926):33–110.

Faye, Stanley. "Privateers of Guadeloupe and Their Establishment in Barataria," *Louisiana Historical Quarterly*, 23 (April, 1940):428–44.

———. "Privateersmen of the Gulf and Their Prizes," *Louisiana Historical Quarterly*, 22 (October, 1929):1012–94.

Fisher, Ruth A. "The Surrender of Pensacola as Told by the British," *American Historical Review*, 54 (January, 1949):326–29.

Forrester, Cecil S. "Victory at New Orleans," *American Heritage*, 8 (August, 1957): 4–9, 106–108.

Galpin, William F. "American Grain Trade to the Spanish Peninsula," *American Historical Review*, 28 (October, 1922):24–44.

Gayarré, Charles E. "Historical Sketch of Pierre and Jean Lafitte," *Magazine of American History*, 10 (October and November, 1883):284–98, 389–96.

Goodrich, Caspar F. "Our Navy and the West Indian Pirates," *United States Naval Institute Proceedings*, 42 (January, 1916):1459–75.

Hamilton, John A. "Jenkinson, Robert Bank, Second Earl of Liverpool," *Dictionary of National Biography*, 10:748–52.

Hardin, J. Fair. "The First Great River Captain," *Louisiana Historical Quarterly*, 10 (January, 1927):27–28.

Henry, Robert S. "Tennesseans and Territory," *Tennessee Historical Quarterly*, 12 (September, 1953):195.

Hunt, Robert. "Sir Alexander Forrester Inglis Cochrane," *Dictionary of National Biography*, 10:159–61.

King, Grace, trans. and ed. "Marigny's Reflections on New Orleans Campaign," *Louisiana Historical Quarterly*, 6 (January, 1923):61–85.

Liljegren, Ernest R. "Jacobinism in Spanish Louisiana, 1792–1797," *Louisiana Historical Quarterly*, 22 (January, 1939):47–97.

Lister, Walter B. "Portrait of a Pirate," *American Mercury*, 7 (February, 1926):214–19.

McClellan, Edwin. "The Navy at New Orleans," *United States Naval Institute Proceedings*, 50 (December, 1924):2041–60.

McCutcheon, Roger P. "Alexander Walker," *Dictionary of American Biography*, 19: 37–38.

Maclay, Edgar S. "Battle of New Orleans Half Won at Sea," *Magazine of History*, 16 (January, 1913):29–34.

Mills, Dudley, Colonel, Royal Engineers. "The Duke of Wellington and the Peace Negotiations at Ghent," *Canadian Historical Review*, 2 (March, 1921):19–32.

Morgan, David B. "General Morgan's Defense of Conduct of Louisiana Militia" (a letter written at Madisonville, April 15, 1817), *Louisiana Historical Quarterly*, 9 (January, 1926):16–29.

Niles' Weekly Register. Baltimore, 1812–1815.

Parsons, Edward A. "Jean Lafitte in the War of 1812, a Narrative based on the Original Documents," *Proceedings of the American Antiquarian Society*, 50 (October, 1940): 205–24.

Rapson, Edward J. "Sir Samuel Gibbs," *Dictionary of National Biography*, 21:264.

Ritchie, Carson, I. A. "The Louisiana Campaign," *Louisiana Historical Quarterly*, 44 (January to April, 1961):13–103.

Ross, Frank E. "William Darby," *Dictionary of American Biography*, 5:73.

"R.S." [presumably Robert Simpson]. "Battle of New Orleans, 8th January, 1815," *Blackwood's Magazine*, 24 (September, 1828):354–57.

Stephens, Henry M. "Sir John Fox Burgoyne," *Dictionary of National Biography*, 3:342–44.

"Subaltern in America," *Blackwood's Edinburgh Magazine*, 21 (January to June, 1827):243–58, 417–33, 531–42, 719–26, and 22 (July to December, 1827):74–82, 316–28.

Tousard, Louis de. "Letters re Battle of New Orleans," *Magazine of History*, 25 (July, 1917):40–42.

Trussel, John B. B., Jr. "Thunder by the River," *Field Artillery Journal*, 39 (July-August, 1949):173–75.

Vetch, Robert H. "Sir Duncan MacDougall, 1787–1862," *Dictionary of National Biography*, 22:992–93.

Wellesley, Arthur, Duke of Wellington. "Letter of Duke of Wellington (May 22, 1815) on the Battle of New Orleans," *Louisiana Historical Quarterly*, 9 (January, 1926): 5–10.

Westcott, Allan. "Daniel T. Patterson,"*Dictionary of American Biography*, 14:301–302.

MANUSCRIPTS

Andrew Jackson's Manuscript, "Story of the Battle of New Orleans" [partially destroyed], Library of Congress.

Andrew Jackson's Military Papers, Library of Congress.

David B. Morgan's Papers, Library of Congress.

PUBLIC DOCUMENTS

Captain's Letters (1812–1815), Naval Records, National Archives.

Great Britain, Public Record Office, *Admiralty* 1, vols. 505–509, inclusive.

Great Britain, Public Record Office, *Admiralty* 2, vols. 933 and 1379.

Great Britain, Public Record Office, *Foreign Office* 5, cvii.

Great Britain, Public Record Office, *War Office* 1, vol. 141.

Great Britain, Public Record Office, *War Office* 6, vol. 2.

Master Commandants' Letters (1813–1814), Naval Records, National Archives.

Post Revolutionary War Records of New Orleans, Books # 6, 7, 89, 91 and 98. Old Army Records, National Archives.

Register of Letters Received, vol. 8. War Office, Old Army Records, National Archives.

Secretary of Navy Letters (1812–1815), vol. 10, Naval Records, National Archives.

INDEX

Nive, Battle of, 19
Nivelle, Battle of, 19
Nolte, Vincent, 103 (in night attack), 119
Norris, Ortho (Lieutenant, USN), 119, 137
Northumberland, HMS, Cochrane's flagship in Leeward Islands, 7
Nova Scotia, 14, 21

Old Army Records, 134
"Old Hickory," 4
Order of the Tower and Sword, 18
Ordnance Department at Pittsburgh, 26, 87, 133, 134
Orleans Island, 60
Orleans Territory, 36
Orthos, Battle of, 19
Overton, Walter (Major, USA, Artillery), 160

Pakenham, Sir Edward (Lieutenant General, British Army), 7, 14 (biographical data, entered army, first amphibious operation in 1799, wounded at St. Lucia), 15 (wounded at Copenhagen in 1807 and at Martinique in 1810, fame in Spain, 1812–13, Wellington's opinion of, Knight of Bath in 1813, assigned to New Orleans expedition), 16 (American myths about late arrival in New Orleans, brilliant staff), 17 (arrival at Villeré Plantation, KIA [Jan. 8]), 19, 69, 74, 75, 93, 107, 109 (takes command landing force), 110, 111, 112, 113, 115, 116, 117, 118 (sends for naval artillery, sends flag of truce), 120, 121 (special secret order), 122, 127, 128, 129, 131 (distrusts dam), 139, 140, 141, 142, 143, 144 (learns of dam collapse very belatedly), 146, 147 (visited by Smith, ordered rocket fired), 148, 150, 153, 157, 158, 159, 166, 167 (news of death reaches London), 177, 178, 179, 180, 183, 184, 185, 186, 187, 188
Parliament, 7, 13, 169
Pascagoula, Miss., 24, 58, 75, 173
Pascagoula River, possible landing point of British, 59, 69
Passamaquoddy Bay, 22
Patterson, Daniel T. (Master Commandant, USN), 9–10 (biographical information, prisoner of Barbary Coast pirates, gunboat duty at New Orleans, 1806–07, marries American

Patterson, *continued*
girl, serves under Porter, command of flotilla of gunboats, promoted to MC, relieves Capt. Shaw in command at New Orleans Naval Station, correspondence with Jackson at Mobile, destroys Baratarian base in 1814, prophetic letter), 32 (opposes Baratarians), 38, 40 (leads expedition vs. Baratarians in September, 1814) 41, 42, 47 (naval defense plans at New Orleans), 48, 63 (meets Jackson), 68 (orders to Jones), 70 (unable to obtain crew for *Louisiana*), 71, 72, 73, 78, 80, 81, 83 (Louisiana legislature votes bounty), 84, 85, 86, 99 (aboard *Carolina*, Dec. 22), 112, 116, 117, 118, 119, 120, 125, 126, 127, 129, 131, 135, 138, 139, 140, 143, 149, 153, 154, 155, 157, 161, 172, 173, 177, 178, 180, 181, 183, 186
Patuxent River, British landing, 25
Pea Island, 14, 81, 89 (British army assembles), 90, 92, 93, 105, 173, 174
"Peace of Christmas Eve," 120
Pearl River, 35, 59, 89
Peddie, John (Lieutenant, British Army, QMC), 90, 156
Peire, Henri B. (Major, USA), 51, 52 (takes flag of truce to Spanish governor in Pensacola), 98, 137
Peninsular War, 15, 16, 94, 95, 131
Pensacola, Fla., 23, 26, 27 (occupied by British), 28, 29, 34, 36, 44, 46, 48, 49, 51, 52 (Jackson captures in November, 1814), 54, 55, 57, 69, 74, 76, 89, 171, 175, 186
Percy, Sir William (Captain, British Navy), 27 (landed British cadre at Pensacola), 29, 45 (defeated at Fort Bowyer), 54, 55, 77, 171
Perry, William D. (Colonel, USA [Ret.]), Battery #5, 137
Petites Coquilles (fort at Rigolets), 65, 68, 72, 83, 86, 98, 110, 172
Philadelphia, Pa., 10, 61
Philadelphia, USS, 9
Pickets, 125, 132
Pickett, Albert J. (American historian), discusses Blue's expedition, 56
Pigot, Hugh (Captain, British Navy), 24 (report to Admiralty), 27, 77, 173
Pinckney, Thomas (Major General, USA), 6 (commands troops in Creek War), 176

Spain, 13, 15, 17, 19, 26, 33, 34, 35, 36, 52, 69, 70, 82, 121, 163, 169

Special units, U.S. forces

Baratarian "marines": *see* Baratarian "marines"

Battalion d'Orleans: *see* Battalion d'Orleans

Beale's Rifles: *see* Beale's Rifles

Dismounted Dragoons: *see* Dismounted Dragoons

"Men of Color": *see* "Men of Color"

Mississippi Dragoons: *see* Mississippi Dragoons

Spencer, Robert (Captain, RN), scouts Bayou Bienvenue, 89, 91

Spotts, Lt. Samuel, Battery #7, 137

Statira, HMS, 16 (brings Pakenham), 93

Stono Ferry, Battle of, 1

Stout, John B. (revenue officer killed by Baratarians, January, 1814), 40

"Subaltern," 106, 108, 150

Surtees, William (British historian), 104, 108, 113, 128, 130, 146

Sweden, 18

Swedish islands, campaign of Pakenham in 1799, 14

Talavera, Battle of (July, 1809), 15

Talladega, Battle of, Jackson's victory (Nov. 9, 1813), 5

Tallassahatchee, Battle of, Coffee's victory, 5

Tangipac River, 59

Tapp, Henry (Captain, British Army), 144, 149

Tarleton, Col. Bamastre (Tory leader), 1

Tatum, Howell (Major, USA), 8, 60 (kept journal of campaign), 68 (comment on topography), 97

Tchifonte, USS (uncompleted blockship in New Orleans), 72

Tecumseh (Indian leader), 164

Te Deum mass (Jan. 31, 1815), 161, 188

Tennessee, governor of: *see* Blount

Tennessee militia, 3, 58, 87, 99, 104, 115, 133, 134, 149

Tennessee Mounted Volunteers, 4, 5, 49, 51, 58

Tensas River, Jackson returns (November, 1814), 54

Texas, 26, 163

"The Temple" (Baratarian magazine), 86, 181

Thomas, John (Major General, Kentucky militia), 58, 83 (ordered to New Orleans in December, 1814), 133, 134

Thompson, Charles (Lieutenant, USN), commanded *Louisiana* (Dec. 28), 117

Thornton, William (Lieutenant Colonel, British Army), commanding 85th, 25 (success at Bladensburg), 93, 94, 143, 144, 147, 148, 151, 153, 155, 156, 158, 159, 174, 184, 187

Tickfaw River, 59

Tohopeka, Battle of, 6

Tonant, HMS (flagship of Cochrane), 8

Torres Vedras, line built by Burgoyne, 18

Toulouse, Battle of, 19

Trafalgar, 32, 186

Treaty of Amiens, 7, 35

Treaty of Fort Jackson, 6, 57

Treaty of Ghent, 19, 120, 166, 168 (news of ratification reached Europe)

Treaty of Greenville, 22

Treaty of Paris, 21

Treaty of San Ildefonso, 168, 169

Tripoli, 9

Tylden, Sir John (Major, British Army), 144, 146, 147

United States District Court: *see* Hall, Dominic[k]

USS *Carolina*: *see* Carolina, USS

USS *Louisiana*: *see* Louisiana, USS

USS *Philadephia*: *see* Philadelphia, USS

USS *Tchifonte*: *see* Tchifonte, USS

Villeré: canal, 106, 129, 139, 143, 153, 172, 187; plantation, 17, 90, 91, 97, 101, 103, 173

Villeré, Maj. Gabriel, 91, 92, 95, 97, 187

Villeré, Maj. Gen. Jacques, 42 (urges pardon for Laffite), 68, 87, 97, 137, 183

Vittoria, Battle of, 18

Walcheren expedition, 19

Walker, Alexander ("historian"), 17, 60, 61, 87, 110, 111

Walnut Hills (Vicksburg), 24

War Office, 13 (British plans for campaign in America with main effort in New Orleans), 14, 74, 75, 76, 166, 169